# WESTERN FRONT

## By the same author

Hawke's Bay: Lifestyle Province

Wonderful Wairarapa

Wellington/Kapiti Coast

Hawke's Bay: The History of a Province

Havelock North: The History of a Village

Napier: City of Style

Kiwi Air Power: The History of the RNZAF

New Zealand's Engineering Heritage

Working Together: The History of Carter Oji Kokusaku Pan Pacific Ltd 1971–93

Battle for Crete: New Zealand's Near Run Affair, 1941

Blue Water Kiwis: New Zealand's Naval Story

Quake: Hawke's Bay 1931

Town and Country: The History of Hastings and District

Desert Duel: New Zealand's North African War 1940–43

Wings Over New Zealand: A Social History of New Zealand Aviation

Italian Odyssey: New Zealanders in the Battle for Italy 1943–45

Pacific War: New Zealand and Japan 1941–45

Rails Across New Zealand: A social history of rail travel

The Reed Illustrated History of New Zealand

Freyberg's War: The Man, the Legend and Reality

# WESTERN FRONT
## THE NEW ZEALAND DIVISION IN THE FIRST WORLD WAR 1916-18

**MATTHEW WRIGHT**

*To the memory of Private Frederick Charles Wright, s/n 9091,
C Company, 2 Battalion, Duke of Cornwall Light Infantry.*

*Front cover:*
Rumour that New Zealanders ate their prisoners prompted great hilarity in mid-1918. These signs appeared in a trench near Gommecourt.
(Henry Armitage Sanders, RSA Collection, Alexander Turnbull Library, PAColl-5311, G-13460-1/2)

*Back cover, left:*
New Zealand graves at Tyne Cot Cemetery, Flanders.
(Matthew Wright)

*Back cover, left:*
One of the New Zealand panels in the Memorial to the Missing, Tyne Cot Cemetery.
(Matthew Wright)

Published by Reed Books, a division of Reed Publishing (NZ) Ltd,
39 Rawene Rd, Birkenhead, Auckland.
Associated companies, branches and representatives throughout the world.

This book is copyright. Except for the purpose of fair reviewing, no part of this publication
may be reproduced or transmitted in any form or by any means, electronic or mechanical,
including photocopying, recording, or any information storage and retrieval system,
without permission in writing from the publisher. Infringers of copyright
render themselves liable to prosecution.

© 2005 Matthew Wright
The author asserts his moral rights in the work.

ISBN 0 7900 0990 0
First published 2005

A catalogue record for this book is available from the
National Library of New Zealand.

Printed in New Zealand

# CONTENTS

*Introduction:* New Zealand and the unknown warrior     7

1    In Flanders' fields …     11

2    Trench culture     35

3    The Somme     65

4    Passchendaele     86

5    Spring offensive     121

6    One hundred days     144

*Conclusion:* The First World War as history     170

*Notes*     177
*Glossary*     191
*Bibliography*     193
*Index*     199

## INTRODUCTION

# NEW ZEALAND AND THE UNKNOWN WARRIOR

*'Honour and Glory in this war is due
first to those buried beneath the sod …'*
— Brigadier-General G.S. Richardson.[1]

On a warm Anzac day of 2004, I stood with my wife under Menin Gate in the Belgian town of Iepr (Ypres), shoulder to shoulder with nearly a hundred other New Zealanders and Australians. We were a long, long way from home, and as the 'Last Post' rang in solemn salute, cadets, young and enthusiastic, stepped forward to lay wreaths. Their great-grandparents had marched out as eagerly, nearly 90 years earlier, to join the fight we now remembered. Many walked to their deaths along the very road on which we stood.

Half a year and half a world away, on Armistice Day, I joined around a hundred thousand Wellingtonians watching the funeral procession of an unknown New Zealand soldier killed on the Somme and brought home to commemorate all our war dead. The estimated size of the crowd was sobering. Virtually the same number of young New Zealand men fought in the First World War. More than 16,000 did not come back.

The First World War spans time and place, a poignant reality for New Zealanders into the twenty-first century. The four-year struggle of our grandfathers helped define New Zealand's twentieth century as a social phenomenon.[2] Yet these people did not really tell us about their war. Few revealed more than the broadest details of their experience, old mates' stories of high jinks on leave or tourists' tales of ancient ruins, French wine and the marvels of Imperial London.

They said little to loved ones of crawling under fire through stinking mud and razor-sharp wire, merely to reach more mud beyond. Many did not choose to remember the death that could strike without warning even behind the front lines. Few spoke in detail of the gas, sweet-smelling poison that left men slowly dying. Few revealed much about the strain that drove some men mad and scarred all, one way or another, for life. They were coy about the temptations of London or Paris, with their soldiers' bars and sixpenny prostitutes.[3] These were hidden realities, so harrowing they could not really be understood by outsiders,[4] yet woven into soldiers' culture, accepted, and silently shared with others who had been through the experience. They never forgot. Even 70 years on, some veterans wept as they recounted the truths of their hell on Earth.

Theirs was a war of unprecedented scale, mind-numbing lethality, and unexpected consequence. At the time it was called the Great War, the Great World War, or the European War. *The Times* correspondent Charles à Court Repington coined 'The First World War' in late 1918 to underline his thesis that the 'war to end all wars' epithet coined by H.G. Wells was premature.[5] Time proved him right, and although technically the first planet-engulfing war erupted in the late 1750s,[6] the four-and-a-half-year struggle that began in 1914 had to be distinguished from its predecessors. It was very different, a war of industrialised economies, new technology and mechanised death. Its bureaucratised participation underlined the declaration of Carl von Clausewitz that war was ultimately neither art nor science, but part of our social life.[7]

Few New Zealand men escaped it. The usually cited figure indicates that 100,444 New Zealanders served overseas during the First World War,[8] but there are many ways of dividing the numbers, and the official tally published in 1921 tells us that 91,941 volunteers and 32,270 conscripts joined the expeditionary force. Of these, 98,080 were embarked and a further 620 joined overseas.[9] They totalled some 42 percent of all those of military age in New Zealand. Just over 6000 re-enlisted during the war.[10] All this came at a time when the national population was just under 1,100,000.[11]

Some 58,014 of those who fought became casualties.[12] Of these, 16,781 died — 10,245 outright, 3958 of wounds, and 2351 of 'other causes', mostly disease. A further 227 died in New Zealand after war's end, before discharge.[13] Put another way, around 12.4 percent of those mobilised were killed.[14] The largest proportion fought with the New Zealand Division on the Western Front. Yet peace did not end the sorrow. Thousands of returned soldiers bore physical and psychological scars. Many were disabled. Hundreds succumbed to the lingering effects of gas through the 1920s, in sufficient numbers to prompt an official enquiry in 1929. However, not all post-war deaths were captured by statisticians, partly because — by contrast with Australia — gas victims were listed among the wounded.[15] One of the tragic realities of the First World War is that we cannot say how many New Zealanders, specifically, were killed by it.

Yet in other respects New Zealand came off lightly. If we take wartime losses as a proportion of males aged between 15 and 49, New Zealand's 5.0 percent ranked third in the British Empire, behind Scotland (10.9 percent) and Britain-Ireland (6.3 percent). Kiwi losses by this measure were also well behind France (13.3 percent), Serbia (22.7 percent), Romania (13.2 percent), Germany (12.5 percent) and Turkey (14.8 percent) among others.[16] New Zealand was one of the more fortunate participants by these figures.

However, this does not diminish the truths of our human tragedy. New Zealand's popular image of the First World War remains the eight-month struggle for Gallipoli. The wider story of New Zealand's three years in Flanders and Picardy from 1916 looms largely in the background. Yet this was the single most lethal part of New Zealand's struggle. Beneath silent, neatly mown grasses in these picturesque corners of Belgium and France lie many thousands of New Zealanders. Many, their nameless headstones tell us, are 'known unto God'. A full thousand died on just one horrific day in October 1917, during the ill-fated attack on the village of Passchendaele.

In a conceptual sense the Western Front was New Zealand's First World War, certainly numerically, and it remains New Zealand's greatest historical tragedy. Nearly half of all New Zealand's war dead were killed there. Its flower — the poppy — symbolises all New Zealand's twentieth-century wars; and it was a soldier from that campaign who was chosen, in 2004, to symbolise our whole military heritage. The experiences in France and Belgium carry wide meaning for New Zealanders, even almost a century later. And that prompts questions. Why was this three-year experience so different? Why did so many New Zealanders sail from the 'uttermost ends of the Earth' to die anonymously and by numbers in muddy foreign soil? What was the essence of their 'trench culture'? And were the tactics really as mindless as climbing out of a trench and walking very slowly towards the Germans until everyone was dead?

This book offers answers to some of these questions, while recounting the tale of the New Zealand Division in Flanders and Picardy. I make no apology for highlighting the experiences recorded in some diaries. The hard edge of war is never pleasant, and we cannot understand its truths without knowing the realities. In the process I take issue with various myths and legends surrounding New Zealand's First World War. However, this does not mean trawling the work of others for trivial discrepancy or supposed omission on which to condemn the worth of the author. History is an inclusive field, demanding generous discussion if we are to reach useful conclusions.

Primary documents remain the key to any historical insight, and the Alexander Turnbull Library holds one of New Zealand's most extensive collections of First World War diaries, letters and reminiscences. My historical work first brought me to this documentation in 1993, and new soldiers' records were still flowing into the collection as research for this book drew to a close in late 2004, underlining the point that archival investigation is an ongoing labour. Extracts from some diaries, letters and reminiscences are published here for the first time, and I am grateful for the assistance of the staff of the Manuscripts section. This material is leavened with a selection from the papers of wartime Defence Minister Sir James Allen and the gigantic New Zealand Expeditionary Force record held by Archives New Zealand.

Private cameras were theoretically forbidden on the Western Front. A few personal images exist, and some have been reproduced here, but the majority of the photographs used in this book are by official photographer Henry Sanders, held by the Alexander Turnbull Library. I am grateful to the staff of the Photographic section for their kind assistance. Other images are from the Kippenberger Military Archive and Research Library, and I am grateful to Dolores Ho for her help in locating them. I also thank Lode Notredame for his assistance in Flanders during a hectic Anzac Day, 2004. I am, as always, grateful to my wife, Judith, for accepting my weekend writing habits and road-testing some of the more harrowing sections of my text.

**Matthew Wright**

# IN FLANDERS' FIELDS …

The winter of 1914 looked to be mildly unsettling for New Zealand. An election loomed, and the pro-farmer Reform Government of William Massey held bare majority over the urbanised Liberal–Labour opposition led by Sir Joseph Ward. Massey's effort to turn industrial unrest into a law-and-order issue the year before had polarised a nation, and politics were tetchy.[1]

Social militarism was all the rage in this age of confident jingoism. Schoolchildren endured daily drill on pseudo-army lines, the senior pupils formally as part of an official cadet scheme. A significant proportion of New Zealand's men spent time practising war with the Territorials. It was compulsory, but most welcomed the chance to play soldiers amid a world that exalted patriotism, flag-waving, honour and glory. All knew they were rehearsing for war against Germany — the self-professed opponent of Britain and its Empire — but few expected fighting to break out. The last real crisis lay two years in the past, and amid an atmosphere of professed peace the simmering tensions of Europe seemed quiescent. Germany's high commanders even went on their summer holiday.

Yet within weeks a near-chance killing by a disaffected student with a pistol threw Europe into war.[2] This bolt from the blue underscored the dire truth — when push came to shove, the ideals of Liberals and pacifists did not overcome Europe's centuries-old grievances, rivalries and jealousies, further fuelled from the late nineteenth century by assertive nationalism and economic rivalry.[3]

The eruption of 1914 can be directly traced to the brief Franco-Prussian war of 1871, when Napoleon III's Third Republic suffered humiliating defeat at the hands of Prussian forces.[4] As a result the French sought alliance with Russia. A unified Germany in turn sought connection with the Austro-Hungarian Empire. Britain, realising that 'splendid isolation' might not cut it in the twentieth century, allied itself with Japan in 1902 and then accepted alignment with France and Russia.

The new world order was not stable. Germany clashed with Britain over trade and with France over the disputed territories of Alsace and Lorraine. The Balkans were internally unstable and a point of rivalry between the Austro-Hungarian Empire and Russia. When Archduke Ferdinand of Austria and his wife were assassinated in Sarajevo at the end of June 1914, Austria-Hungary had the excuse to intimidate the Serbs, and the whole of Europe was swiftly drawn in through the entwined network of alliances. Many of the decisions that followed were dictated by iron-clad timetables. It took weeks to organise the citizen-conscript armies needed for war, but the plans organising that mobilisation took even longer to amend, locking nations into early decisions and near-automatic responses that swiftly overtook diplomacy and — when combined with political intransigence and a sense of brinksmanship — helped tip Europe, alliance by alliance, into war. Monarchs, diplomats and politicians screamed for peace in vain.

Only Britain stood aloof from these dramatic consequences of mechanistic thought, but few doubted that the Empire was in crisis. 'Looks as if all Europe and ourselves will be implicated', New Zealand Territorial brigade commander Andrew Russell scribbled in his diary.[5] First Lord of the Admiralty Winston Churchill assembled the Royal Navy on the strength of Russian mobilisation alone, though as late as 2 August he wondered whether some stroke of diplomacy might yet produce peace.[6]

Britain's motive to join, ostensibly, was supporting 'gallant little Belgium' against German demands to pass an army through it, part of their plan to fight a two-front war by delivering a knock-out blow to France first. Britain had guaranteed Belgian neutrality in 1839, providing a de facto legal argument to join in; but the real rationale, prosecuted by Churchill and some Foreign Office officials, devolved to supporting France. As always, British policy-makers favoured a multifarious continent, by nature more easily malleable than one dominated by a single power. Asquith certainly felt British interests would not be served if France was 'wiped out'.[7] However, there were also arguments to stay clear. Domestic issues entered the mix amid heated threats of Cabinet resignations. Arguably, the prospect of allowing the Conservatives into power — with effects on union relations and Irish home rule — was also a factor in the British Liberal decision to fight.[8]

The final *casus belli* carefully committed Britain only to answering a 'substantial' violation of Belgian neutrality. But this was enough. The die was cast when King Albert refused Field Marshal von Moltke's 3 August request for free passage of the German army on promise of post-war independence. A friend of British Foreign Secretary Edward Grey found him standing at his office window as dusk fell over London that evening. German troops were pushing into Belgium. 'The lamps are going out all over Europe,' Grey muttered. 'We shall not see them lit again in our lifetime.'[9]

## Jingoes and patriots

The news reached New Zealand on 5 August. Plans were well established to raise an expeditionary force from the Territorials, but this did not prevent men flocking to recruiting offices, leading a flood who registered in the hope of being called up. It was an Empire-wide phenomenon. Niall Ferguson has argued that British men volunteered mainly to avoid unemployment in wake of an economic crisis that followed the outbreak of war. In New Zealand, by contrast, a self-image of exaggerated Britishness and the emotive pull of the 'good old mother flag' gave power to Imperial patriotism.[10]

Men from all walks of life flocked to fight, even lawyer Robert Watson, lately graduated with an LLB from the University of New Zealand; education did not guarantee rank and he was signed on as a corporal.[11] Some, such as N.E. Hassell, joined up later on news of their compatriots overseas.[12] Tourism also entered the mix, particularly the prospect of being able to see England at someone else's expense. This was true for journalist Aubrey Tronson, who joined for what he called patriotic reasons — but also saw war as fulfilling his love of adventure. He feared he might miss out and pestered the recruiting officers.[13] Others saw it as duty, among them Territorial commander Andrew Russell who 'Wired offering services' on 7 August. On the 10th he was made wartime commander of the Rifle Brigade. 'It is a great compliment,' he confided to his diary, 'must do my best'.[14]

Enthusiasm dimmed only a little as the war went on. 'Left Wanganui to become a soldier,' Clarence Healey penned in early 1916. 'Big hero. Big mug.'[15] But he still volunteered. So did many Maori, whose leaders hoped a contribution might raise their profile.[16] Around 2200 Maori officially joined, though more served than could be recorded. Apirana Ngata — then a Reform member for Parliament — asked for a return in 1916 and was told numbers could not be estimated because a 'large percentage of Maoris and half-castes have registered under European names'.[17] Other New Zealanders were overseas when war broke out, and many gravitated to London in the hope of joining British forces. But the Kiwis were seldom welcomed, and Napier nurse Louisa Higginson reached London in early 1915 to discover that New Zealanders were widely regarded as over-enthusiastic jingoes.[18]

Few really understood what war meant. The last all-engulfing struggle between Britain and a major power had ended in 1815. Regular 'little wars'

School cadetship was typified by pseudo-military rank and discipline. This is the Wellington College shooting team, 1913. Standing: E.T. Hogg, Sergeant G.W. Bramwell, Private R.H. Nicholl, Corporal E.M. Meredith, Private G.P. Rayward. Sitting: Corporal J.C. Williamson, Major D. Matheson, Private F.H. Smith. Centre: Professor W.R. Kell.

(Photographer unknown, E.H. Salem Collection, Alexander Turnbull Library, F-151880-1/2) fought around the Empire through the nineteenth century had been portrayed as glorious — and by the 1890s even Lord Cardigan's imbecilic performance at Balaclava had been translated, by poetic sleight of hand, into the heroic Charge of the Light Brigade. War had the imagery of public-school sports matches. Officers were popular heroes. When Gilbert and Sullivan catalogued the 'very model of the modern Major-General' in *The Pirates of Penzance*, everybody knew they were lampooning Garnet Wolseley, chief of the new Imperial General Staff.

This mix of patriotism and fantasy was an Imperial phenomenon, but New Zealanders saw themselves as more British than the British and were perhaps the most enthusiastic 'jingoes' in the Empire. Such idealism stood alongside a feeling of place in the South Pacific, where the next enemy was thought likely to be Britain's ally, Japan. Trying to get the British to take notice dominated New Zealand defence policy-making for years, though the problem was as much internal as Imperial, reflecting New Zealand's dissonant self-image of dual patriotism. Seddon's successor, Joseph Ward, tried to take the high ground

Members of the Mounted Maxim Brigade at Tapawera camp, 1914.

(Frederick Nelson Jones, F.N. Jones Collection, Alexander Turnbull Library, PAColl-3051, G-70774-1/2)

in 1909, forking over more than £1 million for a capital ship to strengthen the Royal Navy. Academic study has shown that his precipitate action was designed to stop Australia stealing a march on the policy.[19] However, the Empire-wide political ruckus that followed galvanised wider defence reform,[20] hammered into reality during the 1909 Imperial Defence Conference.

In wake of this meeting the British Chief of Imperial General Staff (CIGS), General Sir William Nicholson, worked with New Zealand Inspector-General Colonel R.H. Davies to develop a scheme for compulsory national service and a New Zealand territorial army of just over 30,000 men. This was calculated sufficient to deter all but a large-scale invasion, while providing an expeditionary force and enough trained men to support it overseas for an extended period.[21] Assumed loss-rates belied popular fantasies. Infantry losses during the 1904–05 Russo-Japanese War had been up to 95 percent in the first year. Nicholson split the difference between that and more traditional rates to conclude that New Zealand infantry might lose 80 percent, with other units taking less of the brunt.[22]

On the way to Johnsonville: Lord Horatio Herbert Kitchener (1850–1916), First Earl of Khartoum, with entourage during his advisory tour of 1910. New Zealand adopted the recommendations of CIGS General Sir William Nicholson after Kitchener's endorsement.

(Sydney Charles Smith, S.C. Smith Collection, Alexander Turnbull Library PAColl-3082, G-45238-1/2)

This was still a remarkable figure, but the fact that the highest echelons of the British army envisaged mind-numbing casualties went unnoticed by a public dazzled by the imagined glory of battle. However, the scheme was not adopted without debate. Ward balked at compulsory service, and although the Liberal Government enshrined the scheme in the Defence Act 1909, Cabinet did not implement it until after Lord Herbert Kitchener's advisory visit in 1910.[23] Amid a sense of Imperial militarism there were few raised eyebrows when the Defence Amendment Act 1910 established compulsory territorial forces and a school cadet system. By the middle of 1911, some 21,838 Territorials and 29,991 Cadets were on the books.[24]

William Massey's Reform Party did not change Ward's army initiatives when it gained power in 1912, and Major-General Alexander Godley came out from Britain to organise the army and finalise plans for an expeditionary force. As he remarked, the economics of war made it crucial for Europe to fight quickly; and the 'value of assistance' would be 'greatly lessened' by waiting until war actually broke out before planning any contribution. Godley envisaged early deployment 'as soon as it is considered safe', using Egypt as a half-way base where New Zealand forces could train before being despatched to the 'main theatre of operations', wherever that might be.[25]

Lieutenant-General Sir William Riddell 'Birdy' Birdwood (1865–1951) (centre left) and Lieutenant-General Alexander John Godley (1867–1957) (centre right) at Bailleul, 14 June 1917. Godley, a Sandhurst graduate and nephew of Canterbury founder John Godley, came to New Zealand in 1912 to establish the territorial army and organise an expeditionary force. When war came he led that force into battle, and went on to command 2 Anzac Corps. Birdwood led 1 Anzac Corps and remained in close contact with New Zealand Defence Minister Sir James Allen even after the New Zealanders had gone from his direct command.

(Henry Armitage Sanders, RSA Collection, Alexander Turnbull Library, PAColl-5311, G-13398-1/2)

Initial thinking called for a quarter of the Territorials to make up a two-brigade expeditionary force and various supporting arms.[26] This was less than a full division, but the prospects of trans-Tasman co-operation seemed self-evident at a time when the British saw Australasia as a single strategic unit, and when New Zealand had been within an ace of joining the Commonwealth of Australia. Godley went to see Australian Brigadier-General J.M. Gordon in 1913, coming up with a proposal for a joint division of 17,476 men 'of all ranks', to which New Zealand would contribute 6053.[27] These plans were well in hand when war broke out a year later.

## Movement to deadlock: the origin of the Western Front

In the early days of August 1914 many in Britain and its Empire found war a welcome diversion.[28] In an age when popular expectations were largely shaped by Napoleonic memory, the inventions of the dawning second industrial revolution offered pace and lethality beyond dreams. Rail had already transformed the strategic mobility of armies, with results that were evident to European military planners as early as the 1871 Franco-Prussian war. By 1914, Europe's rail networks were even more comprehensive; deployment timetables were built around them, and the motor buses and lorries coming into service provided a new dimension of tactical flexibility for troops pushing out from the railheads.

The battlefield itself was more lethal than ever. Artillery and rifle were longer ranged and faster firing than cannon or musket, supplemented with belt-fed machine-guns that gave two or three men more firepower than whole companies of Napoleon's day. Battle also extended into the skies. Aircraft were reconnaissance machines in 1914, but still better scouts than men on horseback. The superficial implication of all these inventions was speed, and in August 1914 even experienced military thinkers expected sharp but glorious infantry tussles,[29] a heroic cavalry charge here or there, decisive victories in the field, then a fast-negotiated peace. It would all be over by Christmas.

Inevitably, though, this paradise of eighteenth-century idealism and late nineteenth-century technology had its snakes. Bolt-action rifles increased the range of infantry battles from 50-odd metres to over 600, meaning that troops had to cross that distance under fire to take any position. A few heavy machine-guns sufficed to sweep these spaces with leaden death; and when the ground was also laced with wire and mines the battlefield became virtually impenetrable to infantry. This tactical reality had become obvious during both the Boer and Russo-Japanese wars. Yet as late as 1914 many French and German commanders still had the field tactics of 1871, 1856 or even 1815 in mind. Some French units were even dressed in the gaily coloured uniforms of past centuries.[30]

Only the British had really learned from recent experience. The answer to the larger-scale battlefield was fire-and-rush advance by platoon, itself a new organisational unit. The method demanded teamwork, and a small professional service such as the British army was better able to introduce it than the huge citizen-conscript armies of the continental powers. Marksmanship also came in for attention; some commanders even paid out of their own pockets for extra training ammunition.[31] The results were extraordinary. By 1914 the average British soldier was capable of firing up to 15 aimed rounds per minute from the classic Short Magazine Lee Enfield (SMLE).[32] When combined with a vigorous *esprit de corps* the result was a force with great endurance and hitting power for its size.

In 1914 most units were also wearing camouflage. The new khaki battledress could hardly be considered as sharp as the red shell jackets, shakos and brass buttons that some regiments retained as late as 1908. But it was practical wear for a modern battlefield. Nor were other lessons missed by British planners. The Field Service Regulations of 1909 warned of the defensive powers of trench and wire, urging commanders to break the enemy at the weakest point with concentrated artillery, machine-gun and infantry. The focus on cavalry as a fast-moving arm to exploit any breakthrough was also not the retrograde step it might seem. Cavalry may have been vulnerable to machine-guns; but even after tanks appeared, the horseman remained the sole fast-moving punch available to land forces.[33]

For all these reasons the British were in a better position to fight a modern war than continental armies in 1914. And the seven division-strong British Expeditionary Force (BEF) under General Sir John French needed all the advantages it could get in the face of the huge German force that pushed into

Belgium — though the oft-repeated claim that the Kaiser considered the BEF a 'contemptible little army'[34] was actually a morale-builder from the War Office.[35]

The massive German assault on their northwestern neighbour was a consequence of plans to handle a two-front war with an army that was not strong enough to carry an offensive on both borders. Initial thinking in the wake of the 1894 Franco-Russian alliance called for defence in the west while pushing east. But in 1906 the Chief of the General Staff, Count Alfred von Schlieffen (1833–1913), projected a lightning campaign to knock France out in six weeks, a risk thought possible in light of ponderous Russian mobilisation plans. He envisaged flanking French defences by advancing through Belgium, then wheeling to encircle Paris. This plan became doctrine, though the details did not. Germany deployed 87 divisions in 1914, but von Schlieffen's successor, Helmuth von Moltke, compromised the thrust in favour of strengthened eastern defences.[36]

The French war plan, devised by Marshal Joseph Joffre, envisaged an advance into Alsace-Lorraine. The scheme was up to revision XVII by 1913 and included an option to push into Belgium. To achieve these aims the French army deployed 62 infantry and 10 cavalry divisions.

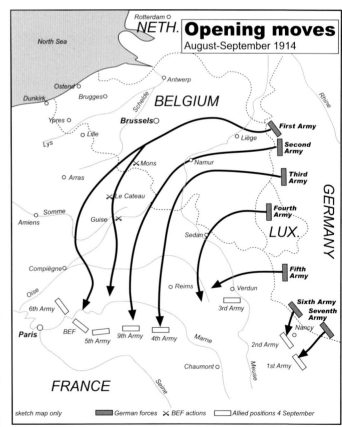

The scene was set for a whirlwind struggle, but in the event, the plans of both sides soon came adrift. Brussels was protected by mighty ring-fortresses at Liège and Namur. First Army commander Colonel-General Alexander von Kluck blasted them with huge howitzers, including monster weapons forged in the Krupp and Skoda works, legendary guns with such ironic names as 'Dicke Bertha' (Stout Bertha) and 'Schlanke Emma' (Slim Emma);[37] but the larger pieces did not prevail and it was 20 August before the Belgian capital fell. The French, too, had trouble. Joffre launched a counter-offensive into Alsace-Lorraine, but the advance drizzled to a halt on 20 August with the loss of 300,000 men. This was still enough to prompt von Moltke to strengthen his left wing at the expense of the crucial right.[38]

By this time the BEF was in southeastern Belgium, and on 22 August they ran into von Kluck's forces near Mons. It was the first time British soldiers had been in action on the continent since 1815, and in this juxtaposition of 'euphoria and reality', as one historian put it,[39] the Germans received an education in 'mad minute' rifle fire.[40] But the British could not prevail against von Kluck's juggernaut, and General French ordered a retreat. Lieutenant-General Sir Horace Smith-Dorrien nonetheless threw 2 Corps against the Germans at Le Cateau on 24–26 August, without orders — a controversial action that probably saved the BEF, but which met little favour from his superiors. Lanrezac slowed von Below's Second Army at Guise three days later, and in the face of these setbacks, von Kluck turned his First Army early, dropping Moltke's modified Schlieffen plan without encircling Paris.[41] Sir John French still intended to pull the BEF behind the Seine, but Joffre now planned a counter-attack on the Marne, less than 40 miles (65 km) from Paris, and persuaded the reluctant Englishman to put the BEF into the line. Reinforcements included the newly formed French 6th Army, whose spirited dash from Paris in commandeered taxis and buses seized headlines around the world. The four-day battle began on 5 September and proved decisive; by 10 September the Germans were in full retreat to high ground above the Aisne.[42]

Both sides then began a dash to the north in the hope of turning the other's flank, and while Joffre's men clashed with German forces along a growing line of trenches, General French side-stepped the BEF through Compiègne, Abbeville and St Omer. He toyed with the idea of fortifying Boulogne, but finally swung towards Ypres. They were just in time. A German effort to short cut the race through northern Belgium was slowed at Antwerp by the Belgian army, backed by Winston Churchill's Royal Naval Division (RND); but they could not hold for long. New Zealander G.S. Richardson was there long enough to watch the 'forts … crumble under the fire of the German heavy howitzers … I saw the sufferings of women & children and the desolation of a country by war. Although a soldier it made me regret that war was necessary.' He left one jump ahead of the Germans and 'narrowly escaped' being made prisoner.[43]

The Belgian army fell back into the western corner of Flanders, and on 24 October, as the Germans pinned them remorselessly against the Channel coast, King Albert ordered the Nieuport flood-gates opened. Water rolled into the Yser valley, forcing the German Fourth Army to swerve towards Ypres and the BEF. The thin khaki line held; a final German attack north of the Menin Road was repelled on 11 November, and the Germans pulled back to higher ground, leaving the British in possession of a rough crescent around the medieval trading town.

Both sides envisaged new offensives in 1915. The German General Staff intended to tackle Russia, but planned a final assault against Ypres before turning to the defensive in the west. The British also wondered about the salient. The 'contemptibles' were still flowing from colonial posts, and Haig launched an attack on Neuve-Chappelle in early March

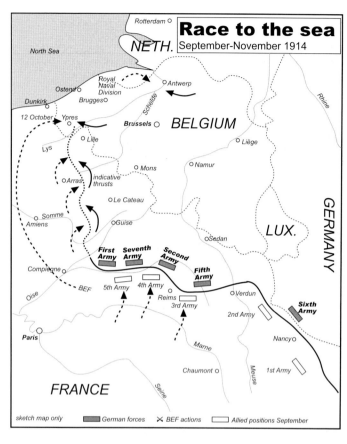

1915 with the aim of taking Aubers Ridge. However, during three days' heavy fighting the BEF suffered 12,000 casualties without taking the objective.[44] Smith-Dorrien had intended to follow up with an attack against Wytschaete, but the Germans responded with a push into St Eloi. This was held by 27 Division, including regulars from the Second Battalion of the Duke of Cornwall Light Infantry, lately brought across from Hong Kong. There was skirmishing on the 13th and intermittent action during the night. Late next day the Germans set off two mines near the brickworks, blowing in the trenches as prelude to a massive assault backed with heavy artillery. They took the village; but next day 82 Brigade counter-attacked, retaking St Eloi in a bitter-fought battle.[45]

In late April the Germans launched their main offensive, heralded by a sickly green cloud of chlorine that drifted across Canadian and British lines

Lieutenant-General Sir Horace Lockwood Smith-Dorrien (1858–1930). Survivor of Isandhlwana, Boer War commander, Harrow old-boy and career officer, Smith-Dorrien's controversial handling of 2 Corps during August and September 1914 did much to stem the German advance, but his disputes with Sir John French led ultimately to his dismissal in April 1915.

(Photographer unknown, Barbara Basham Collection, Alexander Turnbull Library, F-111350-1/2)

near Langemarck. The fighting that followed was generally known as the Second Battle of Ypres, but Germany's liberal use of gas did not produce a breakthrough; and on 1 May the men of 15 Brigade kept up steady fire despite being enveloped in chlorine.[46] Fighting stuttered to a halt in the face of Joffre's equally ineffective Artois offensive.

Nobody knew what to do. Sacking French and promoting Haig to command the BEF — though satisfying to politicians and army heads — did not resolve the deadlock. The main difficulty was that multi-layered trench, wire entanglement, minefield and interlocking machine-gun positions were near-insuperable barriers to infantry. As one historian has remarked, 1914 technology could whisk soldiers to the battlefield, but it could not move them on it.[47] The obvious answer — an armoured fighting vehicle — had yet to be developed, though armoured 'land ships' had been popular in fiction for years, and the Holt caterpillar tractor — already used to haul artillery — seemed an obvious starting point for a heavy cross-country vehicle. But in Britain the concept had to be sold to a conservative Department of the Master General of the Ordnance.[48] Churchill finally took direct action in early 1915, spending around £70,000 of the naval budget to get the ball rolling, without authorisation from either the Admiralty or the War Office.[49]

The second tactical problem was communications. As Haig discovered at Neuve-Chappelle, industrial-scale warfare took battles out of voice range; but commanders lacked portable field radio, and telephone was hard to extend to troops advancing through the field. Semaphore, rockets and messengers were only a partial answer. As a result, exploitation was often reduced to solo efforts, uncoordinated with other units. Officers frequently lost touch with their own artillery. Many of the apparent blunderings of the Western Front can be put down to this difficulty.[50]

All of these problems could be solved given time, but by early 1915 plans were afoot to bypass the stalled front altogether. The volcanic First Sea Lord, 74-year-old Admiral Sir John Fisher, wanted an amphibious assault on Germany's Baltic coastline. This was kite-flying, particularly as no ships were available for the purpose. The Cabinet authorised Fisher's huge construction programme, but nothing could be done quickly and his political counterpart, First Lord of the Admiralty Winston Churchill, believed the Turkish entry into the war against Britain created more immediate possibilities in the Balkans.

This, too, had aspects of fantasy about it, but the idea gained momentum in British command circles. Fisher, mindful of cordite shortages and the slender margin of naval superiority in the North Sea,[51] was one of the few dissenters; he consented only 'with hesitation',[52] urging a joint assault on Gallipoli. However, his voice was lost amid a mood of jingoistic optimism over the power of the Allies' floating arsenal.[53] By early February British plans revolved around a naval expedition under Vice-Admiral J. de Roebeck. A fleet largely made up of older battleships would hammer the Dardanelles forts into submission, sink the Turkish battlecruiser *Yavuz*, née *Goeben*, put Istanbul under the guns of the fleet, and invite the Turkish government to surrender.

It sounded too good to be true, and it was. The Allied fleet failed wholly to silence the forts on 19 February. A second attempt on 18 March did little damage, and Turkish mines took a toll of the battleships. Fisher urged Churchill to 'press on the military co-operation',[54] and after a few days, Hamilton and de Roebeck decided to launch the combined operation.

Plans were already in hand to assemble a land force for operations in Hungary. New Zealand and Australian forces training in Egypt were tipped to join the Royal Naval Division and 29 Division — both deployed from England — to form the Mediterranean Expeditionary Force (MEF) under General Sir Ian Hamilton. The new plan called for Hamilton's MEF to invest the peninsula, and the assault went ahead in spite of ongoing Admiralty concerns that the Dardanelles draw-off threatened slender superiority in home waters.[55] Both 29 Division and the RND were so hastily despatched that their stores had to be reorganised in Egypt, and they joined the Anzacs in an assault against well-emplaced and thoroughly alerted Turkish defences.

## Anzac and the death of glory

In many respects New Zealand's Middle East experience, including Gallipoli, was prelude to the Western Front campaign that followed. Kiwis getting together in Egypt had opportunity to contrast themselves for the first time with other cultures and societies. They found brothers-in-arms among the Australians, and to this extent Cairo was as much an arbiter of the Anzac phenomenon as Gallipoli. At the same time the Gallipoli experience introduced them to the style of warfare that they had to endure later. However, none of this was anticipated when the Main Body of New Zealand's expeditionary force reached Egypt in November 1914 and settled into Zeitoun camp, more than half-way to their expected final destination in France.

Many soldiers had found it traumatic to leave home; N.E. Hassell had to choke back tears as his transport pulled away from the wharfside crowds.[56] But the sense of loss was soon replaced with comradeship and wonder. Most of the men were overseas for the first time and Egypt was an exotic land of ruin and sand. George Bollinger thought Heliopolis magnificent, and was amazed by the pyramids.[57] Frank Campbell had a 'great day' visiting the Sphinx and pyramids over Christmas 1914.[58]

Off to war: members of the Mounted Rifles Regiment ride through Nelson, 18 August 1914.

(Frederick Nelson Jones, F.N. Jones Collection, Alexander Turnbull Library, PAColl-3051, G-26531-1/2)

*Left*
Elements of the New Zealand Expeditionary Force moving along the Hutt Road, 10 October 1914.

(Photographer unknown, Alexander Turnbull Library, F-2507-1/2)

*Below*
New Zealand soldiers' farewell; the *Limerick* leaves Wellington, 1914.

(Joseph Zachariah, Alexander Turnbull Library, F-70041-1/2)

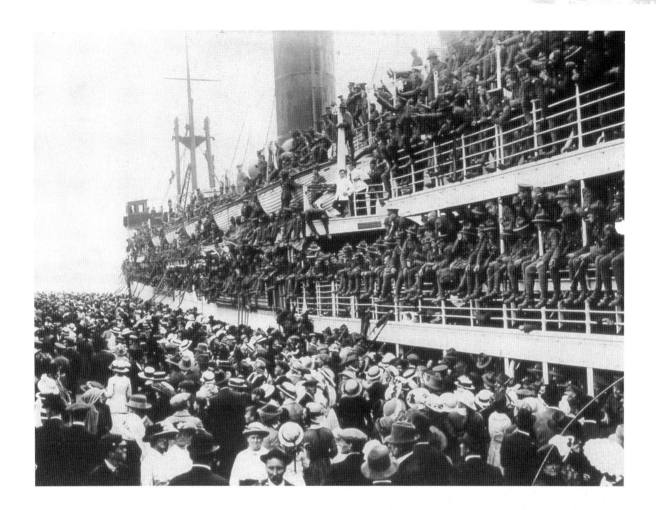

Off on the great adventure; soldiers of the New Zealand Expeditionary Force depart amid sadness and excitement, 1914.

(Photographer unknown, *The Press* [Christchurch] Collection, Alexander Turnbull Library, G-8265-1/1)

The mysteries of the ancient world paled beside Cairo.[59] The New Zealanders were 'very anxious' to see the city,[60] though few anticipated the depth of culture shock amid this riotous, teeming, crowded metropolis of 600,000 with its endless procession of bars, stalls and brothels. The assault on the wallet began as the men entered and were 'besieged by an army of juvenile boot-blacks'.[61] None had much experience in the trade practices of street hawkers, or knew much about the food, drink and cigarettes they could buy at knock-down prices from dark eating houses reeking of exotic smoke. Rumours soon circulated that traders were attempting to poison the young soldier-tourists. Bollinger was convinced he had been offered drugged cigarettes during one visit to Cairo in January 1915.[62] He was not alone.

All this was a recipe for trouble, though it is misleading to reduce the motive to racism, as suggested in the late 1980s.[63] Anachronism is a poor substitute for analysis, and the attitudes of the First World War cannot be accurately described by terminology that has such specific meaning in a later context. In fact the ethnocentrism of 1915 New Zealand was part of a mix of attitudes as complex and wide-ranging, in their own way, as their inverse in the late twentieth century. The real question is more subtle. The British shared New Zealand's derogatory attitudes to the Egyptians,[64] but had been doing so for several decades without much trouble. Yet the Anzacs soon generated ill feeling that boiled over into large-scale violence. The crisis peaked in the 'battle of the Wazir', a riot by Anzac soldiers in the red light district on Good Friday 1915. It was not quelled until British military police and regulars opened fire.[65] At least two soldiers died, and the dismaying affair reduced the Anzacs to 'mud in the eyes of the Imperial authorities'.[66]

The incident was explicitly triggered by disaffection with prostitutes; the main target was a brothel. But a wide-eyed innocence in the face of Middle Eastern trade practices played a role, as did the novelty not just of Egypt, but of being away from home and country. Many soldiers were also disappointed. Cairo did not live up to its magical expectations; within a month Bollinger classified the city as filthy,[67] while Tronson thought it squalid.[68] To this was added the 'larrikinism' that reputedly filtered into New Zealand lines through comradeship with Australians. The behaviour that followed drew official attention as early as December 1914 from Birdwood, who told 1 Australian Divisional commander Major-General W.T. Bridges it was 'up to the men themselves to put a stop to it by their own good feeling'. The problem was that Cairo was 'full of temptations' and 'some ... of the most unscrupulous people in the world'.[69]

Godley was copied the letter and took a harder line: '...it is quite time that we began to think of nothing but making ourselves really fit to take the field in France alongside our comrades of the regular army'.[70] However, plans to fight in France evaporated in the face of the Turkish threat to Egypt. 'We have just heard that we will be going to the front in four weeks,' John W. Muldoon wrote just after Christmas 1914, 'and you can imagine the boys are all very pleased.'[71] New Zealanders were despatched to deal with Bedouins in late January 1915,

Members of the Pioneer Battalion, possibly the Third Maori Contingent, wait to depart. Tropical dress suggests they are en route to Egypt. Maori leaders hoped a contribution might enhance the status of their people back in New Zealand, but in the event the soldiers were used as a labour force.

(Photographer unknown, Alexander Turnbull Library, F-11079-1/2)

Laurie Mackie was among many New Zealand soldier-tourists, eager to see the world as much as to fight. He was also one of the few with a camera, taking this snap of fellow soldiers returning to camp after an expedition to the pyramids, probably early 1915.

(Laurie C. Mackie, Alexander Turnbull Library, PA1-0-308-6-3)

struggling through appalling conditions.[72] More serious fighting flared in Palestine during February, giving the barely trained New Zealanders their first taste of warfare, though even in March Bollinger was able to describe it as fun.[73]

Then orders came to prepare for the Gallipoli campaign. The New Zealanders joined the Anzac Corps under Lieutenant-General Sir William Riddell Birdwood, a force that included both 1 Australian Division and Godley's composite two-brigade New Zealand and Australian Division. It was deployed to the northernmost landing zone on the Gallipoli Peninsula and tasked with cutting off the Turks from the main landings further south. The transports came ashore off course, north of Ari Burnu, in a rugged 'small bay' with 'steep cliffs, almost down to the water's edge'.[74] It was an unlikely place, but the seasoned soldiers of the Turkish army reacted sharply. Lance-Corporal Frank Campbell recalled that:

> *Our men had rushed the trenches & driven out the enemy at a fearful cost & pushed them back for 3 miles over a second ridge, which was wooded & offered excellent cover for snipers, the warships did their best to silence their batteries who were pouring shrapnel onto the beach where many men were hit, boats coming ashore being often hit & several men shelled & wounded, the naval officers were loud in their praise of our men's work.*[75]

Bollinger saw men falling as the New Zealanders tried to get to the beach.[76] Campbell found a 'fearful sight when we got ashore, dead & wounded everywhere laying [sic] in clusters'.[77] One early casualty was pre-war fantasy. 'I've seen sad sights here,' Campbell wrote as early as 29 April, 'held a few dying hands & I'm satisfied war is no good. I've seen a big battle & I've seen the results. Our list must be bigger than the retreat from Mons.'[78]

These feelings did not improve as days turned to weeks. Bollinger recorded the intense heat, swarming flies and stench from the dead in his diary, wondering whether anybody in the wider world realised what they were going through. The smell was still getting to him a few days later. 'We see such scenes as this and still some newspapers have the audacity to suggest we like this life.'[79] Yet this war seems to have been fought without rancour. Selwyn Chambers

Realities of war. Glory vanished amid the terror of fighting on Gallipoli, the first introduction many New Zealanders had to the truths of twentieth-century conflict. This classic image highlights conditions in Anzac Cove during the landings, late April 1915.

(Photographer unknown, Alexander Turnbull Library, PAColl-4318, F-32248-1/2)

found the Turks 'quite friendly' during a short armistice on 24 May, arranged to let each side retrieve and bury their dead.[80]

On Gallipoli, trench fighting was a novelty. But the job still had to be done, and in August the New Zealanders led a final push to try and take the peninsula. Against all odds, the Wellington Battalion under Colonel William Malone reached their objective on Chunuk Bair. His heroic effort became one of the key pillars of the Anzac legend; but in the face of staunch resistance his forces could get no further. Godley was given command of the Anzac Corps as the year drew to a close, while Russell was promoted major-general to lead the New Zealand and Australian Division, confusingly renamed the Anzac Division. Russell took up the post in November, but his first significant duty involved bringing the force back to Egypt. The evacuation in early December went 'like clockwork'.[81]

New Zealand suffered 7452 casualties on Gallipoli, of whom 2721 were killed.[82] As British Prime Minister Herbert Asquith put it, the Anzacs had 'shed their blood like water'.[83] It was a horrifying introduction to twentieth-century warfare; New Zealand nurse Louisa Higginson, tending some of the survivors in Cairo, mourned the lives sacrificed for nothing.[84]

## The New Zealand Division forms

The Anzac Division arrived back in Egypt during December 1915, concentrating initially at Moascar, adjacent to the Suez Canal. It took some time; as one soldier put it in his diary, units were scattered.[85] There was thought of reorganising the Anzacs for action against the Turks in Syria. But in late January, Mediterranean Expeditionary Force commander General Sir Archibald Murray decided to add new units drawn from base reinforcements to create five Australian, one New Zealand and one mixed Anzac division. Birdwood liked the idea, but as he warned Allen on 4 February, a 'great deal of improvisation' would be needed to 'get our formations right'. He had to raise 16 Australian and 4 New Zealand battalions: '… the point upon which I feel the greatest apprehension is … involving you in the responsibility of keeping up drafts for this increased force …'[86]

This was a tricky question indeed. New Zealand planners had banked on 25 percent casualties per month for infantry, less for other arms, on the basis of a two-brigade force. This implied drafts of some 3000 men every two months, and although war experience prompted a few amendments, this schedule was broadly locked in.[87] British planners expected the war to last another three years, and New Zealand, a nation of a little over a million souls — of whom around 160,000 were of military age in 1915 — could not afford profligacy. 'To put units into the field which waste away for want of Reinforcements is entirely opposed to the principles laid down by the Imperial Government,' Colonel C.M. Gibbon of the New Zealand General Staff penned in 1915. 'We must prepare for a long war, and it is essential that we should count the cost, and make sure that our resources of men are organised in such a manner as to last to the finish.'[88]

Allen thought the only answer was conscription.[89] However, there were already three brigades' worth of New Zealand infantry in Egypt, and the Massey-Ward coalition tacitly admitted British authority over their forces.[90] Allen agreed to supply what was needed, though he felt 'very large demands are being made on us'.[91] In the event reinforcements could not be obtained for the third brigade until August, nudging the government towards Allen's long-standing vision for conscription as a planning tool.

The Australians left Moascar at the end of February, and on 1 March the remaining units were designated the New Zealand Division. 'The division will I am sure do well under Russell,' Birdwood advised Allen, 'and I think you have every reason to be exceedingly proud of them.'[92] The division was organised to the 1915 New Army plan, though it initially lacked a cycle company and machine-gun battery among other minor units.[93] The original force became 1 Brigade; 2 Brigade was formed; and Russell's Rifle Brigade became 3 (Rifle) Brigade — though still often referred to by its old name.[94]

To this were added a headquarters unit, divisional artillery, a squadron of the Otago Mounted Rifles, and a Pioneer Battalion. This last was a fighting labour force. They were principally drawn from the thousand-odd Maori who

A view from the train taking the New Zealand Division through France from Marseilles to the front, April 1916.

(Laurie C. Mackie, Alexander Turnbull Library, PA1-0-310-6-2)

had been despatched to Gallipoli, with the addition of nearly 150 Niueans, around 50 Rarotongans,[95] and elements of the Otago Mounted Rifles.[96] This seems extraordinary from the modern perspective. Maori had given British regiments a run for their money 60 years earlier in the Waikato and Taranaki wars. The Maori Contingent discharged themselves brilliantly on Gallipoli. But such realities counted for little in the face of the mind-set of 1916. Non-Europeans were lumped together and, as in civilian life, given menial tasks.[97]

The division was quickly caught up in a strategic reshuffle. The Russian entry into the war against Turkey relieved the pressure on Egypt just as fighting on the Western Front seemed to be taking a turn for the worse. The British reorganised their forces accordingly, and the New Zealanders embarked in early April for Marseilles,[98] leaving the Mounted Brigade in Palestine with the Anzac division. From Marseilles the New Zealanders took to the railway for a 58-hour journey to Picardy. The French flocked to welcome the Kiwis as they rolled past. 'We have been getting a great hearing,' Clarence Hankins wrote in his diary, 'at Lyon I managed to get a bottle of wine.'[99] They reached Armentières under steely skies.

# 2

# TRENCH CULTURE

In some ways Armentières in 1916 was a return home for the New Zealanders. The division once again came under Godley's 1 Anzac Corps. But all else was new. The Anzac Corps was part of the Second Army of Lieutenant-General Sir Herbert Plumer. He looked the archetypal Colonel Blimp, a round-faced soldier with a great white moustache that emphasised his receding chin. Russell met him for the first time on 21 April, discovering a 'well preserved man of about 60' who talked 'sense' and seemed to be a 'good soldier'. But Russell was wary — 'don't know whether he is a heaven born strategist'.[1]

Plumer was actually one of several commanders who understood the tactical issues of the day. And tactics were the thorny problem in that spring of 1916. The failure of Gallipoli brought home to Allied command the point that there was no way around the Western Front; yet efforts there also seemed doomed to failure. The battle for Loos drizzled to a halt in November 1915 with the loss of more than 48,000 British soldiers. In December, British, French, Russian and Italian army officials gathered at Chantilly to discuss strategies. The plan that emerged called for a three-pronged offensive on the Italian, Russian and Western fronts, though it could not be launched quickly. The Russians had been hammered in 1915; and Kitchener's New Army was still being trained.[2] Perhaps the biggest problem was that, after the disasters of 1914, both the British and French armies lacked experienced commanders.

Haig wanted to attack from Flanders, but the risk to the vital channel ports if the push was defeated seemed too great,[3] and after a good deal of diplomatic to-ing and fro-ing he agreed to a mid-year offensive on the junction with French forces at the Somme. The line was held by General Rawlinson's Fourth

Army, facing the German Second Army of General Fritz von Below. There was time to bring new officers up to speed and refine artillery techniques, including the 'walking' barrage designed to screen advancing troops. Haig was a convert to this system.[4] Front-line units also began receiving Fullerphones, a secure telegraph that was effective even if most of the signal was leaking to earth through damaged wiring.

In the event, however, these tactical innovations ran second to the concept of the *bataille d'usure*, a strategy to wear out the other side by drawing its soldiers into battle, then massacring them. No civilised nation, the logic went, could long withstand the human cost. The strategy was ruthless but expected. As early as 1911, Haig had predicted that any war would begin with a clash, continue to a wearing-out phase, then end with one or more decisive battles. The problem in 1915–18, as he remarked in hindsight, was that the war brought millions to the field, backed by the power of empires. The wearing-out phase was extended and Haig, still in hindsight, saw the events of 1916–17 as one great battle.[5] At the time, the strategy was thought war-winning on the basis that the Allies had a higher population base than Germany. Commanders keen to justify the slaughter took the German collapse in late 1918 as proof that it worked.

In fact, while Germany sought peace that year for a variety of reasons, running out of soldiers was not one of them. As Winston Churchill pointed out in the 1920s, Germany inflicted far higher casualties on the Allies than it received.[6] More recent analysis suggests the ratio was 35 to 50 percent in Germany's favour, more than enough to offset the population differential. Furthermore, the number of Germans turning 18 in any year of the war exceeded field deaths by a factor of at least 1.5.[7] As Churchill noted, German conscripts were still plentiful at war's end, and the prognosis for 1919 was even better.[8] Nor did a huge death toll on both sides lead to the collapse of unit morale. Niall Ferguson has shown that the British regiments that were hardest hit, mostly Scots, did not suffer failure of spirit.[9] This was also true of the New Zealand Division, which broadly kept its chin up despite suffering one of the higher casualty rates.

General Sir Herbert Plumer (1857–1932), left, with New Zealand Brigadier-General William Garnett Braithwaite (1870–1937), May 1917. Despite appearances, Plumer had a sharp understanding of the tactics needed on the Western Front.

(Henry Armitage Sanders, gelatin dry plate negative, RSA Collection, Alexander Turnbull Library, PAColl-5311, G-13388-1/2)

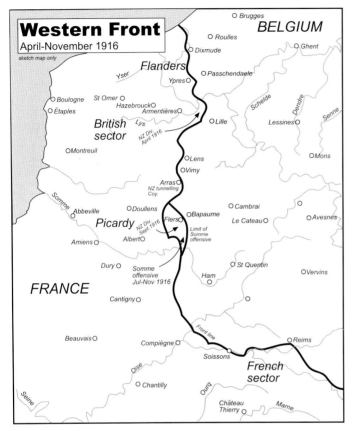

However, these realities were not evident in 1915–16, when the reduction of war to an accounting exercise had seductive logic in the face of the tactical deadlock. It occurred to both sides at about the same time, and was made feasible by the expanding bureaucracies of the period. Governments were capable of conscripting young men at ever-increasing rates while simultaneously organising other citizens to produce the arms and logistics to support them. Britain alone had just over a million men in the field by February 1916.[10]

The New Zealand Division, organised on British lines and fighting alongside British or Imperial forces, shared the experience. But it was not quite what myth suggests. Popular memory tells us that tactics devolved to a slow walk in line abreast towards enemy machine-guns, on the order of imbecile generals who were safely tucked away in distant chateaux.

In fact there is good evidence that most generals had a good picture of the field conditions.[11] Most also had a personal style. 3 Australian Division commander Major-General John Monash, for instance, never visited the front line, preferring to use maps and photographs to get a handle on what the men faced.[12] Russell, by contrast, went forward three or four times a week — this despite coming under frequent fire. He was not alone. 'This is a very big show,' New Zealand Brigadier-General G.S. Richardson wrote in 1916, 'and it is difficult to get into touch with people unless you are actually near their units — I certainly take an interest in the men, having risen from the ranks myself, my sentiments are sympathetic to the men in the ranks. Everything I do and every order I give is influenced by what I first consider will be its effect on the men in the Ranks …'[13]

Richardson ended up commanding the New Zealand forces in England; but many officers up to Richardson's rank or beyond habitually led from the front.

Their casualty rate was commensurate. New Zealand lost three general officers through the war, and Russell himself was 'nearly ... bagged by a sniper' in mid-1917.[14] His very narrow escape prompted alarm in New Zealand. 'Napier Johnston tells me you yourself run too many risks,' Minister of Defence James Allen admonished. 'I hope you will not do this in future.'[15] But Russell saw no option in light of his need to plan effectively and keep control of his battles.

Given the hands-on command style that New Zealand officers shared with many of their British counterparts, we have to find other explanations for the high death rate. One of the main causes was politics. As late as April 1916, with plans for an attrition offensive well advanced, the British government was wondering about resolving the war without great cost in lives.[16] But Haig bent to the demand for a decisive victory, and the result was a disastrous tactical compromise. As Rawlinson argued during the build-up to the Somme offensive, attrition demanded that the British strike only hard enough to draw von Below's three Corps on to well-prepared defences. But this would not bring the tactical victory Haig needed.[17] And so the attrition war became a succession of efforts to obtain a decisive breakthrough. The two goals were not compatible, and the price was paid in blood — British and Imperial as well as German.

Tactical problems compounded the difficulties. We have seen how lack of communications hampered co-ordination on the new larger-scale battlefield, but this was not the only issue. In 1914 the 'contemptibles' fought in platoon-based 'fire-teams', leapfrogging forward under cover of rifle or machine-gun fire. This emerged after the Boer War and was suited to the longer range battlefield. However, as has been argued, Kitchener's New Army of 1915–16 was trained by instructors unfamiliar with the new methods. Nor was there time to develop citizen soldiers to the levels needed to make fire-and-rush effective. So the army reverted to the old Napoleonic method of advance by wave.[18]

New Zealand's forces followed suit, and the lesson had to be re-learned the hard way — though most commanders were experimenting with new tactics before the Somme battles were over. Platoon-based organisation was enshrined in regulation by early 1917. Even so, it was 1918 before the techniques matured. In part this was a matter of practice making perfect, but commanders also had to cope with emerging technology. Devices such as portable field wireless were in their infancy in 1916, and until they matured there was no real answer to

## Landships

The tank was a British invention, though it cannot be credited to any individual. H.G. Wells popularised armoured 'land ships' in fiction as early as 1903, and the mechanical components — particularly the all-terrain combination of internal combustion engine and self-laying tracks — were all available. However, it was another matter to bring the concept to reality. Proposals were put forward by Colonel Swinton and Captain T.G. Tulloch in January 1915, but fell on deaf ears at the War Office, and first Lord of the Admiralty Winston Churchill finally spent naval funds without authorisation to get the ball rolling. The broad mechanical concepts were worked out by talented Director of Naval Construction, Sir Eustace Tennyson-D'Eyncourt; and the details were developed by Sir William Tritton and Major Wilson.

The first design was effectively an armoured box built atop a Holt tractor, similar to the vehicles used by the British to haul artillery; but early experiments revealed a shortfall in trench-crossing capability. A total redesign produced the classic rhomboid with tracks running around the exterior of a structure shaped to create the mechanical equivalent of a 20-metre-diameter wheel. It was too tall to carry a top-mounted turret, and the prototype emerged with casemate-mounted six-pounder naval guns, an all-up weight of 28 tons and a bellowing, unmuffled Daimler motor. Rather ironically — or aptly — it was given the official epithet 'Mother'.

The Mk I tanks that fought alongside the New Zealanders at Flers were soon superseded by the Mk IV. Variants included close-support 'Female' tanks with machine-guns. Despite being optimised for the trench environment, examples often became trapped; later trench-crossing aids included 'unditching' beams and 'fascines', great bundles of wood which could be rolled off the tank roof into a trench.

Iron centipede: a disabled Mk IV tank, February 1918.
(Malcolm Ross, Malcolm Ross Collection, Alexander Turnbull Library, PAColl-5192, F-17536-1/4)

communications beyond elaborate systems involving telephone, flare and messenger. None was reliable. Clarence Hankins, a signaller with the New Zealand Field Artillery, discovered the difficulties when he went forward to the firing line in June that year. Contact with his artillery battery was intermittent, so he repaired both phone and wire; but:

> *Communication went again about 1.30 at night. Went out with Withell on open mound bullets flying all ways. Luckily neither of us were hit. Found no fault & got thro [sic] alright after about an hours [sic] work. Don't want many more trips like that.*[19]

Tanks and aircraft were so new that nobody knew how to make best use of their strengths. Many lessons were learned the hard way, arguably because a rigid British army hierarchy deterred lower-level innovation.[20] However, the carefully controlled combined-arms tactics that finally emerged in 1918 were decisive not only during the 'hundred day' offensive that led up to the armistice, but also during the Second World War.[21]

This learning experience came at a cost in lives, and was particularly damaging for Britain in 1915–16 because the 'new army' was partly built up of 'Pals Battalions', an outcome of a recruiting tactic that played on local spirit to create new units. In theory, friends and family trained and fought more easily together; but the cost became brutally evident in the first Somme engagements of mid-1916, when the Leeds Pals Battalion was among more than 32 such units that suffered over 500 casualties.[22] Suddenly, the glorious notion of patriotic neighbourhood chums fighting shoulder to shoulder did not seem such a good idea.

New Zealand did not directly share the 'pals' phenomenon. Although battalions were organised on provincial lines, there was a good deal of mixing, in part to avoid shared community tragedy. However, this intent was defeated by a national population little larger than a British county. The army contribution ran to one in nine, of whom more than half were killed or wounded. Many families lost multiple sons over time. Brothers Edwin and H. George Clark died of wounds in 1917 and 1918 respectively. When Oliver Stayte was killed in January 1918 his brother Jesse tried to find the grave 'to send a little of

New Zealand's base establishments in Britain included hospitals and convalescent homes. This is Hornchurch Convalescent Hospital.

(Photographer unknown, Alexander Turnbull Library, F-57935-1/2)

the earth … to mother in NZ for that is all I can send her from him'.[23] Then in late October, with talk buzzing of an armistice, Jesse Stayte was killed. Nor were families always successfully separated. Jim Handley and his brother were among those who died fighting side by side in battle.[24]

There were few degrees of separation even at national level. Eric Spedding discovered common connection with his company captain and the camp commander as soon as he reached Sling Camp in mid-1916. Within two days he had run into two others he knew directly.[25] Later, as platoon commander in 4 Otago Battalion, he found an 'old OBHS [Otago Boys High School] chap who I used to be fairly chummy with', and soon made contact with four old schoolmates.[26] Such experiences were typical. During the attack on Flers, Tano Fama took a stretcher party to rescue a wounded soldier, who 'turned out to be young Booth of Patea and I knew him'.[27] Richard Tuckey was treated by a doctor in the field who had treated his sister back in New Zealand.[28] N.E. Hassell recalled the time when one soldier's insistence that he was 22 was rubbished by another soldier nearby — a former next-door neighbour who knew the young man was but 15.[29] John Harcourt was recognised by Brigadier-General W.G. Braithwaite, who asked after his father.[30]

Partly for these reasons New Zealand shared the British social response to war, both at home and in the field; and the historically important point is that neither Britain nor its far-flung Dominion gave up, despite enduring such shattering loss for years.[31] However, none of this was obvious in 1916, as the British laid plans to fight an attrition battle on the Somme. As it happened, Haig was beaten to the attrition punch by the Germans. In late February, Falkenhayn launched a gigantic barrage against the French fortresses around Verdun,[32] specifically to draw the French army into the mincing machine and force a collapse of morale.

It was at this moment that the New Zealanders arrived in theatre.

## Young Kiwi soldiers at Armentières

France was very different from Gallipoli or Egypt. The New Zealand front sliced through the willow-spotted banks of the Lys with barbed wire and mine. Fertile fields, tended by generations, lay churned by shell, muddy morasses littered with abandoned farm equipment. But grass still flourished in no-man's land, curling around the mines and wire. Other defences were built amid meadow and wood, adding tactical complexity to the battlefield. In this environment, picturesque villages, rising as French villages do with suddenness from surrounding farm and copse, became tactical objectives. By 1916 only about a third of the local population remained.

Russell arrived on 14 April to find nothing ready.[33] He was concerned by the proportion of newcomers in the division, and wanted 'time for officers and men to become fully acquainted with the local conditions'.[34] A cold spring was leavened with icy rain that turned the ground into sludge, and an extra blanket did not much relieve the misery. When the move was finally made into the trenches, the men of 3 (Rifle) Brigade had to go 'without a sufficient supply of steel caps'; and a captured German declared that the local wire was 'rotten'.[35] Those on duty in the fire-trench faced a vigilant enemy across a sixty-odd yard

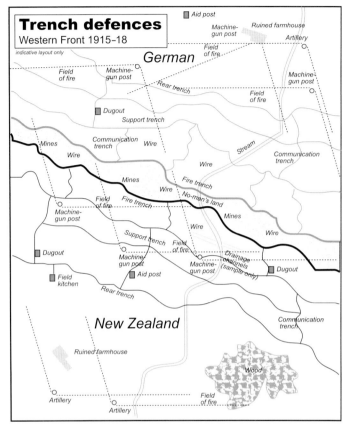

strip of no-man's land laced with tangled wire-and-timber 'gooseberries', mines and booby traps.

The New Zealanders set themselves up in defensive localities along the trenches, separated by gaps that were well enfiladed from the flanks and rear. None of this was achieved easily, and as late as 12 June, Birdwood was 'not too well pleased' by what he saw in the 2 Brigade sector, though Russell thought it was mainly because the work was half finished.[36] It was late June before Birdwood was satisfied.[37]

The men had to get used to new rules. Bollinger found his camera a problem in the face of censorship.[38] Smartness and saluting were another bugbear. 'As yet they are very slovenly,' Russell penned in his diary, 'and make a bad figure amongst the more disciplined soldiers of Europe.'[39] Birdwood wanted action, but Russell knew he had to reason with his men. Saluting and 'general bearing' were not 'matters of discipline … as such', he argued, but did reflect 'self respect'; and while this had little to do with fighting ability it did make a 'bad impression'. This same understanding of the colonial ethos also told him why his countrymen were behaving badly. 'To be smart and alert isn't servility', he declared, and he urged every man and officer to 'walk about as if he had £10,000 a year'.[40] Part of the problem was New Zealand equalitarianism. As late as October 1917 it was possible for Kenneth Luke, a junior officer, to rush up and clap his old friend Harry Holmes on the back, and get a like response — this despite the fact that Holmes was a Brigadier-General.[41]

Adaptation took time, and during the first months in France convictions for insubordination, drunkenness and absences skyrocketed. More than half of those convicted were given field punishment, which could involve being tied to a wagon wheel or tree for up to two hours a day. Seven death sentences were handed out to New Zealand soldiers in August 1916, a quarter of the 28 meted out in the division during the war. Most were commuted, in line with Haig's general aim, but three of the 1916 sentences were carried out. However, the initial rate of offending fell sharply in September,[42] probably driven by the fact that the men were settling, though arguably the officers were also on a learning curve and had found ways of better handling their men.

For all that, disobedience did not mean the New Zealanders had degenerated to larrikinism. Those charged and convicted were a minority, and only a small core did not adapt. Russell wanted to bundle these 'incorrigibles' back to New Zealand lest they demoralise the rest, dismaying Allen. 'I really do not know what we shall do with them … They will only contaminate the rest of the community and create trouble.' His own answer was ruthless:

*Can you not give them the post of honour in the front firing line? It may be hard to say so, but my opinion is this, that they are either better shot trying to do their duty at the front, or reformed if possible by the knowledge that they have been called upon to do the most dangerous jobs.*[43]

Other reports implied that 'incorrigibles' were simply ordinary Kiwis who disliked army discipline, a theme that certainly emerged in some post-war writings. 'Sneered at, pestered by overbearing bullies', at least one New Zealander 'gradually hardened into [a] defiant and reckless trouble seeker, for whom orderliness spelt disguised abuse'.[44] Russell seems to have eventually understood. It was early 1917 before he concurred with Allen's request, and then only after seeing 'incorrigibles' in battle:

*We are not sending back any more incorrigibles. I agree with you that we must make the best of our own bad bargains. The front line, as you suggest, sounds a very fitting spot for some of them, and having actually enquired into the behaviour on the Somme of those who were marked down as very undesirable members of society, I am satisfied that they fight just as well as, though I will not admit better than, those who have learnt, or who know, how to behave themselves …*[45]

The problem was pinned down to a response to military training. 'I see that my rough guess of the percentage of good and bad was a pretty shrewd one … I was rather surprised that the conclusion so far is that the very bad get worse; that the good get stronger and better.'[46]

The other divisional problem was more easily fixed. Most Kiwi soldiers had terrible teeth, and the army went out of its way to deal with it. The work done was an extraordinary indictment of New Zealand's dental health; the 1998 men of the 17th Reinforcements alone received 6335 fillings, 5237 extractions and 854 dentures before despatch, 'leaving 371 fillings, 48 extractions and 32 dentures still to be done abroad'.[47] Some of the false teeth were, as Jesse Stayte observed, 'vomited … overboard' during bouts of seasickness on the way across.[48] A dental hospital was also set up at Étaples, where wounded men were treated before discharge back to their units, and no fewer than five dental establishments were set up in Britain.[49]

These were pioneering efforts, but Russell still found the 'state of teeth in the Division was deplorable' in mid-1916 — something that impacted on fighting efficiency — so he 'concentrated all the [dental] mechanics I could lay hands on, and set up as big a Dental establishment (mechanical dentistry only) as I could in Armentières … They tell me they did £1600 worth of work a week'.[50] The experience helped persuade the government to set up a school dental clinic service after the war.[51]

## The jaws of hell

Trench life on the Western Front had a character of its own. There was better defence in depth than in Gallipoli; rows of diggings extended well back from no-man's land, a network of fire, communications and support excavations that was easy to dent but hard to break. There were dugouts, even roofed areas and spaces for rough bunks. Logistics were better organised than on the peninsula, and field kitchens produced relatively regular meals, sometimes with food scavenged or bought by individual platoons to supplement the ration. Braziers helped keep the men warm, fuelled with coke issued 'on a fairly liberal scale'.[52]

Most garrisons lived under threat of shell, bullet, mortar or gas. The skies buzzed with aircraft, friend and foe; and the men felt naked under their gaze.[53]

Enemy aircraft ranged far behind the lines, often strafing or bombing known billets. They did not fly much after dark, but night brought new reason for fear. 'Ares, the Great God of War, stalked,' one New Zealand soldier recalled nearly two decades later; 'you could see him pass as you peered into the black night.'[54] Even the glow of match or cigarette could become a target for enemy snipers. Sentries were doubly alert in the gloom, demanding passwords from those moving even short distances along the fire trenches. The call 'Who goes there?' was pregnant with anticipation: would it be death at the hands of an arriving German raider, or would it be life, as a friend slipped into view?

Much of the environment reflected the way the race to the channel had played out in 1914, when the British were left at the bottom of a succession of watercourses and slopes. Sandbags had to be laid to bring the parapet up to a useful height in the Armentières sector. Here and in the Ypres salient the men slithered over duckboards at best, waded ankle-, calf- or thigh-deep in sludge at worst. 'Trench foot' was endemic, not much alleviated by the efforts of fatigue parties tasked with bringing each man a fresh pair of socks daily from giant laundries set up behind the lines. The men recognised the physical contrasts, as John Fraser mused in 1916:

German prisoners of war carry wounded soldiers into Spice Farm, Ypres salient, after the successful New Zealand assault of 4 October 1917. The muddy wasteland beyond typifies conditions across virtually the whole front.

(Henry Armitage Sanders, RSA Collection, Alexander Turnbull Library, PAColl-5311, G-12932-1/2)

> By Jove, lots of mothers would not have known their own sons after being up at the front line for a week or so, and we were absolutely covered with mud, dirty and unshaven. I often laughed at myself and thought how funny it would be to walk into the house with my old muddy clothes and boots on.[55]

Mud was, however, the least of the problems. The same low-lying land and high water table made waste disposal difficult, however carefully or deep the latrines were dug. At worst the men fought amid their own sewage. Those who fell wounded risked infection — this in pre-antibiotic days. Others became ill with 'trench fever' or other disease. Lice were also endemic, and the fact that the experience turned 'lousy' into a pejorative was small comfort to those who had to suffer.[56] These were not the only unwanted companions. 'Rats,' Dr A. Martin declared, were 'very plentiful' in the Houplines trenches.[57] Clarence Healey found other rats in Armentières.[58]

Stretches of line were riddled with the remains of the dead, soldiers who could not be retrieved during battle or who had been buried in too-shallow graves. Martin saw the 'feet of a dead German sticking out of the ground' in

New Zealand reinforcements heading for the front near Kansas Farm, Ypres salient, the day after the disastrous attack on Passchendaele.

(Henry Armitage Sanders, RSA Collection, Alexander Turnbull Library, PAColl-5311, G-12933-1/2)

New Zealand trenches during September and later found a 'badly decomposed' German in a dugout. These sights attracted ghoulish attention from some quarters. Martin discovered the New Zealand sector full of sightseers, and not just Kiwis, feeling it was a 'lesson to the soldiers to see these trenches'.[59]

The appalling environment made an impression on all who had to live in it, among them J.R.R. Tolkien, serving with the 11th Lancashire Fusiliers. He penned the first words of his Middle Earth mythos in the trenches, and his Dead Marshes were a direct echo of front-line conditions in Flanders. Like Tolkien's marshes, the grotesque morass in which the New Zealanders had to fight wrinkled noses miles behind the line.[60] It was palpable, tangible — to Claude Weston, even capitalised: 'the Stench'.[61] Lime chloride did little to relieve the problem.

To give army authorities their due, divisional commanders never put all their units into the lines, and formations that had to commit reserves during pushes were relieved quickly if possible. New Zealand's 23 straight days in combat during the Somme campaign later in 1916 were unusual, and most soldiers spent more time out of the trenches than in. Even so, men who had been rotated out knew they would soon be back. They had to find ways of enduring both place and the terror of being under fire; and they adapted, burying old ways under a veneer of the new. The transition came over weeks or months; Jesse Stayte was horrified by his first visit to the trenches in October 1917,[62] but by mid-1918 his attitude was more relaxed.[63]

As with all social phenomena, 'trench culture' had its built-in contradictions. It was a coping mechanism rather than a way of life; nor did every soldier subscribe to it in every detail. But it was generally shared by British, New Zealand, Canadian and Australian alike.[64] Its standards were not those of the wider world, and the tensions between the value systems caused stress; but for many New Zealanders the adaptation was not difficult. Blokish colonial culture emphasised an indifference to the visceral.[65] The unpleasantness was identified, remarked upon, then accepted. 'There is a beautiful odour in the possie where we are,' H.G. Clark wrote to his family, 'but [I] am quite used to it now as one has to acquire a nose for this sort of thing.'[66] Another soldier refused to describe the 'hideousness of this wicked war' in letters home — and with his next breath declared: 'however, we had a job to do'.[67]

*Opposite above*
Brave face for the photographer. Men of 3 Battalion pose with a wounded companion amid duckboards and sludge near 'Clapham Junction', Ypres salient, late November 1917.
(Henry Armitage Sanders, RSA Collection, Alexander Turnbull Library, PAColl-5311, G-12979-1/2)

*Opposite below*
Battle behind the lines, this time against trench foot. The men at the front were issued with fresh dry socks daily, demanding an industrial-scale laundry operation not too far back from the trenches. This particular laundry had a staff of 20, all over 45 years old, who produced 4000 clean pairs of socks daily.
(Photographer unknown, RSA Collection, Alexander Turnbull Library, G-13179-1/2)

Depersonalised death was part of the mix; after a while, bodies were part of the scenery. When one soldier went souvenir-hunting in Delville Wood later in 1916 he found 'pieces of men on the ground, an arm here & leg & head there', added 'it is a horrible sight', and carried on with his hunt for spent munitions.[68] One unit even used part-buried bodies as navigation waypoints.[69] By 1918, some thought little of using thinly buried Germans as an observation platform — gruesome, as one soldier put it, but 'a good stand'.[70] All recognised the environment as horrible, few wanted to come back to it, but they still consciously called it 'home'.[71]

Niall Ferguson has argued that many British soldiers had little difficulty killing Germans,[72] and New Zealand soldiers apparently shared this mind-set. It was a learned response. On Gallipoli, many Kiwis felt very sorry for the Turks; but as the Western Front developed, few worried much about an enemy depersonalised as 'Hun', 'Bosche' or more usually 'Fritz'. One motivator seems to have been revenge, fuelled by field comradeship. As one soldier put it in 1918, 'We were all naturally nervous at the start but once we started and saw our mates going down all fear vanished and our one aim was to get to them with

The funeral of Sapper J.F. Haynes, New Zealand Engineers, early May 1917. Adaptation to life in the trenches did not reduce the sorrow when comrades died.

(Henry Armitage Sanders, RSA Collection, Alexander Turnbull Library, PAColl-5311, G-12761-1/2)

our bayonets.'[73] Another candidly declared in a letter home that: 'Brian had a cobber of ours killed near him and ... got into the Huns' trench and he DID kill. Hands up and running away ... He is a good shot — 'nough said.'[74] The pseudonymous 1920s prison inmate Dawes Bently[75] recounted the 'maniacal hatred' spurred in the minds of men such as Doug Stark by the death of a comrade in 1918.[76]

The risk of being killed seems to have been accepted. Some were resigned to it. 'I am never likely to see New Zealand again,' one soldier declared in a dismally frank admission to his family.[77] But others were more optimistic. 'We were practising an attack today,' Stayte declared in mid-1918, 'and everything points to a Stunt shortly ... We don't mind as long as there seems to be a reasonable chance of getting through.'[78] Eric Spedding put it clearly in 1916: 'We make an advance this afternoon, and with God's guidance and protection I hope to win through all right. I feel quite calm, and am anxious to do my bit.'[79] Spedding was killed next day. But as Tano Fama related, although some wondered whether 'I'll be next', there was little time to 'dwell too much' on 'such morbid thoughts' in the heat of battle.[80] He was not alone. John Harcourt

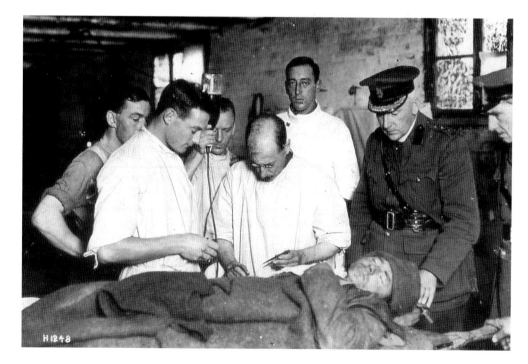

Members of the Second New Zealand Field Ambulance administer a gum infusion to a wounded soldier.

(Photographer unknown, RSA Collection, Alexander Turnbull Library, G-2076-1/1)

was 'absolutely cool' during action in early 1918, despite being 'windy' beforehand — and was well aware of the mechanisms, remarking later on the curious psychology of it all.[81]

Even wounding was just part of this environment, often neither sought nor avoided. 'One Hun plane passed over our huts,' Heseltine penned in 1917. 'The searchlight was on him and aircraft shells were bursting all around him, pieces were dropping in our camp on top of our tents, but we didn't care, a chap might get a Blighty if a piece hit him in the right place …'[82] Others took the risks in their stride. 'If we got killed it wouldn't matter where it happened and if we didn't get killed the more places we saw the better!'[83] Even in quieter periods the risks of the front did not spur drama:

> *A pair of mules were just in front of me when one mule fell over, it appears the mule was hit in the flank by two stray bullets from a machine-gun some Australians were practising about half a mile away, the poor mule died an hour after. I was walking quite close up behind the mules, another two feet further or I would have stopped the bullets, but my luck was with me …*[84]

Such laconic words betray the matter-of-fact life of the trenches. But it could be nothing else; it was too horrible for words; it had to be normalised. Most soldiers succeeded. Intense emotion usually came only during the hours after battle. It was here that the terror became real, that the strains of the unanswered 'fight or flight' reflex had to be met; here that men had time to recount these feelings in their diaries or letters home. 'It is the dizzy limit and I hope I never see the rotten place again or such ghastly sights as I have seen down there,' John Fraser wrote after leaving the New Zealand lines on the Somme.[85] But he had endured it.

The dark hours made the death of mates difficult to take. H.G. Clark found a casualty list while in camp during mid-1917, and 'my word it was hard as some of the boys I knew personally'.[86] Most soldiers were saddened, dismayed and upset at the loss of friends, brothers, cousins and comrades; 'poor old Frank Wilson',[87] 'poor kid',[88] 'a finer chap one could not wish to meet anywhere'.[89] In 1917 James Evans lamented the loss of Frank Hare, 'wounded by a

The road to hell — Menin Road, leading out of Ypres, probably during 1917. Hessian-cloth screens helped shield man and beast from being targeted by German shellfire, but this route to the front earned the epithet 'Hellfire Corner'. New Zealand reinforcements heading to the front in 1917 passed along this dire track in their thousands.

(Photographer unknown, Alexander Turnbull Library, F-51945-1/2)

shell at 2 pm & died on arrival at the dressing station — another splendid fellow gone'.[90] Nor was the effect of such loss back in New Zealand forgotten. Letters from commanding officers to grieving family back in New Zealand were riddled with words to cushion the blow: death had been instantaneous or without pain; the lost soldier was killed doing his duty; he died in company of comrades and friends.[91]

In the end, though, even death was accepted as just another element of an environment that all knew to be hell on earth. Many soldiers sustained themselves with the thought of a return to villages with hot food and warm bedding. It was this, and not the trench environment, that elicited the deepest emotions. Heseltine's disgust at being billeted into an 'old shed at the back of a farmhouse' was complete:

*Oh My God I nearly cried, an old shed at the back of a farmhouse, wet stinkin' manure over the boot tops, to get to the door one look inside was enough for me. Two mules at one end and us to live at the other on lousy stinkin' straw. I don't know how our officers can ask to live in such dirty holes, they have white sheets and good beds, but us boys that are fighting for our country, we are nobody, just treat [sic] like pigs and asked to sleep in pigstys. Life is not worth living. I often wish I had been killed and out of the way. Hundreds of our boys pray for their death many a time; dear Mother, I wish you could see the little place where I am now sleeping four of us in a wee farm an old one time pig stye [sic] stink something awful, but it's good enough for us ...*[92]

Their difficulties did not go unnoticed. 'Every day when I see what the men have to put up with in the way of danger and hardships,' Russell reported in 1917 to Defence Minister James Allen, 'it astonishes me with what cheerfulness and fortitude they put up with the very trying conditions they have to meet ...'[93]

Some of that strength was a product of army camaraderie. Cecil Malthus found existence 'more satisfying' than civilian life for these reasons — 'it was corporate, not competitive, and characterised by a sharing and acceptance that banished all worries and cares'.[94] As at least one historian has remarked, gallows humour also played a part in the adaptation to this world.[95]

Like soldiers from all ages, many also drew fortitude from the bottle. The New Zealanders were notorious for their ability to imbibe, in part a legacy of settler-age 'bloke' culture.[96] Wine, beer and spirits were on sale in cafés and estiaments, and the Kiwis were helped by pay rates that began at four shillings a day,[97] a figure which inspired jealousy among Tommies surviving on but one. 'Pay day', J.C. Heseltine exalted in early August 1917. 'Half holiday four of us famous drifters have been drinking glorious beer all afternoon celebrating third year of [the] war.'[98] Some drank in the trenches. A fortifying nip of rum was usually doled out before the men went 'over the top', but the men sometimes brought in more. N.E. Hassell found one group of New Zealanders 'drunk as owls', sitting in a shell hole while shells burst around them.[99]

Leave was another escape valve worth 'much honour and glory'.[100] Soldiers with three or four days in hand could get to London or Paris. The latter was off limits to British forces, but in late 1916 Russell was able to get permission for a 'few men every day' to 'go down for a couple of days' leave'.[101] The men appreciated the gesture. 'It's lovely to be away from the horror stricken battlefields of France,'[102] J.C. Heseltine declared in 1917. Yet the vast majority of

*Above*
Practising for the 'off'; a British picture of troops at exercise, copied into a New Zealand soldiers' album.

(Kippenberger Military Archive and Research Library 2002-7)

*Right*
Dark side of war; a mass grave, probably near the front lines. Verse above the picture in the original album is poignant: 'Before he was aware/The "Verey" light had risen … on the air. It hung glistening … A rifle cracked. A dauntless New Zealander fell!'

(Kippenberger Military Archive and Research Library 1992-760)

soldiers returned when their time was up. It was 'cruel coming back to the war';[103] but as Heseltine put it, 'someone has to do the cruel work'.[104]

This resigned attitude was the key to trench culture and does much to explain how the war could be maintained for so long. The British and their colonial children also seem to have been better at it than the French, who suffered extended mutinies in 1917 at the hands of a disaffected *poilus*. Potentially the 'stiff upper lip' played a part; and in New Zealand's case the image of the tough colonial male probably contributed. Leave, drink, and the knowledge that front-line duty was temporary helped make it endurable. Comradeship was a key part of the mix. One soldier even suggested the loss of that close friendship made some men sorry the war was over — they could never again know their friends in dangerous times, feel the 'joy of hearing the roar of the guns' and know they were playing their part, 'never again to know a friend inside and out, and know that his life would be given for ours as willingly as ours would be given for his'.[105]

For all that, trench culture was not a normal way of life; in the psychological sense it was game-playing, and none could play the game indefinitely. Most New Zealanders survived it to the end of the war, though with increasing difficulty. The reserves of emotional strength on which most drew to make trench culture work were a limited resource. Many of them knew it. 'I could stand up to anything in the way of shell fire for the first couple of years,' one soldier wrote, 'but the last year or so was my undoing. Every burst used to set me all quivering …'[106]

A minority had an immediate reaction, sometimes triggered by small or chance incident, often during the aftermath of battle. The resulting 'combat fatigue' was decried initially as cowardice, prompting a culture of shame. Some internalised the problem. A handful tried suicide; but more often — though still infrequently — those wanting out wounded themselves, taking the risk of often harsh disciplinary action. A small minority walked off the line, sometimes involuntarily. One soldier came under shellfire in his bivouac and 'ran half a mile' to get away from it, then sat down to devise 'ways and means of getting back to New Zealand without getting caught'. Sunrise brought a change of heart and 'by the time dawn had fully arrived I was quite content to go on again'.[107]

Actually walking out was risky. There was virtually no chance of getting away with it, and desertion was very harshly treated. Of the 28 New Zealanders sentenced to death in the First World War 26 were deserters, and 5 executions were carried out in spite of recommendations from GHQ to commute them. It has been argued that three, at least, were victims of combat exhaustion.[108] The New Zealand government finally recognised the issue in late 2000, passing legislation to pardon the men post-fact and 'remove, so far as practicable', the dishonour to the soldiers and their families.[109]

Defection was almost unheard of. The New Zealand Division suffered just one throughout the war — Private W.P. Nimot, who crawled out of the New Zealand fire-trench in early 1916, slithered into no-man's land, and surrendered.[110] There was talk that he had been a spy;[111] but the Germans merely put him into a POW camp.

All this must be put in perspective. Trench culture was a coping mechanism, a palliative rather than a cure. It embodied deep contradictions that could never be entirely resolved, and even those who survived the war without apparent breakdown did not get a free ride. The terrors lurked beneath the surface of conscious thought, often for the rest of their lives.

## Slung into Sling: discipline, tourism and temptation

The trenches were not the only shaping forces New Zealand soldiers faced through the war. British discipline and the sights and sounds of Britain and Europe added to the mix. The War Office made the decision to shift the New Zealand base to Britain in late April 1916, and New Zealand support forces were split between various depots. The No. 1 General Hospital was set up in Brockenhurst in Hampshire; and another went up at Codford, near both Sling in Southern England and the Command Depot in Wiltshire.[112]

For most New Zealanders, though, camp meant Sling — the main training establishment and a place synonymous with privation in the colonial mind, not least because it was 'jolly cold', as Thomas Lynch discovered in October 1917.[113] Another decried the area as dreary.[114] However, its advantages outweighed such matters in the army mind — New Zealand authorities knew the

'Salisbury Plains may sometimes be rather inclement in the winter', but the place at least had huts, which could not be guaranteed elsewhere.[115]

Bryan McDermott arrived by train from Plymouth in 1917. He saw fields flashing past the windows with the 'old typical farmer, dressed in his old fashioned suit cap and walking stick ... looking over his stock'. There were tea urns at Exeter railway station, where the local council gave the New Zealanders a 'paper bag containing a cake'. He discovered Sling was set amid 'miles of rolling, open country ... and the existence of an aerial school a short distance away accounted for so many [aircraft] hovering about'.[116]

The men were 'drafted indiscriminately' to sub-camps. 'I must explain this,' Eric Spedding wrote in August 1916. 'No. 1 [Camp] is 1st Battalion and joins No. 1 Brigade, the old Main Body in Flanders. No. 2 Camp is No. 2 Battalion and No. 3 Camp is the Rifle Brigade. The Rifle Brigade [3 (Rifle) Brigade] get a very poor hearing here — I do not know why, as one is considered unlucky to get into them ...'[117]

School experience and basic training in New Zealand were nothing against British army discipline, with its attention to authority and minutiae of uniform. Both were part of a conditioning process designed to reduce men to automatons in the face of mind-battering fear; but they also reflected British class society, which New Zealand did not really share.[118] By the First World War the approach also had a name: 'bullshit', which had such specific meaning in the context of army spit-and-polish that it became the de facto technical term.[119] 'The discipline ... is much stricter than New Zealand, and many rules that hit us rather hard are strictly enforced,' McDermott grumbled in his Service Diary, adding: 'the angry roars, curses and uncomplimentary remarks of the instructors showed only too plainly that Trentham style was completely out of favour here'.[120] Another was 'mighty glad to get away from the Tommy officers at the school', and 'hope I never have to go to another'.[121]

Formality and the gulfs of rank stood at odds with the relaxed New Zealand approach. Eric Spedding found an old friend among the ranks when he reached Sling in mid-1916:

> *He was invalided with a bad leg from Egypt ... By Jove, he has improved, and what is more he plays the game — whenever I speak to him if there*

*are other officers present he springs to attention and always comes out with 'Sir'. I dislike his doing this, but it shows a chap up in his true light.*[122]

Others did not put up with it. 'One of the Boys are [sic] falling in every day for C.B. for giving cheek to the instructors,' Jesse Stayte remarked.[123] The worst aspect, in the minds of many Kiwis, was the 'Piccadilly Stunt':

*All the troops in Sling are lined up about half a mile away from camp and to the accompaniment of two Bands we have to march past a Saluting point where the Salute is taken by the Colonel, and for the last 200 yards there is a Sergeant or Corporal on each side of the road and they are in pairs every half chain and we march past them they are continually chipping us … 'hold your head up, get the step, correct that slope, do up that button, put up that chin strap etc. etc.', till they would make you wild and if you say a word you are punished for insolence.*[124]

New Zealand officers dine alfresco during a heatwave. White cloth over the trestle table underlines the refined expectations of officer culture; but the New Zealanders never wholly subscribed to the soldier-officer separation in the British sense.

(Henry Armitage Sanders, RSA Collection, Alexander Turnbull Library, PAColl-5311, G-12818-1/2)

It got worse. Spit-and-polish was mere prelude to the real work of training. McDermott received:

> six days in musketry instruction, ... As far as I can remember, I scored 125 points out of a possible of 70, which qualifies me for a marksman. The shooting over we were sent into the bullring, which is a section of the parade ground where bomb throwing, gas resistance, constructing entanglements, bayonet fighting, company drill, and instructions on working the Lewis machine-guns are all taught, a lesson on each subject being given each day for about an hour. The bayonet instructors are particularly keen, and have us doubling about in all directions in order to 'liven us up'.[125]

Sling was not without compensations. The camp was a little part of New Zealand, half a world away from home, and a giant Kiwi carved into the chalk hillside above created a distinctly antipodean air. And there were opportunities to play tourist. Edwin Clark and several friends took a three-day weekend jaunt to Portsmouth in early 1916. He had 'not been there before' and 'quite enjoyed it'. Even the Salisbury Plains had appeal. One weekend Clark 'went to Salisbury … and it is a very pretty place … the remarkable thing about it is the way the houses are all together … The cathedral is a very pretty one …'[126]

## Tourism and temptation

The Kiwis at Sling were not the only ones just a skip and jump away from the delights of Britain. The First World War was largely fought on Britain's back doorstep, and New Zealand soldiers could be in combat one day, take a train and fast cross-channel packet to England overnight, and be eating breakfast in a London hotel by 8.30 a.m. next morning. Ormond Burton thought it dislocating,[127] and he was not alone in such sentiment. 'Arriving in London and seeing and being among our own spoken people is just like a dream to me,' Heseltine declared in July 1917, 'passing from one world to another.'[128]

Other New Zealanders went to Paris, 'gay Paree' to Charles Kerse, 'a glorious city, you can't possibly imagine the lovely streets and shops, etc …'. He found

Paris in summertime, 1918. High life went on in the city of romance even at the height of the war, and New Zealanders were occasionally able to get leave there — a special privilege that was not shared with the British. Kiwi soldier Charles Kerse thought the city 'glorious'.

(Laurie C. Mackie, Alexander Turnbull Library, PA1-0-311-1-3)

the windows of Notre Dame 'the loveliest sight you could care to imagine'.[129] Perhaps with the Wazir experience in mind, British authorities were reluctant to allow antipodean troops to visit, and Russell only turned the issue by arguing that the trips were educational. Even so, he was 'warned afterwards by the provost marshal' that 'in the case of the slightest trouble' the visits would end.[130]

Paris, however, ran second to Britain. At a time when New Zealanders fancied themselves to be more British than the British, London was the centre of New Zealand's cultural world. Many soldiers volunteered in the hope of seeing it, and long-held anticipation did not dim the wonder of the bustling metropolis, 'a great eye opener to us new chums ... mighty London'.[131] Despite the intermittent attentions of high-flying Zeppelins and monstrous Gotha bombers, the city was barely touched by war. 'London is the place for me,' Heseltine penned in his diary.[132] Others found it curious. James Evans was 'Very much taken with the quaint old customs'.[133] Many enjoyed the entertainments of the West End. Jesse Stayte found the House of Commons disappointing, but was 'astonished at the fearful amount of traffic in the streets' and 'much taken with the internal beauty of Westminster Abbey'. He had just four days in the city but thought 'it would take a year to see it and I was thinking all the while how I should have enjoyed the sights if Mother was only with me'.[134] The lure of the city outstripped that of his hotel:

> It is so long since I slept in a nice bed that I felt like staying in all day, but four days' leave soon flies and I want to see all I can, so I had breakfast and went off down Holboro ... Petticoat Lane on a Sunday morning. I cannot describe this place better than comparing it to a

*thousand cheap Jacks all talking together. You can buy anything in this world there.*[135]

Most soldiers stayed at the New Zealand YMCA facility, or the New Zealand Soldiers' Club. This, Stayte declared, was 'the best place I struck and the cheapest. The food is splendid and the beds good. Tariff, bed eightpence, breakfast eightpence, dinner one shilling and ten pence'. Officers could afford hotels. Many went to the Royal Overseas Officers Club, established in the 'magnificent building' of the Royal Automobile Club. The stiff civilian entrance fee of fifty guineas was waived.[136]

Some found accommodation elsewhere; Eric Spedding hoped to see London, was called up to the front, but still managed to see the city briefly before hastening to France. As an officer he had the cash to stay at a 'ripping hotel', the Regents' Palace in Piccadilly; but it was full and he instead went to the Cecil. He lost no time sightseeing. St Paul's was a 'glorious place', but he was most impressed by the Tower of London. 'Ye Gods! It is worth seeing. We went through all the old dungeons and saw captured cannons, models of kings in armour, etc etc …'[137] Others found the streets and markets magical. Kenneth Luke went through Rotten Row and Hyde Park, amazed to see 'all these much talked about places'. For him the main impact of London was the sight of women smoking and drinking in bars — a novelty for someone from New Zealand with its near-exclusively male pubs.[138]

Only a few Kiwis were disappointed with the Imperial capital,[139] but many arrived with more on their minds than the scenery. Ormond Burton remarked that London teemed with women — and the Kiwi soldiers were eager to experience the 'glamorous mysteries of life'. True romance seldom flourished; some women developed genuine relationships with the New Zealanders, but the practical reality was that most men found their way to seedy locales where, as Burton delicately put it, the 'semblance of love' was 'bought and sold'.[140]

It was often cheaply bought. One New Zealander discovered the going rate in Dublin was sixpence, though he 'never became a purchaser', and the soldier wondered how a living could be made out of it.[141] It was about $2.50 in early twenty-first-century money. However, there were hidden costs at all levels, not least for women often driven unwillingly into prostitution by financial necessity. The biggest practical problem was disease. The average rate of venereal disease (VD) in British forces was 4.83 percent per annum,[142] but New Zealand's was higher, perhaps a reflection of the access made possible by their higher pay rate. In the three months between November 1917 and February 1918, for instance, 2.77 percent of 4680 New Zealand soldiers sent on leave in London contracted it; and 2.82 percent of 920 soldiers on leave in Paris suffered the same fate.[143]

It was a worry to government and army, reducing the number of men fit to fight and carrying moral connotation in that age of social purity. Popular wrath exploded when expatriate New Zealander Ettie Rout began distributing contraceptives to soldiers on leave. Her motives were practical and cynical. 'You cannot keep soldiers away from girls by making speeches to them or playing cards with them in the evening,' she argued in early 1917. 'We must take facts as they really are and not how some of us wish them to be. By all means let us try to maintain ethical controls, but these things have become shadows in these abnormal times … Don't, don't, DON'T rely on "moral suasion" alone.'[144]

Rout's analysis was cynical but also brutally realistic, her campaign perhaps the only practical one under the circumstance, but it ran against the abstemious ideals of social purists whose cause had been intensified by the war; and Rout did herself no favours by buying into their argument, even condemning 'English Puritans' as the 'most poisonous form of organic life'.[145] Tempers ran high, and as Allen remarked to Russell, it was 'difficult to restrain some … from making violent attacks'.[146] Russell merely urged Rout to act 'in strict accordance with regulations', on the logic that 'those with whom she comes in contact will undoubtedly connect her and her actions with New Zealand'.[147] However, his own recommendations were surprisingly similar:

> We must admit that Venereal Diseases exist and that prostitution exists, and that, in spite of all that has been done by Chaplains and Officers from the moral standpoint, we have failed and will fail to prevent the men from consorting with the latter and becoming the victims of the former. I am, therefore, entirely in favour of the issue of prophylactics and would even go further than General Richardson in that I would make the issue to men going on leave … obligatory; at the same time

*saying that he … can either throw it away or give it back on his return, and that, if he plays the man, he will have no need for it … I am of this opinion because many a young fellow starts out on leave without the least idea of self-indulgence, but the temptations he meets, both in London and Paris, are unknown to him … The above appears to me all the action that can be taken by the military authorities. Moral on the part of the Chaplains and Officers, medical on the part of the N.Z.M.C., practical in the provision of prophylactics …*[148]

Allen did not think Russell's pragmatic reconciliation of reality with moral fortitude would get far. Massey was 'against the use of prophylactics but I asked him to suspend judgement until he saw for himself the conditions prevailing in France and England'.[149] Russell raised the matter with the prime minister, but quickly 'desisted because evidently Massey has very strong opinions on [the] subject at variance with those which I hold myself, and I did not think I could do any good'.[150] Massey's sentiment highlighted the gulf between civilian life and the attitudes of the front; and by mid-year Allen, too, had decided against compulsory issue of prophylactics, reminding Russell of the 'necessity of stiffening up the moral fibre of your soldiers, especially with regard to the question of immorality'.[151]

# 3

# THE SOMME

In June 1916 the New Zealand Division was administratively transferred to 2 Anzac Corps, again coming under Godley — though he was not wholly in favour by this time. Allen aired his concerns to Birdwood. A 'good deal' had been 'said about him in New Zealand … For some reason or other Godley was never popular with his staff in New Zealand and he is not popular with the Expeditionary Force now.'[1] Neither Birdwood nor Allen doubted Godley's abilities, but the issue rankled for months, even drawing parliamentary questions in New Zealand.

The division was not the only New Zealand force in France. There was also a company of tunnellers under Major J.E. Duigan, who reached the theatre in March.[2] They were despatched to join 3 Division at Arras, where British engineers were burrowing under the German lines. The New Zealand excavations embodied place-names from home, broadly arranged from north to south. Few Germans could have guessed the sequence behind Russell, New Plymouth, Auckland, Wellington, Nelson, Blenheim, Christchurch, Dunedin and Bluff.[3]

An advanced New Zealand base was set up alongside the British base in Étaples — a 'stinking hole' to one New Zealander who passed through in mid-1916.[4] Another decried it as 'a few sand-hills and thousands of tents', cursed by its denizens because of the 'gruelling days in the notorious "bull ring"'.[5] The division entered Corps reserve at the beginning of May, headquartered at Estaires; but within the week orders came to relieve 17 Division, four miles (6.5 km) east of Armentières. 1 Brigade began moving to the l'Epinette sector. 2 Brigade moved to Houplines, squaring up with the river Lys on one flank, leaving 3 (Rifle) Brigade in reserve at Armentières. It was very much an Anzac effort; the Third Australian division of Major-General John Monash held the next sector along.

Conditions were very different from Gallipoli. New Zealanders rotated out of the line were often able to rest in billets, sometimes with proper beds and sheets. Some lived in Armentières, famous as the subject of Edward Rowland's adapted marching ditty; but it was too close to the front, and Clarence Hankins found the once bustling town 'deserted except for a few little shops that still keep open'. Most sold 'stuff that soldiers will buy' or were 'eating houses';[6] and although the four shillings a day paid to private soldiers did not stretch particularly far,[7] it was still better than the single shilling paid to the typical Tommy. Cafés were commandeered or became associated with particular units. The men made friends with remaining villagers, were welcomed into homes, and did what they could to help. But the town was often under fire, half ruined, its clock frozen at 11.30,[8] and part of the enduring tragedy of the war came when new friends were killed by barrage or bomb.

Men of the New Zealand Tunnelling Company in their bunks. This unit reached France in March 1916 and began work on a massive series of excavations around Arras.

(Henry Armitage Sanders, Making New Zealand Collection, Alexander Turnbull Library, F-1984-1/4-MNZ)

## The battle of the Somme

German forces opposite the New Zealanders held ground rising back to the Perenchies Ridge, itself part of the defences of nearby Lille. Their trenches were drier, in places even concreted and equipped with electrically lit bunkers, and their effluvium drained towards the New Zealand positions. The Germans soon discovered who they faced, and in late May a rifle grenade rattled into the New Zealand lines bearing a note: 'What time is it, Anzacs?'[9] A few days later a placard appeared, taunting the New Zealanders about a British defeat at sea — the first news of the Battle of Jutland. It could not be refuted; the Admiralty initially released the official German communiqué to the British public.[10] Martin called the revelation a 'cold douche … out here we feel very blue.'[11] But better news came next day, and New Zealand soldiers were able to hoist a chart showing actual losses.

These assaults on morale were sometimes accompanied by informal truces — particularly at mealtimes. In fact the New Zealanders developed a particular

Laurie Mackie photographed this field cookhouse on the Somme in mid-1916. Army authorities tried hard to make regular hot meals available to the men in the front lines, although everything from shellfire to gas could foil the effort, and meals were often lukewarm or cold by the time they reached the long-suffering troops in the fire trenches.

(Laurie C. Mackie, Alexander Turnbull Library, PA1-0-310-16-1)

relationship with the Saxon divisions, a 'fairly friendly crowd as far as conditions of war would allow and we were always pleased to meet up with them again', as one soldier put it.[12] There was nothing like the sports matches of the infamous 1914 winter truce, but the Saxons usually announced themselves with a chalked sign, and as the New Zealanders 'held no grudge' the trenches often fell quiet. New Zealand infantry even hurled occasional 'humorous messages across in bully-beef tins'.[13]

Such fraternisation was frowned upon by the officers. In any case truces were inevitably broken, and a kind of informal currency soon emerged; if German artillery fired a round, New Zealand's fired two, duly reciprocated. These brief paroxysms of action punctuated an otherwise dull existence.

At the end of June 1916 the New Zealand Division joined a general effort to draw German attention away from the battle of the Somme. The British had high hopes for this offensive. Haig committed 25 divisions to the push, hoping that unprecedented artillery would smash wire and trench, allowing General Sir Henry Rawlinson's Fourth Army to break the German line. Lieutenant-General Sir Hubert Gough's Reserve Army would then exploit the gap. It was an ambitious plan, though flawed by confusion between goals. To some officers, as Major-General Archibald Paris remarked, the real objective was to 'kill and capture Bosches'.[14] However, the tactical plans for breakthrough belied such aim. A week-long barrage began on 24 June, but when lines of 'Tommies' went 'over the top' between the Somme and Ancre on 1 July they found the wire still uncut. The British Army suffered 57,470 casualties in 24 hours,[15] of whom 19,240 died[16] — the worst day in its history. Tactical victory was arguably unattainable after this rebuff.[17] However, Haig pressed on, throwing Gough's army into the fray.

At this stage the New Zealanders were limited to diversionary raids. Aerial photographs became a staple planning tool, and the Kiwis even built replica trenches in which to practise. Divisional artillery registered targets on and behind German lines, including known billets; and over an 18-day period from 24 June fired up to 3000 rounds per day. The Germans often replied, sometimes in prelude to a raid of their own, forcing the New Zealanders to scurry for cover — and occasionally units even slipped into no-man's land to escape the fire.

The men of 3 (Rifle) Brigade launched the first raid on the night of 25 June. It was presaged by a sharp artillery bombardment, and then 72 men under Captain A.J. Powley surged into the German fire-trenches, capturing nine prisoners along with a good deal of equipment and papers. Powley won the MC, and two of his officers the Military Medal. A week later, 1 Wellington Battalion launched another raid into a junction between two German divisions. The preliminary bombardment cut the wires and 81 men advanced to find German infantry 'cowed by our artillery fire'. Two New Zealanders were killed and one wounded,[18] but they took their toll and Russell was pleased with the outcome.[19]

A raid by 2 Wellington Battalion failed the following night — the 'Bosch had an inkling and was prepared'.[20] This did not diminish the effort; Sergeant-Major W.E. Frost was recommended for the VC, and in the event received both DCM and Medaille Militaire. Later raids were prosecuted with equal verve. Sergeant J. Courtney distinguished himself in the first week of July, leading a foray into no-man's land and then returning alone to look for the wounded and missing.[21] The Germans responded on 8 July with a ferocious bombardment against the Mushroom, a bulge in the New Zealand line. The 'monstrous tumult' left Cecil Malthus buried under timber and earth and was prelude to a raid that left the Germans temporarily in possession of the Mushroom.[22]

Godley's call for nightly raids was never met, but by the time action fell away in mid-August the New Zealanders had launched 11 assaults. Casualties and personal sacrifice were high, particularly on 13 July when the Otago Battalion threw more than 200 men into the fray, of whom but a handful returned unwounded. Malthus calculated that he had only had about 30 minutes' sleep a night during his eight-day stint in the front.[23]

The New Zealanders were partially relieved by 18 Division early in the month and relieved altogether during the third week of August, when 51 (Highland Territorial) Division took over the sector. The Kiwis moved by rail to the 'delightful rolling country' of Abbeville for a rest and further training.[24] New Zealand's stint at Armentières cost some 2500 casualties, including 375 dead and 30 missing.[25] Fresh forces were brought from Sling to fill the gaps, among them Eric Spedding. Although his 14th Reinforcements had only arrived in August, he and a dozen other officers were called to the front at the beginning of September. Spedding 'wanted to see London first' but 'got quite excited at the prospect of … having a "smack" at the "great push" which is coming soon'.[26] In the end he was able to spend ten precious days in the Imperial capital, and by the third week in September was attached to a company of the Hawke's Bay Regiment.

## The attack on Flers

In September 1916 the New Zealand Division joined Major-General G.S. Horne's 15 Corps, part of General Sir Henry Rawlinson's Fourth Army, for the battle of Flers-Courcelette that was intended to extend the Somme offensive towards the Ancre River and Bapaume. Flers lay amid three layers of defences. The southwestern defence — and the first New Zealand objective — was Switch trench complex. Its supporting excavations lay less than a thousand yards south of Flers. The second line, the Flers trench system, ran through the southern outskirts of the town and northwest past Eaucourt Abbey. About a thousand yards beyond, protecting the village of Gueudecourt, lay the Gird trench network.

All were designed around interlocking strongpoints; troops who took the outer layers were certain to come under cross-fire from the inner. Tactics were further complicated by rising ground and woods, the latter formidable barriers for horse-drawn artillery and transport. Forty-nine Mk I tanks were also available, waddling into battle for the first time amid the guffaws of the Tommy soldiery.[27] These hulking 28-ton rhomboids with massive side-slung naval guns and unmuffled Daimler motors were production copies of the prototype, 'Mother',[28] and the New Zealanders were intrigued. Like his British counterparts, Tano Fama could:

> *hardly resist bursting into laughter. They were reincarnations of such things as I used to read in my youth in the 'Frank Read' or 'Jack Wright' editions of the Penny Dreadful. The most wonderful thing about them is the mode in which they are constructed, so as to overcome the ordinary difficulties of locomotion over broken or shell pitted ground. They certainly do good work and it is a great pity that we haven't a few thousand of them.*[29]

*Above*
Wreckage of the first tank used in the war, deployed in direct support of the New Zealanders near Flers. These 'land dreadnoughts' were ungainly, slow, dangerous to their crews, and unreliable — but battle-winning when they worked, and the social impact was extraordinary. London socialites watched erotic dancer Regine Flory perform the 'Tanko' in November 1916; there were bawdy music hall songs; and cinematographers deliberately emphasised the abstract Cubist imagery of the rhomboid with its revolving tracks and hard-angled surfaces.

(Kippenberger Military Archive and Research Library 1990-1712)

*Below*
Battle terrain: New Zealand horse-drawn transport files past a giant shell-hole, possibly in the Somme region. Sustained trench warfare quickly reduced the territory well behind the front into this dismal and somehow lunar landscape.

(Henry Armitage Sanders, RSA Collection, Alexander Turnbull Library, PAColl-5311, 13512-1/2)

Fama was not alone in such sentiment. Winston Churchill was deeply critical of the way the first handful were so 'improvidently exposed' when the obvious tactic was deployment *en masse*.[30] In the event, only 32 were mechanically sound enough to fight when the moment came.[31] However, the arrival of the 3rd and 4th Bavarian divisions hinted that Germany was digging deep into its reserves, and there were hopes of a breakthrough. The New Zealanders were one of three divisions deployed for the assault, and Russell went to look at the Somme battlefield on 7 August, finding 'heavy shelling going on but unaimed mostly'.[32]

The engineers and Pioneer Battalion came under 15 Corps engineers, working on trench systems along Bazentin Ridge and into Delville Wood. Russell set up divisional headquarters southeast of Albert, 'all under canvas'.[33] The divisional artillery was divided by brigade and attached to the 14th and 7th Divisional artillery, partly for tactical reasons. John Fraser recalled the journey:

> This last march was about 15 miles, but Lord, it seemed 30 owing to the dust. From this camp at night we could see the Shrapnel shells bursting and hear the roar of the guns at the Somme, our final objective. On Sept 10 at 5 pm we once more started on a march of 6 miles to a hill overlooking the old original front lines of trenches near Firecourt … How our people got them out of those trenches and dugouts is a miracle, as the dugouts were over 30 feet down in the earth, and divided into rooms for sleeping in. In one I climbed down into, there were some dead Huns which did not smell too sweet, so I climbed out to fresh air again.[34]

The New Zealanders reached the front in time to be met by a German barrage, and 3 (Rifle) Brigade deployed into the front on 10 September, settling into former German trenches near High (Foreaux) and Delville Woods — territory so recently taken that the dead still lay where they fell.

By this stage tactical thinking had gone beyond the barrage-and-walk of the early Somme battles, though advance was still by waves. Objectives were carefully laid out, colour-coded, and timed to match a rolling barrage that blasted the ground about 120 yards ahead of the men. No preliminary barrage was planned; the British had learned from bitter experience that this gave away

*Opposite above*
Death's Valley, Somme battlefield.
(Kippenberger Military Archive and Research Library 1990-1712)

*Opposite below left*
This jumbled ruin of shattered debris was all that remained of the main street in Flers after the battle.
(Kippenberger Military Archive and Research Library 1990-1712)

*Opposite below right*
Stretcher-bearers during the Somme battle, from an album of collected pictures and ephemera apparently assembled some time after the war by a former soldier of the New Zealand medical corps. A verse below the picture reads: 'Do you remember the duckboard track, The broken strands of fire, The shell-torn mud – the abandoned trench – Swept by Fritz's fire?'
(Kippenberger Military Archive and Research Library 1992-760)

surprise. The tanks were viewed as mobile pill-boxes — fair assessment given their expected speed through trench and shell-hole of 33 yards per minute (1.8 kph).³⁵ The New Zealand advance from High Wood was geared to help protect the flank, and objectives included both a sugar factory and a trench system on high ground known as Grove Alley.

Russell put 2 and 3 (Rifle) Brigades into the assault, holding 1 Brigade back as reserve.³⁶ Plans were well advanced by the second week of September; he attended a final Corps conference on the 12th, and by next day thought everything was 'on a sound footing'.³⁷ The men readied their fighting kit — '2 days' rations, oil sheet, 2 sand bags, 220 rounds of ammunition, and 2 Mills bombs'.³⁸ It was a hefty load for men who were expected to fight. Mills bombs were in short supply, but there were still 'heaps' of them 'lying around', causing what Martin called 'lots of accidents'. One man was killed when he accidentally released a pin; while, as Martin wryly observed, another soldier from 4 Battery dropped a bag of them. 'There were 15 casualties.'³⁹

The 14th was a difficult night. 'Hope our [boys] win through,' Martin penned in his near-illegible doctor's scrawl.⁴⁰ Russell was worried by lack of munitions — there was 'some trouble getting flares and [Mills] bombs'.⁴¹ The reserve infantry arrived in Fircourt Wood, 'sleeping there under what was left of the trees';⁴² and the eight companies from Auckland and Otago battalions ordered to make the assault were in place by midnight. The sector was surprisingly quiet and sleep might have been possible in the forward trenches, but few men snatched more than a brief rest. In the pre-dawn gloom they were served breakfast and a swig of rum. By 6.00 a.m. the soldiers stood, tense and nervous, waiting in the fire-trenches with fixed bayonets. Twenty minutes later the artillery spoke, a rolling bass thunder punctuated with the calico-tearing scream of shells.

The New Zealanders surged up the scaling ladders and over the top into the dawn mist. They embraced the barrage, advancing in waves of eight platoons along the churned wake of the plunging shells, pausing to fire, then moving again. The defenders fired back, but within a few minutes the New Zealanders ran over the outlying defence line, Coffee Trench, and into Crest Trench, where about 200 Bavarians were put to flight.

Switch lay 150 yards beyond; but as the New Zealanders advanced — now ahead of the British forces to their right — they came under raking machine-gun fire. Soldiers fell like mown grass. Eighty or ninety men lay dead in a few minutes, and 26-year-old Sergeant Donald Forrester Brown and J. Rogers crawled forward to deal with it, silencing the gun in the first of the actions that won Brown a Victoria Cross. But men continued to fall, and one soldier recalled that by the time the fourth and last wave arrived, the combined force was scarcely larger than one of the original waves.[43] They surged into the Switch trenches, wanting to 'get at' the Germans 'with bayonet',[44] and a furious melee erupted.

Men found themselves doing things they might never have considered in peacetime; one soldier used the dead body of a German as a ladder to vault himself out of a trench, then coolly shot and killed another who was running away.[45] By 6.50 a.m. the New Zealanders were in possession of the Switch system.[46] Elements of 3 (Rifle) Brigade came up, ready to move to the next objective. They were supposed to have tanks with them, but the huge vehicles were still plagued with breakdowns. Lack of armoured support did not daunt the New Zealanders, and the men of 4 Battalion sang as they moved through Switch. They were on the second objective by 7.50 a.m., backed by 2 and 3 Battalions and apparently undaunted by artillery shells crashing around them. The Germans had been caught by surprise; 6th Bavarian and 50th Divisions were in the throes of relieving the 3rd and 4th Bavarian when the barrage began.

Tanks were meant to lead the attack into the outskirts of the Flers trench network, but were still not in position when the moment came, and New Zealand infantry again pushed ahead without them. But then 3 Battalion ran

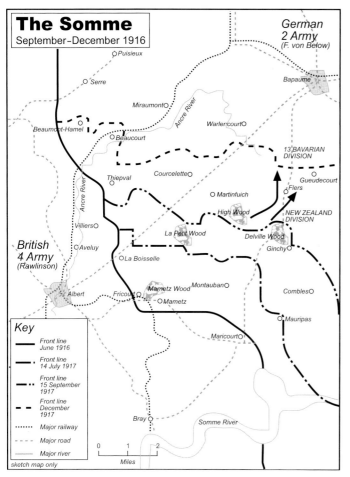

into intact wire nests ahead of Flers trench and stalled. machine-guns blazed from behind the barrier, sending the New Zealanders diving into shell-holes. Efforts to breach the obstacle with wire-cutters were foiled by the heavy fire, but around 10.30 a.m. two tanks finally snorted up, and the crew of the first dealt with the problem by driving over it, crushing both wire and machine-gun nest.[47] The vehicle then provided cover for the New Zealand infantry, who advanced in the lee of its steel walls into the Flers support trench.

By mid-afternoon the New Zealanders were settling into their objectives. But they were thin on the ground, and in the face of a looming counter-attack, Brigadier-General W.G. Braithwaite sent 2 Wellington Battalion into action on the outskirts of Flers, backed by the tank 'Diehard'. By day's end the advancing forces, British and New Zealand, were in possession of Flers and the trench systems to each side.

It was not a cheap victory. The New Zealand Division took more than 2500 casualties including 'a good many officers',[48] and had yet to reach final objectives towards the Gird trenches. One soldier approached Flers to find the town reduced to a heap of rubble:

> … up a sunken road lined on either side with broken wagons, smashed guns, dead Huns, mangled horses and mules … the whole scene being a horrible one to view … Probably no smell on earth can be compared to the awful sickening sweetness (I use the word deliberately) that hovers for weeks over a battle field. The fumes from cordite, ammonal, gun-powder, poison gases, and decaying mules and horse all combine to make one hideous smell that is peculiar to the battle field alone, and one that sickened me far more than any of the pitiful sights did.[49]

Soldiers and medical corps alike laboured to ferry the wounded from the field. 'High wood (or what was left of it) was a veritable shambles,' N.E. Hassell wrote, 'with mangled bodies or small parts of them, in all sorts of grotesque and hideous positions, here a body with no head, here a half body only, here a leg and foot … details too hideous to recall. We picked many men up only half dead and sent them back on the limbers. I don't suppose many of them lived but it was all we could do.'[50]

*Above*
A captured German trench with New Zealand regimental aid post, during the first day of an unidentified offensive, possibly the Somme, September 1916.

(Henry Armitage Sanders, RSA Collection, Alexander Turnbull Library, PAColl-5311, G-13497-1/2)

*Right*
An advanced New Zealand dressing station on the Somme.

(Henry Armitage Sanders, RSA Collection, Alexander Turnbull Library, PAColl-5311, G-12928-1/2)

Even prisoners were called in to help. Tano Fama had 'four hefty German [prisoners] helping me and they seemed mighty pleased to do it too. Poor devils, they had the life terrified out of them through the vigorous distribution among them of "iron rations" by our guns.' Ambulancemen were cut down as they worked, and it hurt Fama to see 'our own stretcher bearers lying dead on the track … chums who a few moments before were full of life and vigour now lying dead beside the patient they were carrying'.[51] Doctors, too, died under fire, among them Martin, killed while 'bandaging a wounded man'. Fama was impressed. 'All the doctors displayed a disregard of their own personal safety when there was work to be done, that provoked our highest admiration.'[52]

A renewed attack was planned next day, beginning with a long barrage. A company-strength German counter-attack partly disrupted the push, but the New Zealand attack broadly got under way at 9.25 a.m., led by 1 Wellington Battalion. All did not go well. The men failed to reach their first objective, and then 41 Division failed to capture Gueudecourt. Rain began spattering from grey skies late on the 16th, filling the trenches with water and sludge. Fama later recalled that:

> *It sometimes took us several hours to get a wounded man in from Flers, a distance of about three miles. No one … can have any conception of the state of the country. Closely pockmarked with shell holes the ground soon became sodden and muddy. Wet through and mud covered from head to foot, we had to toil night and day with very scanty chance of a sleep or a wash. I had not had a shave or a wash for nearly a fortnight when I arrived in hospital … We seldom came through the German barrage of fire without losing one or two of our own stretcher-bearers and the question uppermost in each one's mind was 'will I be next?'*[53]

The strain began to tell. Hassell saw his first case of 'shell shock', a man who acted normally until they jumped into a sap, then 'went all to pieces and began scrabbling around in the dirt and yelling fearfully'.[54]

These were the conditions in which the division supported an effort by 3 Corps to take a ridge on the left of the New Zealand sector. It was topped by a trench known as Goose Alley and had to be taken before Gird trenches could be tackled. Even getting to the starting point was hazardous:

*Well, off we started, and didn't we get it going up; of course there were no saps to get cover in so it was a case of just marching along a road that Fritz was shelling very heavily. Up this road I saw sights that I never want to see again. It was awful, dead and wounded lying round everywhere. One shell landed about 2 yards from the end of our Company, wounding about 11 men of my platoon, they dropped all round me, how the pieces missed me I don't know. The boy next to me got a piece of shell in his hip, and one on my right had his left arm shattered … we reached a sunken road in what was left of the village of Flers, and had 10 minutes' spell.*[55]

A soldier on the Somme, probably 1916.

(Photographer unknown, Alexander Turnbull Library, F-89217-1/2)

They had to run the gauntlet of a machine-gun post, but finally reached the start point around 1.00 p.m., half an hour before they were meant to launch the assault. Then word came that the '"stunt" was off as the troops on our right had failed to take their objective'.[56] The men dug in:

*The weather changed again to rain and very cold, and Lord, the mud, it was over our boot tops, there was no 'bivvie' to sleep in, so it was just a case of sleeping standing up. The old trench started to fall in on the sides, Hell, it was the limit. Then our rations and water went astray, I never craved for a drink of water like I did in this trench, tucker we could do without, but water, no. However, next day some of the boys went foraging and managed to get 2 gall. [gallon] tins of water and a few loaves of bread. The water tasted of benzine but it was not too bad. On the morning of the 20th about 4 a.m. we were relieved by our 2nd Brigade and made our way across the shell-torn country to a place where our cooker was and had some tea and stew, our first meal of anything hot for three days. By jove, it was good too, a great stew, fresh meat, pork and beans, and potatoes, tell you I did have a gorge.*[57]

Other efforts to push the line at its eastern end were frustrated. C.H. Weston recalled a desperate night on 18 September in steady rain, lit by the flashes of shells illuminating a 'long string' of men bent under loads, struggling forward on soggy ground. He moved past a dressing station to see 'many helpless wounded' lying soaked to the skin. Unburied corpses were scattered about, and 'the Stench followed us'.[58] It was a scene from hell. However, Russell remained optimistic. 'Am I satisfied with the result?' he asked himself on the 20th. 'Yes.'[59]

Fighting flowed around Flers for another fortnight, finally stalling amid increasingly stout resistance from 13 Bavarian Division. Wet weather hampered everything. 'Communication trenches very wet and muddy and must get duckboards down,' Russell scribbled on the 21st. Real progress had to wait for fine weather,[60] but the New Zealanders laboured on. Spedding led 50 men to lay railway lines up to the trenches. 'We were shelled heavily by the Huns … HE [high explosive][was] dropping all round and so I had to withdraw [my] men.'[61] Although Gueudecourt fell on 26 September there was still no breakthrough. 'We are still at it, hammer and tongs,' Russell wrote to his sister on the 29th. He was disturbed by the loss of life, but believed the 'Boche is

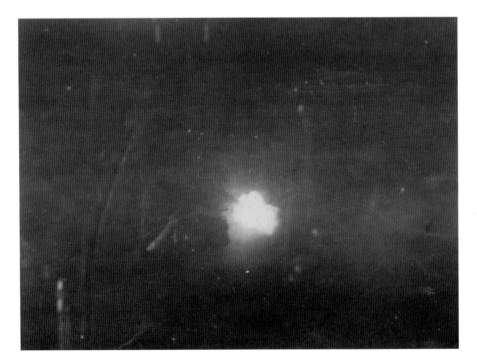

Gun-flash at night on the Somme front during the 'big push', September 1916 — another of Laurie Mackie's images. In theory private cameras were forbidden on the Western Front; Mackie's collection is a rarity.

(Laurie C. Mackie, Alexander Turnbull Library, PA-0-310-11-1)

getting pretty tired'.⁶² In fact the Germans were replacing their worn-out defenders with a fresh division, 6 Bavarian.

This stood in contrast with the weariness of the attackers. The New Zealanders nonetheless played a part in a final effort to take Eaucourt l'Abbaye on 1 October. 'The NZ Divn. have a comparatively small objective,' Russell remarked after a Corps conference to discuss the advance on the 30th, 'but a somewhat difficult one depending as it does on the success of the adjoining [47] Dn. who have the major operation.' He took Horne up to the Switch trench to show him the terrain.⁶³

The assault was scheduled for 1 October and preceded with a hefty barrage, including bursts from oil-mortars. Eric Spedding was optimistic: 'We make the advance this afternoon and with God's guidance and protection I hope to win through all right. I feel quite calm, and am anxious to do my bit. Au revoir for the present.'⁶⁴

The guns roared, and 2 Canterbury Battalion pushed three companies into low ground between Goose Alley and the portion of Gird trenches still in German hands, under cover of machine-gun fire. They took the trenches with heavy losses. Otago Battalion attacked from the southern end of Goose Alley trench and mowed into Circus, but were held up by a machine-gun. Sergeant Donald Brown crawled forward until he reached the point where he could tackle the crew hand to hand. The gun was silenced; but Brown fell to an anonymous bullet. He was awarded a posthumous Victoria Cross.⁶⁵

Spedding was wounded late in the action and brought into an ex-German trench that the New Zealanders were using as a dressing station. He was 'a real hero', another soldier wrote, 'pretty badly knocked about and had to remain there some time — but never uttered one complaint and absolutely refused to drink until thoroughly satisfied that we had ample for ourselves. We did everything possible for him.'⁶⁶ He died on 2 October.

Russell was dismayed by the British performance. 'The division … entrusted with the taking of Eaucourt l'Abbaye made a mess of it, and our flank was very much up in the air.'⁶⁷ The men of 3 (Rifle) Brigade laboured knee deep in mud as they tried to consolidate, relieving the exhausted and decimated 2 Brigade. By this time the whole New Zealand Division was tired; and 41 Division relieved them on 3 October. The New Zealanders had fought for 23 days and achieved spectacular success by the standards of the campaign, although losses were commensurate. Some 7000 men were casualties and over 1500 died.[68]

Part of the divisional artillery remained in contact with the Germans through October, and New Zealanders serving with British forces fought on under increasingly difficult conditions. One of these soldiers produced Britain's last gain of the campaign. A final effort to take Beaucourt in November would have ended in stalemate had it not been for a young Wellingtonian serving with 63 (Naval) Division. With his men falling around him, Lieutenant-Colonel Bernard Freyberg improvised a new plan, securing Beaucourt on 19 November at the cost of serious wounds to himself — wounds so dire he was first laid out with soldiers expected to die. His outstanding performance won him the VC and was classified by General Sir Beauvoir de Lisle as 'the most distinguished personal act of the war'.[69]

## North to Messines

In mid-October 1916 the New Zealand Division — still minus its artillery — was ordered to relieve 5 Australian Division at Sailly, facing 2 Bavarian Corps. This sector was north of the main Somme battlefields, but Russell did not want more casualties than he could help. 'Men's comfort and safety first', he declared after a divisional conference on 21 October.[70] A channel had been cut to the Lys, but with his experienced pastoralist's eye Russell did not think 'full advantage' had been taken of the fall and it did not 'relieve us as it might'.[71] Later, near the stretch held by 2 Wellington and 2 Otago battalions, the divisional engineers dammed some of the ditches into no-man's land, backing water against the German trenches.[72]

As winter closed in during November the New Zealanders settled down to the familiar round of patrols, raids and skirmishes amid temperatures lower than any recorded for 33 years; and the Germans remained alert. Clarence Healey was in one fatigue party that got 'badly shaken up' when the Germans opened fire on them.[73] The soldiers slipped and slid across icy mud, and artillerymen had to take picks whenever they went to water the horses.[74] Christmas arrived wet and cold, sprinkled with shellfire. 'Had rotten Xmas dinner,' Harold Foley scribbled on Christmas Day. 'Wish I was in NZ.'[75]

Field cemetery. Thousands of New Zealand dead were buried in temporary graves such as these. Comrades made sure graves were as well tended as possible under the circumstances. After the war, all were reorganised by the Commonwealth War Graves Commission into orderly cemeteries.

(Henry Armitage Sanders, RSA Collection, Alexander Turnbull Library, PAColl-5311, G-12762-1/2)

It was mid-February 1917 before the weather began to pick up, and the tired Kiwis were relieved by 57 Division — though not before 3 (Rifle) Brigade launched a large-scale raid against 77 and 78 Landwehr Regiments. Some 500 men of 2 Auckland Battalion under Major A.G. Mackenzie rehearsed for weeks against mock trenches. Detailed preparations even extended to padding the duckboards in the front fire-trench to prevent the Germans being tipped off by the noise. Some 88 artillery pieces ranging from 4.5-inch howitzers to 60-pounders were deployed for the assault, backed by mortars and machine-guns.

The attack began with a short but sharp barrage in the dawn hours of 21 February, and 2 Auckland Battalion went 'over the top'; but the plan went awry at once. Amid pre-dawn mist and smoke the Kiwis overran the first objective, a derelict trench hardly discernible amid the torn ground, and surged directly into the German fire-trench, which many soldiers mistook for the derelict. A fair number of men pushed on and were caught by the New Zealand barrage. The cost was 18 killed and 76 wounded, and though Russell thought the affair 'fairly successful', he took Godley to inspect them on a 'very foggy' 21st, and felt it was 'easy to see from their eyes they had been thro [sic] a severe strain'.[76]

The division took over a stretch north of the Lys in late February 1917. The trenches were in poor order, and 3 (Rifle) Brigade arrived just in time to be met by a German raid. Shellfire cut the telephone line, and an SOS by Very flare went unmarked in the morning mists. The New Zealanders had their work cut out to make the sector defensible, but had not long begun when orders came to step north, relieving elements of 36 (Ulster) Division while part of 57 Division picked up the gap in the Australian part of the sector to the south. This put the New Zealanders into the St Yves, Messines and Wulverghem sectors at the south end of the Ypres salient.

Flanders was very different from Picardy; low, softly rolling, and — before 1915 — sprinkled with attractive farms and hedgerows. The highest hill available to the New Zealanders, Rossignol, stood 63 yards above sea level, a mountain by Flanders standards, and virtually the whole British defence of the southern Ypres front pivoted around it. Russell thought the hill was 'not a bad proposition — lends itself to defence'.[77] Wire rather than trees provided the main obstacle in woodlands blasted by months of artillery fire. Like Picardy, the Ypres salient was also a land of mud, fed in the New Zealand sector by the Steenebeek Stream and Douvre River. Rumour had amplified its nastiness. Most of the Kiwis found the place no worse than the Somme.[78]

New Zealand soldiers looking at the ruins of the Ypres Cloth Hall, 4 October 1917. The medieval trading town had been under German artillery fire for almost three years by this stage in the war.

(Henry Armitage Sanders, gelatin dry plate negative, RSA Collection, Alexander Turnbull Library, PAColl-5311, G-13129-1/2)

At the end of February Russell was told the division would be expanded to four brigades, each of four rather than three battalions. This was the outcome of some slightly fractious Imperial politics. Massey had bragged about the size of New Zealand's reinforcement pool to Haig during his visit in October; and a few weeks later the British asked New Zealand to form a second division. However, the idea did not go down well in Wellington. The problem was eking out manpower. Allen argued the toss, but in light of British hints that they intended a mid-year push finally buckled, compromising with a fourth brigade on the proviso that 'our monthly number of reinforcements should remain exactly as it is'.[79]

Russell's objections echoed those flowing from New Zealand. 'I think it is a mistake,' he confided to his diary, 'and it were better to use the Division more freely and absorb its reinfts [sic], in place of casualties.'[80] He was well aware of the rate at which men could be lost, and the extra brigade was not always under command — the British envisaged it as gap-filler or labour resource. To form it he was obliged to strip the other brigades of 'many of their senior and experienced Officers and N.C.O's in order to ensure that, when the Brigade comes over, it may be able to take its place either in the trenches or in practical operations at once'.[81] He was still trying to find them at the end of March, grumbling that 'new officers in big numbers' were required.[82] Other changes in the officer line-up did not help. 'We never seem to get straight and keep straight for any time.'[83]

The use of the brigade flew in the face of Allen's proviso that it would be 'attached to the New Zealand Division',[84] but the British habitually mixed and matched forces to create larger formations. It was a legacy of the Victorian-age regimental system, and worked well when Imperial fire-fighting was handled by brigade-sized forces. But the system stumbled on the larger scale of the Western Front, and fell over altogether when it came to handling Dominion forces with their separate administrative arrangements. From Russell's perspective the ad hoc loss of units created a planning headache and was an obstacle to a solid *esprit de corps*. He was not alone in such sentiment; and when New Zealand prepared for the Second World War 20-odd years later, one of the main concerns at divisional and government level was setting up mechanisms to ensure the experience would not be repeated.[85]

# 4

# PASSCHENDAELE

New Zealand's second full year in France was shaped by the tumult that followed the Somme campaign. Staggering losses shook the British spirit. Germany, too, was in difficulties. German Chancellor Theobald von Bethman-Hollweg approached US President Woodrow Wilson with a request for mediation in December 1916; but the effort foundered on belligerent pride, and the German administration — influenced, in practice, by Field Marshals Paul von Hindenburg and Erich von Ludendorff — decided instead to continue the war.[1]

Haig was promoted Field Marshal; but new Prime Minister David Lloyd-George, though determined to push the war to a conclusion,[2] wondered about the attrition strategy and openly questioned Haig's capacity to command.[3] The French did not seem much better off, and Joffre warned that his nation had but one major offensive left in them. Haig's plans revolved around an attack from Ypres, partly to relieve the abysmal tactical position — they were suffering around 7000 casualties a week merely to hold the salient. However, Lloyd-George preferred an Italian push into Austria, and Allied powers held a conference in Rome during early January 1917 to discuss it.

Here the decision was taken to launch another offensive in the west.[4] Lloyd-George backed it with caution; Birdwood found him 'cheery and confident' when he visited France soon afterwards, but without 'undue optimism about speedy victory, which so many people have foolishly entertained for months past'.[5] Haig still hoped to attack from the Ypres salient in February, but Nivelle insisted on an April thrust north of the Aisne. The British government concurred, and the pressure to make these efforts winning blows went on in early February when Germany began unrestricted submarine warfare. A revolution toppled the Russian monarchy in March, and while the new administration of Alexander Kerensky was grudgingly pro-Ally, Russia's domestic trouble was far from over and a separate peace with Germany did not seem far away at times. Russell, for one, was dismayed, telling Allen mid-year that:

> *Only a few short weeks ago I felt confident that the war would be over this Summer. I had counted without the Russian Revolution and all that it has entailed. As it is I see no hope of an end this year and am afraid that we must wait for 1918 …*[6]

Although the Germans were occupied in Russia, an offensive in the west could not be ruled out. Russell reported in February that the 'Bosche in our front has proved very mild and I think would leave us entirely in peace if we allowed him to do so'.[7] But by mid-March he had heard talk of a 'determined push by the Bosche' to take Calais, 'in which we must and will stick our toes in'.[8]

In fact Ludendorff was aware of his vulnerability north of the Aisne; he laid plans to fall back on what the British and French called the Hindenburg Line, and authorised the withdrawal as soon as Nivelle's plan was leaked to him.[9] The new line was a formidable obstacle, shorter than the old and far tougher. Nivelle, undeterred, proposed to flank it from Champagne while the British attacked Vimy Ridge. Assault preparations had been going on here since 1916 with the help of the New Zealand Tunnelling Company, and General Edmund Allenby's Third Army attacked in early April, principally using Canadian and Highland troops.

The assault delivered Vimy Ridge into Allied hands, but the same could not be said of an Australian attack at Bullecourt, while Nivelle's effort from Champagne was disastrous.[10] In early May the distraught and demoralised *poilus* of one French division mutinied, and the rot spread like wildfire until more than 50 divisions were affected.[11] Many agreed to defend their trenches but refused to attack; some raised the red flag and tried to dictate terms; others sent representatives to Paris; and more than 20,000 deserted.[12] Nivelle was sacked, and while Marshal Henri Petain eventually re-created an effective force, there was no chance of a major French offensive in 1917.

Against these dramatic turns the British fell back on Haig's plan to push from the Ypres salient. Germany had built a complex array of defences here, mostly based around concrete bunkers — and as Russell declared after a Corps conference on 7 March, the retreat to the Hindenburg Line released forces to 'harden things up our way'.[13] Haig decided on a step-wise plan, first taking Messines Ridge, then breaking the lines beyond and pushing into Belgium with the objective of denying Germany its U-boat bases at Zeebrugge and Ostende. And so the stage was set for what the British usually called the Third Battle of Ypres.

The New Zealanders knew it by its other name — Passchendaele.

## Bite and hold: the Messines offensive

The attack on Messines was code-named the 'Magnum Opus' in divisional paperwork,[14] and Russell put a great deal of thought into it. The division had not come up to his exacting standards, and at one stage in late March both he and Brigadier-General B. Napier Johnston inspected the artillery on a daily basis.[15] A whole British formations was put on relief duty, allowing Russell to rotate his brigades out for training at Tilques. Even so, it was the end of April before he felt satisfied, and he thought one exercise by 2 Brigade, under Brigadier-General W.G. Braithwaite, was 'very good indeed'.[16]

Messines Ridge was held by the German 20 Corps, part of Army Group Wytschaete, itself part of the force under Crown Prince Rupprecht. These units could flank British formations advancing from Ypres to the north, and the British had to take that high ground as an essential prelude to pushing hard east across a gently rolling vale towards Passchendaele. However, Plumer had no intention of over-stretching and with a new strategy dubbed 'bite and hold', envisaged taking Messines Ridge and straightening the line south of Ypres — but nothing more. He also intended to use every weapon at his disposal to get it, including 20 of the two dozen gigantic mines that engineers had been assembling under German positions on the ridge since early 1916.[17]

His plan projected a two-mile (3-km) deep advance along a ten-mile (16-km) front, via a series of tactical objectives — mainly trenches and strongpoints — dubbed the Blue, Brown, Black, and Black Dotted lines. The final objective

New Zealand forces in training for the attack on Messines Ridge.

(Photographer unknown, RSA Collection, Alexander Turnbull Library, G-12753-1/2)

was the Green or Oostaverne Line, running north from St Yves to Hill 60; and the New Zealand Division had the task of occupying Messines village, then advancing to the Black Dotted line. The distances were not great, but the Germans held a salient above the Steenebeek Valley that had to be taken to protect the New Zealand flank, and 25 Division were given the task.

Russell began considering his part of the operation in late March, working near the front line and even spending one afternoon 'on Hill 63 examining Messines Ridge'.[18] By early April a plan was 'beginning to take shape in my mind'. He envisaged using the 'smallest number of men possible' to leave a 'reserve for future developments',[19] and had a draft plan ready by 3 April.[20] Plumer liked it.[21] Russell's main problem was likely losses, and after one conference in early May he warned gloomily that 'At the end of the operations as outlined by the Corps Commander this morning, I will have expended my entire Division and will have no troops in hand.'[22] Some of his brigadiers, however, felt that such casualties were acceptable. 'It is far better to use up the whole Brigade,' Braithwaite argued, 'and gain our furthermost objective, than to fail to reach the last objective and yet have troops intact.'[23]

A good deal of work had to be done to prepare for the attack, made all the harder because, as Russell put it, the Germans were:

> *on the rim of the saucer, while we were at the bottom. Consequently, all our preparations in the way of improving our communications and assembly trenches had to be done at night. Every man in the Division had to spend his nights working, and getting what sleep he could during the day. This in itself was a severe tax on the men's endurance ... with the enormous concentration of artillery, life on the slopes in front of us had become practically impossible.*[24]

Engineers laid tramlines and dug assembly trenches with names such as Otira and Auckland. Russell was pleased, although as late as mid-May he felt there was still 'want of liaison' between 'infantry working parties' who were helping the gunners.[25] Munitions were stockpiled in mountainous dumps ready to feed the voracious maws of the artillery. Some 3,552,090 rounds were brought forward for 102 guns in the New Zealand divisional sector alone.[26] The allocation for 2 Anzac Corps included more than 200 weapons, ranging from

New Zealand guns in Ploegsteert Wood, mid-1917.

(Henry Armitage Sanders, RSA Collection, Alexander Turnbull Library, PAColl-5311, G-12769-1/2)

6-inch howitzers to one monster 15-inch gun. Tanks were also brought forward, under Corps command, and special efforts were made to conceal them from German observation.[27]

The artillery whirlwind began on 3 June, and drew retaliation. New Zealand forces assembling near Hill 63 had to wear masks as gas shells plunged around them. Russell attended the final pre-attack Corps conference on 5 June, then toured his commanders to find them 'all serene'.[28] Much rested on the mines, and though nobody quite knew what the effect would be on the Germans, few doubted the scale. More than one million pounds of ammonal lay under the ridge. 'Gentlemen,' Plumer reputedly told his commanders, 'we may not make history tomorrow, but we shall certainly change the geography.' Russell felt the men were 'extraordinarily confident of success', and later told Allen he could not 'speak too highly of the spirit displayed by everyone'.[29] By 2.00 a.m. on 7 June most of the 'cheery and confident' New Zealanders were assembled in the fire-trenches.[30] Seventy minutes later the British blew the mines.

It was the largest conventional explosion yet contrived in the history of warfare. One of the mines failed to go off, but it made little difference. The colossal blasts tore the forward slopes of Messines Ridge asunder and hurled the

New Zealand Lewis gunners in the front line, mid-1917. This semi-portable machine-gun was one of the key infantry weapons by this time, offering two or three soldiers a moderately mobile firepower well in excess of half a dozen riflemen.

(Henry Armitage Sanders, RSA Collection, Alexander Turnbull Library, PAColl-5311, G-19461-1/4)

very substance of the earth skywards on pillars of flame.[31] Carefully planned fortifications, concreted machine-gun nests, interlinked outer trenches, observation posts and dugouts vanished in a flash, reduced to rubble or overturned by the almost unthinkable forces dancing about the ridge. Shocked observers on nearby Kemmel Hill even saw a complete pillbox, dozens of tons of steel and concrete, spinning into the heavens. The tortured earth twisted and slumped, a 'big earthquake' hammered the waiting New Zealand soldiers,[32] nearby villages shook, windows rattled, and northern Europe trembled. Munitions workers near London, 130 miles (209 km) away, paused as the ground shook. David Lloyd-George, working into the small hours, felt the jolt in his Downing Street study.[33]

Some 10,000 German soldiers died in moments, crushed or asphyxiated as debris came thundering down. There were even casualties among British forces when tumbling clods slammed to earth among soldiers pushing into no-man's land.[34] They were keyed up to tackle the enemy, but found only broken men, young German soldiers stunned by blast and trembling from shock, their minds and bodies undone by the concussion. The New Zealanders, whose advance skirted the mighty Ontario Farm mine, cut the trouser buttons from their prisoners and sent the stunned Germans hobbling back to Allied lines.

Shells bursting on the New Zealand front line during the battle for Messines Ridge, 14 June 1917.

(Henry Armitage Sanders, RSA Collection, Alexander Turnbull Library, PAColl-5311, G-13399-1/2)

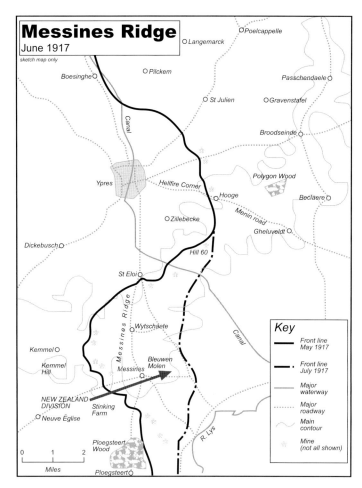

There was more resistance beyond, but the Kiwis quickly came to grips with the men of 40 (Saxon) and 3 Bavarian divisions; and in just over a quarter of an hour the New Zealanders were swarming past the front-line German trenches. They struggled up the ridge through ground churned by blast. The light was growing by the time they reached the Brown Line on the edge of Messines village, finding shell-holes occupied by tenacious Germans, toughened men who had held on through the shattering power of blast and quake, and now hurled fire towards their Kiwi attackers. A melee erupted, and then part of 3 Battalion came under heavy machine-gun fire from the direction of Messines as they reached the Brown Line trenches. Former Blackball miner Lance-Corporal Samuel Frickleton led a platoon through the barrage to take the gunners with grenade and bayonet. Then he charged on to take a second machine-gun post and dugout. This extraordinary performance earned him a VC.[35]

The tanks began rattling forwards around 4.00 a.m. One crashed through a farmhouse north of Messines, putting the garrison inside to flight. Messines village lay ahead, on naturally strong ground and fortified with wire and machine-gun. The attack was timed to the minute, given to 4 Rifle and 2 Canterbury battalions, each stiffened with a company from the reserves, and they advanced about ten minutes after the Brown Line fell. It was not easy; Canterbury were blocked by machine-gun posts in the Oxonian trench. There was more fire in the town from 'very strongly re-inforced concrete dugouts', but the main opposition came from the Institution Royale, 'strongly concreted and prepared for all round defence'. There was no easy answer, or an approach cheap in lives, and the building was finally taken by a single platoon in a 'regular hand-to-hand fight',[36] a bloody struggle that had the appearance of a massacre and produced two posthumous VC recommendations.

Just two men survived this re-introduction to the horrors of urban warfare.

The advance continued. Beyond the blast area it devolved, as always, to the grit of the attackers versus the doggedness of the defenders. Around 5.00 a.m. 1 Brigade advanced to the Brown Line, ready to push ahead to the Black Dotted Line. The first objective was Ungodly trench line southeast of Messines. 1 Auckland Battalion surged into it as the artillery lifted, finding the Germans had fled. Another company leapfrogged them, pushing beyond to seize two guns. There was other resistance northeast of the town where a machine-gun and observers had been set up in the Bleuwen Molen, a prominent mill. This was rushed by a squad from 1 Wellington Battalion under Corporal J. Fernandez. More than 50 prisoners were taken, but elsewhere New Zealanders began falling to German snipers. The next objective was Fanny's Farm, nicknamed by British forces, which was tackled by New Zealanders in the October Support Trench due north of Messines. They advanced into bitter opposition and were finally stalled by another well-fought machine-gun. Private John A. Lee rushed ahead to deal with it, capturing the four gunners.

Within 20 minutes the Black Line was in New Zealand hands, and the men began digging in under cover of an hour-long barrage. Damp ground and brisk counter-battery fire made the task difficult. One trench collapsed into a muddy pile, while shellfire brought another to complete ruin, burying a gun crew and knocking out their weapon. The other forces prosecuting the advance — 3 Australian Division and the British 25 Division — closed up. So did the tanks, which had so far been unable to advance with the infantry over the broken ground. At 8.40 a.m., the New Zealanders began advancing to artillery positions and strongpoints dubbed the Dotted Black Line.

The Germans, caught off balance by the mines and swift follow-up, did not counter-attack in strength until noon, by which time the British, New Zealand and Australian troops on the ridge were well dug in. The New Zealanders spent the rest of the day bringing forces up. They were not scheduled to advance further — Plumer had no intention of opening decimated companies up to a counter-attack. The new thrust fell to fresh Australian units, which moved on to the Green Line with New Zealand artillery support.

*Right*
An aerial view of Messines after the battle; a battered, cratered wasteland pocked with shell-holes.

(Kippenberger Military Archive and Research Library 1992-760)

*Below*
Courtyard of the Institution Royale, apparently taken during the German occupation early in 1917. A New Zealand platoon was virtually wiped out taking this building.

(Kippenberger Military Archive and Research Library 1992-757)

Stretcher bearers with wounded near Ploegsteert Wood, Ypres salient. This scene was repeated many thousands of times through the war.

(Henry Armitage Sanders, RSA Collection, Alexander Turnbull Library, PAColl-5311, G-12899-1/2)

It had been a tough morning's work, and the advance was achieved without close reference to divisional headquarters. Telephone was erratic, pigeons, rockets and semaphore more so. Russell complained of 'very bad communications'.[37] He went forward on 8 June to talk with 1 Brigade commander, Brigadier-General C.H. Brown; but an artillery bombardment began as they met and Brown was killed right in front of Russell. Efforts were under way to thin the line and keep casualties to a minimum; but losses continued to mount, and by the time the advanced New Zealand brigades were relieved by 4 Australian Division on the night of 9 June, total casualties had risen to some 3700 men.

Russell was nonetheless delighted with the result, telling Allen that the battle '… was won through the weight of metal thrown on to the enemy positions, and the mettle of the men who advanced to attack them'.[38] His officers concurred. 'The success,' one wrote, 'was due I think to … Very careful preparation and training beforehand … [and] The dash and elan shewn [sic] by all ranks in the … attacking force.'[39]

New Zealand Pioneers build a corduroy road through the slush near Messines Ridge, mid-1917.

(Henry Armitage Sanders, gelatin dry plate negative, RSA Collection, Alexander Turnbull Library, PAColl-5311, G-12772-1/2)

The news went down well in New Zealand, and though Allen was 'sad' about the casualties, he was also pragmatic: 'we know that there must be losses in this terrible game'.[40]

The first phase was not yet over. Godley wanted to secure the line south to Basseville and as far east as the Lys, where it turned north of Armentières. The front here was held by the New Zealand 4 Brigade, which moved into it on 10 June. Russell went to have a look and escaped death by a whisker when a bullet slammed through his helmet.[41] Then a burial party found that the Germans had evacuated several trenches. By the 12th the 2 Canterbury and 1 Otago battalions — both tired from their push into Messines, but still able to garrison a line — were established in positions formerly held by their enemy.

Next day the men of 4 Brigade cautiously advanced north of the Armentières–Warneton railway towards the river. It looked as if German forces had pulled back, and Braithwaite was ordered to find out. He had to use the two tired battalions, joining the 4th Rifle Battalion in a cautious advance on the night of 13 June. A company of 2 Otago Battalion reached Unchained Trench in the darkness, only to come under fire from a machine-gun nest in a ruined cabaret on the junction of the Basseville–St Ypres road. They had made no progress by dawn and dug in on Knoll 30, then made another effort later in the day. The attack was short, expensive and decisive, sending the surviving garrison fleeing up the Basseville road.

Russell was pleased. His forces were 1000 yards beyond planned position and he thought the new trench would 'serve *pro tem* as the new front line'.[42] German forces still held the Warneton Line in strength. The New Zealanders might have been able to tackle it, but at a Corps conference on the 16th Russell was ordered to 'stand fast on [the] present line' and make it 'strong and comfortable'.[43]

The wisdom of this decision became evident over the next few days. An effort to raid the German trenches at Warneton did not go well on the night of 20/21 June, largely because the barrage overshot the mark.[44] Another attempt

Lieutenant-General Alexander John Godley reviewing the New Zealanders after the battle of Messines, 21 June 1917.

(Henry Armitage Sanders, RSA Collection, Alexander Turnbull Library, PAColl-5311, G-12874-1/2)

two nights later was more successful, but the Germans retaliated with a hefty dollop of gas and high explosives — to which New Zealand artillery could not easily reply because most of the heavy guns had been sent to join the Fifth Army.⁴⁵

Many found the losses of the previous fortnight hard to take. Sergeant Edwin Clark arrived in Messines on the 20th:

> *Got the casualty list though while there and my word it makes it hard as some of the boys I knew personally, and they were the whitest of the white, and they have had to pay the penalty. H. Burrows also was amongst them, and a finer chap one could not wish to meet anywhere … Also met H. Obee, in fact was in the same hut as him while there so had quite a yarn with him, he was lucky being out of the stunt …*⁴⁶

Enthusiastic Kiwis watch the Boxing Championships of the New Zealand Contingent, early July 1917.

(Henry Armitage Sanders, RSA Collection, Alexander Turnbull Library, PAColl-5311, G-12853-1/2)

## 'Gas! Gas! Gas!'

The New Zealanders in France had to face a new and indiscriminate weapon — gas. Both sides toyed with lachrymatories during 1914. But in April 1915, Canadian and British soldiers in the line near Langemarck were suddenly enveloped in a lethal cloud of chlorine, released from hundreds of canisters stashed in German lines and borne into British trenches on a fateful breeze.

It took the British just four months to issue gas masks, a response that was far from laggard in view of the technical difficulties. Even later models were uncomfortable — yet potentially life-saving, and a vast step up from the cotton pads dipped in bicarbonate of soda or the urine-soaked handkerchiefs with which desperate soldiers had been forced to meet the initial attacks.

Anti-gas tactics became an integral part of training at Sling. 'I had my first experience in what is called the bull ring,' Thomas Lynch wrote soon after reaching camp, 'by jove they shake a fellow up in there.'[47] New Zealanders reaching France in 1916 were given further training in a dirt amphitheatre near Etaples. 'We had a lecture on gas,' Eric Spedding declared in mid-September 1916:

and then went through a trench filled with gas. Of course we wore helmets but they are beastly things. Afterwards we exploded a shell filled with lachrymatory gas, and I can tell you it is no nice job to be near the gas, as it gets into your eyes and 'bites some'.[48]

Tear-gas and chlorine were nasty, but chemists on both sides were soon searching for more lethal concoctions. Germany introduced the Allies to phosgene (carbonyl chloride) in December 1915. Chloropicrin, stannic chloride, dichloromethyl ether, diphosgene, ethyl carbasol and even hydrocyanic acid joined the range of chemicals flung by each side at soldier and civilian alike. One New Zealand doctor was among those caught in Estaires by a gas alarm. The streets were filled with running townsfolk, and while the phosgene did not roll over the town, it was 'heavy on the trenches only three miles away'.[49]

However, even phosgene paled into insignificance beside the compound Germany deployed in mid-1917. Chemists called it dichlorodiethyl sulphide, but the men had a more evocative term — 'mustard gas',

## The Third Battle of Ypres

Haig's main offensive of 1917 was launched on the back of the successes at Messines and known generally as the Third Battle of Ypres, eight interlinked battles that reached their climax for New Zealand in the attack on Passchendaele. Tactical planning throughout was generally good; Plumer's 'bite and hold' was a practical counter to trench defences, and the British were getting a better handle on artillery arrangements.

It was still flawed. Gough — an ex-cavalryman — did not concur with 'bite and hold', and the decision to leave the follow-up to the Messines assault until though to some it smelled 'garlicky' or even close to petrol.⁵⁰ Mustard gas could migrate through clothing and acted over a dozen hours to raise crippling blisters. Victims were blinded, choked, suffocated and developed infections. Nor was the threat ended when the cloud dispersed; the gas was dispensed as a liquid, which could puddle over a cold night and evaporate when warmed by the sun next morning. All the men could do was add chloride of lime to the puddles before shovelling over untainted earth. If left to dissolve the liquid tainted the pug, burning soldiers who crawled through it. It stayed on clothes where it had been splashed, polluted drinking water, and gas-tainted mud could even be brought into otherwise gas-proofed dugouts on boots. 'For the removal of mud from boots,' one instruction declared, 'a stiff broom and a pail of water should be kept outside dugouts'.⁵¹

Mustard gas seldom killed directly; but those caught in it sometimes wished they were dead. James Evans 'got a good dose as a shell landed on parapet of my shell hole before I was able to get my box respirator on' in October 1917. He hoped he would be all right, but within a few hours was 'feeling awful', waking at 4 a.m. next morning 'with fresh pain in my eyes & at 6 a.m. found my sight was badly affected'.⁵² He was evacuated that day and spent the next two months in hospital.

Evans' experience underlined the main German rationale for deploying the gas — in the ruthless world of war accountancy it was more expensive for the Allies to spend resources on medical care than to deal with a body. Yet in the end the gas did prove to be lethal. Even those who apparently regained their fitness often succumbed, sometimes years later, usually after a long and painful illness. The cause was not always the old scars on lung and throat; in a final ironic twist, mustard gas also turned out to be a powerful carcinogen.

Gas is estimated to have caused nearly 1.3 million casualties in the First World War, nearly a third of them Russian. The effects were so appalling that, by international agreement, gas was rendered illegal as a weapon of war in 1925. This did not prevent the development of even more horrific gases later. Nor did it relieve the legacy of unexploded gas shells beneath Belgian fields. Many remained, rusting and lethal, into the twenty-first century.

---

the end of July gave the German Fourth Army under General Sixt von Arnim plenty of time to establish themselves on the Passchendaele ridge, backed with fresh forces from the Eastern Front. Once again the British had to mount an uphill attack into a close-linked network of trenches, pillboxes and strongpoints.

Part of the delay was political. Haig viewed Messines as a stepping stone towards Bruges, denying Germany the U-boat havens of Zeebrugge and Ostende. However, he did not provide Downing Street with full details of his plan until 19 June.⁵³ Lloyd-George was not convinced, and debate was coloured by the gloomy predictions of the First Sea Lord, Admiral Sir John Jellicoe, beset with worry over the U-boat menace, who declared that Zeebrugge had to be taken. A divided government argued the toss for days. Haig initiated the preliminary bombardment, but it was 25 July before the War Cabinet finally gave its assent.[54]

Rain set in while these arguments went on, the heaviest seen for decades, and millions of shells completed the destruction of the drainage systems. Soil became effluent-tainted sludge.[55] Pools of water spread from shell holes and low-lying areas, so deep in places that a heavily laden soldier who slipped off the duckboards risked being drowned or suffocated.[56] Although more than 250 Mk IV tanks were due to be deployed, commanders such as Colonel C.D. Baker-Carr wondered whether their heavy vehicles could even move through the stinking pug.

The offensive opened with an attempt to take territory between Langemarck, Broodseinde and Polygon Wood. This was Gough's idea,[57] and although the advance was divided into four his aims were still highly ambitious. Seventeen divisions were committed to the attack, the bulk from Gough's Fifth Army, but they pushed through the ruins of Chateau Wood, Sanctuary Wood and Shrewsbury Forest against increasing German fire. Some objectives were beyond artillery range. By the end of July Gough's motley Fifth Army had struggled only as far as Pilckem Ridge. Nearly a third of the 100,000-odd men committed to the advance became casualties.

Like other elements of Plumer's army, 2 Anzac Corps was given supporting tasks designed to divert German artillery — in New Zealand's case, tackling Basseville and raiding the Douvre Valley towards Warneton. It was subsidiary to the main assault, but no less hard-fought, and Lance-Corporal Leslie Wilton Andrew won the Victoria Cross during the battle.[58] Conditions remained appalling. Evans came back to the New Zealand trenches after leave to find the 'weather worse & dug-outs flooded out. All ranks having a very rough time … The whole of the trench system is flooded out — in places up to the knees in mud & slush.'[59]

Gough wondered about shutting the assault down. But Haig urged him on. The fresh advance on 16 August, usually dubbed the Battle of Langemarck, did not reach the objectives Gough had hoped to make on 31 July. By the end of August the Fifth Army had been effectively gutted, and Gough was relieved of his command. But Haig was determined to continue in spite of signs that, as J.F.C. Fuller has observed, the battle was 'tactically impossible'.[60] A somewhat reluctant Plumer took the field, envisaging another careful application of 'bite and hold'. Four divisions would advance on a 4000-yard front towards objectives well within artillery range, itself built up to unprecedented density. This would allow them to move in four steps to the Gheluveldt Plateau.[61] With a perhaps healthy appreciation of the odds, Plumer also wanted to spearhead the thrusts with his best troops — the Australians and New Zealanders.

The assault opened on 20 September. Its first phase, the battle of Menin road, lasted five days and set the whole of 1 Anzac Corps, among other forces, against the defences. The assault troops took the objectives at a cost of some 21,000 casualties — sending Downing Street into a spin. Lloyd-George even toyed with sacking both Haig and the CIGS, General Sir William 'Wully' Robertson.[62] Nor were the Germans idle; on the 25th, forces from Group Wytschaete slammed into the British 33 Division in the first of a series of counter-attacks. It was not enough to derail Plumer's plan. Next day, seven divisions — including another two Australian — pushed into Polygon Wood. The bitter struggle lasted nine days, a blood-drenched hell of mud, slaughter and gas that cost some 15,000 British and Imperial troops killed or wounded. But they reached the base of the Passchendaele rise. Plumer now envisaged a staged assault on Passchendaele, again led by the Anzacs. This time Godley's 2 Anzac Corps got the job; and while 3 Australian Division was relatively untested, the New Zealand performances at Flers and on Messines gave cause for hope.

## Broodseinde Ridge

The New Zealand Division spent much of September preparing for 'another smack ... like Messines'.[63] The hard lessons of the campaign were absorbed and digested; new tactics included 'worm' attacks on pillboxes, using small columns.[64] The division began moving towards the front in the third week of the month. The men were on foot or horses, but the road was 'alive with red cross cars and motor lorries travelling backwards and forwards' — as one soldier observed, the 'motor traffic never stops day or night'.[65]

After a six-day march the division settled into their new digs. The nearest village was Poperinghe, 'some distance away', but still within lorry range.[66] One soldier found it 'nearly all estiaments, we had a few drinks and look around, the place was full of troops'.[67] Others went forward, eager to see 'what was left of' Ypres. As one soldier recorded:

> Ypres is a big town one mass of ruins, it's an eye opener I can tell you to see what shell fire does, there isn't one intact building in the whole town, it's cruel to see such a lovely town in ruins …[68]

Many had been warned about conditions in the salient; but while some remarked on the corduroy roads and liquid mud, few found it worse than any other area. The biggest problem was the Menin road, 'one of the most desolate sights one could imagine and … a real deathtrap to all who had to traverse it

New Zealand soldiers move down a corduroy road on 4 October 1917, the day of the first big divisional push towards Passchendaele.

(Henry Armitage Sanders, RSA Collection, Alexander Turnbull Library, PAColl-5311, G-12938-1/2)

'... The German artillery had its range to a nicety, and used to land "five-nines" on it with amazing persistence ... the man who successfully ran the gauntlet had something very real to congratulate himself upon.'[69]

The combat elements went forward into the St Jean sector between 1 Anzac and 18 Corps, west of Gravenstafel. The CRA, Brigadier-General Napier Johnston, was given overall command of the artillery in his sector and had a lavish array of weapons at his disposal. Guns supporting the New Zealand positions alone included 180 18-pounders and 60 4.5-inch howitzers. Feeding them was a labour of Sisyphus. The shells were brought forward, eight or a dozen at a time, on the backs of pack animals, a task that was hard on man and beast alike. One night J.C. Heseltine walked his struggling horses 'about three miles through mud knee deep in many parts,' and was 'fair done for ... when I reached the guns ... the sweat run [sic] off me like water from a froggy's pump'.[70]

They worked under the near-constant scream and thump of shells. 'Plenty of smell from the dead and plenty of shells,' Harold Foley scribbled on 30

Wreckage of war — trenches in the Ypres salient after a push. In the background, S.D. Rogers of 2 ANZAC Corps, back to camera, tapes mule tracks in order to bring supplies forward.

(Photographer unknown, Alexander Turnbull Library, F-51947-1/2)

'Duck for dinner', reads the original caption in this New Zealand soldier's album. Men scramble for cover after coming unexpectedly under fire, apparently part-way through preparing a meal. This dugout was probably an advanced aid post.

(Kippenberger Military Archive and Research Library 1992-760)

September.[71] Krupp steel even rained into the rear areas, and the artillery and munitions dumps regularly came under fire. Russell had to move his headquarters twice. He first set up at Hazebrouck,[72] moved to Wateau early on the 27th,[73] then he discovered the attack had been put forward two days. The plan called for an advance by the Fifth Army towards Poelcapelle, while 1 Anzac Corps pushed to Broodseinde. The two divisions of 2 Anzac Corps — of which the New Zealanders were the only experienced force — had the job of protecting the southern flank of 1 Anzac Corps. The New Zealand objective was Abraham Heights, a section of the Gravenstafel spur jutting from Passchendaele Ridge. These hills were held by 4 Bavarian Division, and the plan involved a two-step advance by 1 Brigade to Stroombeek Stream, and by 4 Brigade to Berlin Farm beyond the heights. The ground was unsuitable for tanks, and in an effort to achieve surprise, the guns were restricted to a lightning bombardment at zero hour, though practice barrages were fired daily during the lead-up.

Russell spent the last days of September liaising with other divisional commanders, and by 2 October felt his division was in good shape. 'I fancy we have got most of the work done and everyone seems confident.'[74] This was not quite true. Handlers were still bringing the guns up, and Heseltine recalled:

> *We had a devil of a job to get the gun where it was wanted for shell holes and bridges across old trenches and drains. I shall never forget our experience this morning. Fritz was shelling our battery position nearly all night and I can tell you I didn't feel too safe, but the guns have to go into position at all costs …*[75]

Some guns were positioned amid scattered corpses,[76] an ominous reminder of the war. Nor was there any respite. The Germans 'shelled us throughout the day,' James Evans wrote the day before the attack, 'to which our guns replied tenfold'. The final practice shoots came on top of it and were 'a sight worth seeing'.[77] Light rain began spattering down as night fell on 3 October, reducing the front trenches to a 'quagmire', and was still drizzling from leaden skies before dawn on the 4th as 1 and 4 Brigades moved to their starting points. But they were, as Evans put it, in 'good spirits'.[78]

The men were keying themselves up to go in the pre-dawn gloom when the German guns suddenly erupted — by coincidence, the Germans had planned an attack of their own that morning against 1 Anzac Corps and Polygon Wood. Three of von Arnim's fresh divisions were massing when the British bombardment began,[79] and 'hell' was 'let loose'.[80] Shells did fearful execution among the clustered troops. Men of 1 Auckland quickly found 500 German corpses along their advance. Others were alive but stunned, and 'all glad to get in & all more or less suffering from shell shock caused by our barrage'.[81] Counter-fire began plunging down soon after the New Zealanders 'hopped the bags',[82] scything through the Wellington Battalion. Then the men of 4 Brigade had a difficult time moving towards Otto Farm — but as the men of 3 Auckland Battalion pushed ahead, the garrisons in pillboxes south of the farm surrendered. Other emplacements in the north were swamped by a group from 3 Otago under Private D. Mackenzie, which took 35 prisoners.

The task was made all the harder because each man was burdened with munitions, tools, sandbags, rations and Mills bombs. Most sank to their knees in boggier ground. Yet despite these weights the New Zealanders toiled up to the Hanebeeck Stream, reduced to a quagmire by the shellfire and under observation from pillboxes up the slope. Here the barrage paused, providing cover while the men picked their way across the sludge in the grey light of the misty dawn. The ground beyond rose to the Abraham Heights, and the men hammered ahead to tackle pillboxes and strongpoints built in pillboxes and ruined farms. One particularly powerful emplacement at Van Meulen was bypassed for later reduction.

All went like clockwork. The 3 Otago and 3 Auckland battalions reached the Red Line on the gentle forward slopes of Abraham Heights 'on the tick of 7 a.m.', as Evans put it, and began consolidating for a planned 90-minute pause. They 'got fairly well dug in before the Hun started to shell us but when he did shell he made it fairly warm'.[83] Soon afterwards, 3 Wellington and 3 Canterbury battalions passed through them to tackle pillboxes and defences on the slopes, digging into the 'Blue Line' between Berlin Farm and Berlin Wood around 9.10 a.m.

All had gone well so far; but 1 Brigade had less fortune as it pushed northeast. The men of 1 Auckland Battalion angled into a British sector, which meant that their front to the Red Line was covered by the adjacent 1 Wellington Battalion. The latter rose to the occasion, taking on pillboxes with heroic disregard for safety. One machine-gun nest was taken out solo by Sergeant K.A. Goldingham, who rushed it under cover of rifle grenade fire from his men, and bayoneted the four gunners. Another gun was knocked out by Private T. Geange and another soldier — no minor feat given that Geange had only his service revolver to hand.

The Wellington Battalion reached the Red Line and came under fire from pillboxes on Korek, some 120-odd yards beyond Gravenstafel. This had to be dealt with quickly, and a composite squad from 1 Wellington and 3 Otago battalions, under Sergeant F.E. Chappell, pushed ahead despite the barrage, plastering the pillboxes with Mills bombs. A party cautiously entered the largest to find only dead Germans inside the blood-spattered outer chamber. Others were alive inside, setting fire to secret papers.

Once again the men committed to the first objective were not required for the second, and after a period to consolidate, 2 Auckland and 2 Wellington battalions pushed on to Korek, a pile of rubble that was strongly held by German forces. Soon afterwards, 2 Wellington drifted left, approaching the Stroombeek Stream where the objective was covered by German gunners operating from the ruins of Kronprinz Farm. This was taken by a group under

Sergeant Foot, who had won the DCM at Basseville. The New Zealanders now connected with the adjacent 48 Division and began consolidating under cover of artillery fire.

These guns were one of the key arbiters of the battle, denting German positions and forcing their heads down; but the barrage was kept up only by heroic efforts on the part of munitions handlers, who had to cope with mud, shell holes, old trenches and finally air attack as they brought the 'iron rations' forwards. Heseltine recalled:

> *About eleven o'clock one of Fritz's aeroplanes came over our guns and dropped three bombs quite close to our guns, right on our track and killed three horses and wounded three, also wounded two of our drivers, one chap had his legs badly smashed. I was lucky, I was only about fifty yards from where the bombs dropped, I got a fright I can tell you, the ground was very soft, therefore pieces of shell and earth didn't fly very far; there were dozens of horses and men around our guns unloading their shells at the time, it's marvellous how so few were hit.*[84]

Gravenstafel Spur lay in British hands. Plans to push further were abandoned because British forces had not been able to achieve their aims. For all that it had been a good day for the New Zealand Division, and the men knew it. 'We went over the top at Ypres, Pachendale [sic] and took Abraham Heights,' T.R. Preston wrote in his diary. 'We made a good success & only had 32 casualties in my company.'[85] Evans, too, marvelled at the low loss rates 'considering the extent of the operation'.[86]

That evening Russell estimated New Zealand casualties to be '1500/2000', a remarkably accurate figure.[87] In fact New Zealand suffered some 1853 casualties during the attack, including 330 dead and 200 missing. Edwin Clark was among the dead.[88] So too was Boer War veteran Hugh Boscawen, who had joined up just weeks after war broke out.[89] Yet these losses were surprisingly low under Western Front conditions.[90] Polygon Wood, Broodseinde, Gravenstafel and Zonnebeke were occupied. British commanders believed they had delivered a crushing blow, though this was not the view among the Germans.

Rain set in during the afternoon of 4 October, hampering efforts to bring munitions forward. And from their new emplacements on the Gravenstafel Spur, the men of 4 Brigade looked across at the ruined village of Passchendaele. Some forces were withdrawn quickly, relieved just hours after the battle; and for most, rum and hot food behind the lines a few hours after the battle was 'extremely welcome'.[91] Rain continued to pour down 'in sheets',[92] but the forward troops were relieved by 49 Division on 6 October and, gratefully, marched west through Ypres for their billets. As Heseltine recalled, 'we were not sorry to leave the Ypres sector'.[93]

But they were not gone for long. A week later the Kiwis were back; and this time fortune did not smile.

## The attack on Passchendaele

The New Zealand attack on Passchendaele was to be a disaster. The death toll exceeded the loss of the *Orpheus*, the Tarawera eruption, the Hawke's Bay earthquake, the Tangiwai rail bridge disaster, the loss of the *Wahine* and the DC-10 crash on Mt. Erebus combined.[94] On a per-capita basis, against a 1917

New Zealand soldiers move towards the front amid blasted woods, 11 October 1917.

(Henry Armitage Sanders, RSA Collection, Alexander Turnbull Library, PAColl-5311, G-12939-1/2)

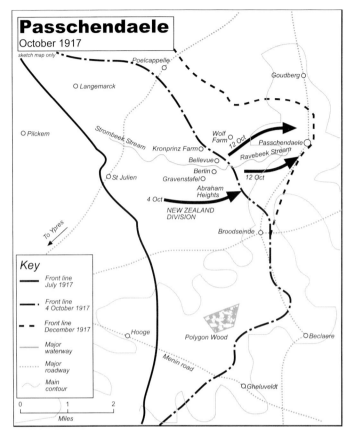

population of just over 1.1 million, it was an even greater catastrophe. Deaths in those black 24 hours on 12 October 1917 amounted to six percent of all New Zealanders killed in army service during the First World War and just over three percent of New Zealand's total killed in all theatres of all wars. Virtually every family in the country was touched — some, mercifully, only by proxy through degrees of separation.

In many respects the battle was a victim of prior success. Plumer's cautious strategy had achieved results up to 4 October, but as autumn turned to winter he wondered about closing the front down until spring. Haig disagreed, and in any case all British commanders were delighted by the results of 4 October — a victory that Plumer, exuberantly, considered as important as the Marne.[95] Passchendaele beckoned, and there were good tactical arguments for taking it, if only to strengthen the line and provide a launch-point for a spring offensive. The current positions were not good, and a retreat to Messines unthinkable.[96] As the official historian has noted, there was also political motive.[97] Reports that German prisoners were dispirited suggested that opposition would not be intense, and there is evidence that this was not wishful thinking at command level. J.C. Heseltine saw prisoners march by his camp all day on 4 October, declaring them a 'miserable lot half boys and dressed very poor, some of them look quite happy. I bet they are not sorry to be captured.'[98]

Von Arnim's 4th Army, it seemed, was scraping the bottom of the barrel; but the landscape was saturated by autumn rain, and as one report declared, 'the operations of the Armies in this locality were greatly hampered by adverse weather conditions, heavy and continuous rain rapidly rendering the ground impassable'.[99] The new plan was built around a two-step attack, starting with a combined 11-division assault on the 9th. In the north of the line, 14 and 18 Corps would push towards the ruined Houthulst Forest and Westroosebeke, on the ridge north of Passchendaele. Meanwhile, forces from 49 and 66 divisions, on 2 Anzac Corps front, would take two spurs separated by the Ravebeek valley and open the way to Passchendaele. Then there would be a further push on the 12th, led by the New Zealanders and 3 Australian Division, to take the village and heights around it. As before, the New Zealanders were given the left and the Australians the right.[100]

The incessant rain turned the Ravebeek Stream into a wide obstacle surrounded by bogs. But Haig's keenness was infectious. By the 7th, when the downpour eased, only Birdwood and 18 Corps commander Lieutenant-General Ivor Maxse were opposed to the effort. Haig should perhaps have listened. The skies opened up again late next day, drenching the field as the Tommies struggled over slimed duckboards to the 2 Anzac Corps assembly areas. When the forces detailed to take Bellevue Spur pushed over the line into a slushy morning they were enfiladed with machine-gun fire, then came up against uncut wire. Forces from 66 Division reached Keerslaarhoek on the other

Conditions in the Ypres salient, 12 October 1917 — the day of the disastrous New Zealand attack on Passchendaele.

(Henry Armitage Sanders, RSA Collection, Alexander Turnbull Library, PAColl-5311, G-12944-1/2)

spur, came under fire from the German positions on Bellevue and had to fall back. The result was that only the first objectives were taken, just 500 yards from the start-point,[101] and British casualties totalled more than 5700 men.[102] Wounded were still being retrieved from the battlefield two days later.

As a result of this calamity the rest of the 9 October objectives were added to those already scheduled for the 12th, and to cap it off Russell was uneasy about the pace. He had been suffering a 'pretty bad' cold all week and was not able to get out to check the ground. His concerns redoubled when Brigadier-General Johnston visited him just after lunch on the 11th to warn that artillery preparation was 'inadequate'.[103] Johnston's guns were actually in a terrible position, deployment hampered by roads that remained deep, sticky quagmires in spite of Herculean efforts by the Pioneer Battalion. Man and beast strained to haul the guns forward, among them J.C. Heseltine, who recalled as early as 3 October that:

> *We got home about three o'clock this morning after a strenuous night's work getting our gun into action. We had a devil of a job to get the gun where it was wanted for shell holes and bridges across old trenches and drains.*[104]

Another gun crew spent five hours dragging their weapon forward through the pug.[105] The Steenebeek became a formidable obstacle under these circumstances, yet movement was only the first problem. Mud had to be cleaned off the shells before they could be loaded, slowing the rate of fire. Firing brought its own issues. Many guns had to sit near-axle deep in the sludge, and the recoil rammed their trails deeper into the bog, with dire effects on range and accuracy. Wooden gun platforms proved unstable in the mud. Nor was the supply of ammunition guaranteed. As Heseltine recorded on the 4th:

> *... twelve of our waggons were out carting shells from the dump to within half a mile of our guns, then us with packs, took it on to the guns through shell holes all the way. I did eight trips with my two horses and took in 132 rounds of ammunition my horses were very tired when I had finished, so was I ...*[106]

*Above*
Wire, mud and fire; the reality of the Western Front. Soldiers had to cross this bullet-torn wasteland before they could come to grips with the enemy.

(Kippenberger Military Archive and Research Library 2002-7)

*Left*
Ambulance scene, from the album of a soldier in the New Zealand medical corps.

(Kippenberger Military Archive and Research Library 1992-760)

The New Zealanders began assembling for the attack under leaden skies, among them Jesse Stayte who had only lately arrived in the Morbeque reinforcement camp, near Hazebrouck, with 3 Auckland Battalion. He reached Poperinge on a wet and cold 11 October to see trainloads of wounded being taken away — not an inspiring sight.[107]

Russell's plan called for 3 (Rifle) Brigade to take Bellevue Spur in two bounds on a narrow front. The fourth battalion would push forwards behind the lead troops, largely to be on hand for a possible counter-attack.[108] The final objective was atop Goudberg Spur. Meanwhile 2 Brigade would repeat a similar manoeuvre on the other spur, aiming for Meetcheele. Here they would be leapfrogged by Australian forces, who would take Passchendaele.

Drizzle began falling in the pre-dawn hours of 12 October. Then a German bombardment erupted and shells screamed down amid assembled troops. Returning New Zealand artillery fire was ragged. The semi-liquid terrain swallowed many projectiles without detonation; and those that did burst were muffled. Shells plunged around the troops as they advanced. The rain hardened, and the New Zealand infantry struggled forward through the pug, rolling from shell-hole to shell-hole in the hope of finding cover. There was no chance of rushing the machine-gun nests, and the men of 3 (Rifle) Brigade fell like mown grass as they laboured up Bellevue, leaving the field behind scattered with the wounded and dying.

When the lead elements finally reached Wolf Farm they could see silhouettes of German soldiers ahead on the ridgeline, apparently retreating; but the machine-gunners remained in their stout pillboxes, and the New Zealanders again came under heavy fire as they reached the wire. Lieutenant-Colonel Edward Puttick arrived at Wolf Farm at around 8.00 a.m. and realised his exhausted and decimated units could get no further. Although 1 Battalion remained unfought, he ordered the survivors to consolidate and directed two platoons into the Ravebeek Valley in the hope of flanking the German positions.

The 2 Brigade effort on the southern spur was equally catastrophic. The men of 2 Otago Battalion struggled through their own muddy inferno, but finally stalled at a gap through the wire along the Gravenstafel road, which was well covered by machine-guns. Major W.W. Turner died cutting the wire, and the fortunes of the following 1 Otago Battalion were no better. Two pillboxes in the

Ravebeek Valley were finally taken by a platoon under Second Lieutenant A.R. Cockerell, who captured 80 prisoners. Cockerell won the DSO; but it was small victory against the wider battle, and 1 Canterbury Battalion lost Lieutenant-Colonel George King and most of its headquarters staff to a chance shell burst. Finally the men dug in, part way along the ridge and well back from the first objective.

Elements of 3 Australian Division nevertheless pushed towards Passchendaele and managed to reach the outskirts of the shattered village; while part of 9 Division, to the north, also reached final objective. The New Zealand failures left both forces with exposed flanks, and Russell took the decision to renew the attack at 3.00 a.m. Braithwaite protested; the men were pinned in full view of German pillboxes and snipers. Russell repeated the order, and only in the last hour changed it to a push by 3 (Rifle) Brigade alone.

Minutes before the attack began, fresh reports from 9 Division and 3 Australian revealed they were in a precarious state. Russell cancelled his own attack, but the order came too late to stop the artillery, and 'shorts' began falling around the New Zealand positions. Evans' unit remained around Abraham Heights until 9.00 p.m., when they were 'pulled out on account of heavy shelling of our positions but not before we had suffered many casualties'.[109]

It was the final blow on a disastrous day. The sun set on a grey, muddy field littered with corpses, nearly 1200 of them New Zealanders. Another 1900 were wounded, and more Kiwis fell during the next few days, including labouring Medical Corps staff trying to bring the wounded off the battlefield.[110] This 'extremely difficult' task involved 'a 3 and a half mile carry over tracks under heavy fire from Artillery, machine-guns and snipers, and rendered a quagmire by the heavy rains'.[111] Stayte 'saw many wounded being carried out' on 12 October.[112]

But it was only next day, as the weather closed in 'miserable cold & wet', that the men began to realise 'what a sad failure yesterday's attack had been'. The wounded began pouring back 'in great numbers', made possible in part by a tacit truce around the spurs. Evans was impressed. 'If it hadn't been for this our casualties would have been considerably heavier.'[113] Extra bearers arrived from 4 Infantry Brigade, and they all struggled through the mire to rescue their comrades, working on until they collapsed from exhaustion. Evans' battalion was among the units pushed forward to relieve the battered 2 Brigade on the

*Above*
New Zealand forces moving forward over the Ypres Canal, heading for the front line, 18 October 1917.

(Henry Armitage Sanders, RSA Collection, Alexander Turnbull Library, PAColl-5311, G-12929-1/2)

*Right*
Heavy going near Kansas Farm, 20 October 1917.

(Henry Armitage Sanders, RSA Collection, Alexander Turnbull Library, PAColl-5311, G-12931-1/2)

14th, and 'it was then that we fully realised how the 2nd & 3rd Bde has suffered'.[114] Some 2500 wounded were passed through the advanced medical units up to 20 October.[115]

The Germans began a day-long barrage on the 15th. Evans thought 'it was hell, and easily the heaviest shelling that I have experienced since I arrived in France'. Next day the Germans began using mustard gas, catching many Kiwis before they could get their respirators on — Evans among them.[116] Stayte went forward to find the area 'strewn with war debris and pieces of dead men', recording dismally in his diary on 16 October that:

> *Life is not worth a minute's purchase here and some of our men are being killed and blown to pieces every few minutes. Our Batteries are all around us and Fritz is shelling and trying to get them and of course he is getting us at the same time.*[117]

Supporting forces continued to work under fire. 'The weather is wet and the trench is very wet and muddy and the weather is bitterly cold,' Jesse Stayte recorded on 21 October. 'My feet are continually half frozen and we cannot get anything hot to eat as our food comes up to us during the night and it is icy cold when it gets here. We dare not light a fire.'[118] He did not get away for another four days, waking on the 26th to the 'welcome sound of church bells instead of the awful roar and carnage of the guns'.[119]

The New Zealand attack on Passchendaele was a shattering disaster. Russell was in no doubt about the cause, writing afterwards that it 'goes to show the weakness of haste'.[120] The failure to cut the wire with artillery had been crucial, and when he had opportunity to air his views to BEF command a few weeks later he:

> *... explained as well as I could what appeared to be the obvious lessons of the 4th and 12th. The chief one, applying more especially to Divl. Staff and Self, is that under no circumstance in war is one justified in assuming anything which can possibly be verified — and that where there are certain known conditions necessary to success it is a great risk, however justifiable, to attack before they are fulfilled.*[121]

New Zealand troops at Ypres, 20 October 1917. Rail made all the difference when it came to getting troops quickly from one place to another; but they often faced jolting lorry journeys or harrowing route-marches after disembarking.

(Henry Armitage Sanders, RSA Collection, Alexander Turnbull Library, PAColl-5311, G-12925-1/2)

Later he took his commanders to task about 'our failure and its lessons', particularly the 'crime of the Division in assuming the wire to be cut' — something he felt 'ought to have been verified'.[122] However, Russell's recriminations were those of hindsight. He did not make his objections known to higher command at the time; though even had he done so, his opinions would have carried little weight in the face of higher-level optimism.[123] Haig, with what Fuller called 'inexcusable … pig-headedness',[124] was unswervable. Godley perhaps did not want to let Haig down,[125] and both Russell and Monash had to conform.

The failure nevertheless niggled in the face of New Zealand's reputation for success. Allen was '… sure that no possible blame can be attached to the New Zealand Artillery. From all I can hear they did all that human beings could do to get their guns out, and I do not propose to enter into a discussion as to the wisdom of the attack under such circumstance.' However:

> *Rumours have been circulating through parts of New Zealand that the situation was not properly appreciated and that it was known to some senior officers ... that it would be impossible for the artillery to clear up the wire and to preserve the barrages ... I lay no blame on you, nor indeed, do I blame anybody, but there is a feeling of unrest and I have it myself. There is no use denying it ... No serious criticism has arisen in New Zealand at present, but as letters come out from officers and men who saw service on that occasion I suspect there will be some complaint.*[126]

The point was driven home by the way Passchendaele was taken three weeks later. The Canadian Corps took over the New Zealand front on 18 October, but had a full week to prepare and were given less ambitious objectives. With support from New Zealand artillery, they finally took the Goudberg Spur and surrounding territory on 6 November. To this extent, the attack of 12 October was a salutary lesson in the dangers of over-extending. Weather and mud compounded the problem; and the New Zealand attack lacked not only proper artillery support but also tanks — though these could not run in the bogs of the Ypres salient. Yet as the battle of Cambrai showed a few weeks later, tanks in sufficient number could be decisive,[127] and on this basis we could question the whole wisdom of attacking from the Ypres salient.

But such an observation is one of hindsight; in 1917, the tactical reasons for tackling the Germans around Ypres seemed compelling. The likely cost in lives was accepted — though few anticipated the way that a combination of weather, terrain and flawed tactics would compound that toll. Nor could the effort be abandoned even after it had become clear how expensive it was becoming in lives. The tactical realities of terrain made it impossible to stop the battle halfway; once British forces had struggled to the feet of the Passchendaele ridge, the only option was to continue or withdraw, and nobody was prepared to waste the lives that had been sacrificed getting that far. The likely cost of finishing the job had to be accepted, and New Zealand, like all Britain's Imperial children, paid that price in blood.

# SPRING OFFENSIVE

New Zealand's gruelling struggle amid the mud ended a few months after the slaughter at Passchendaele. The fighting that came with spring 1918 was very different, taking the division in a dramatic — though long-expected — direction. But these turns of fortune were not obvious as the winter of 1917 closed around the battered force.

In late November 1917 the New Zealanders were sent to 1 Anzac Corps' sector in the south of the Ypres salient, near Polygon Wood. The men were exhausted by the horrors of Passchendaele. Snow lay across the blasted landscape, and they huddled around stoves in their dugouts. Russell was not happy with the position — 'tracks badly laid and in bad repair — roads non-existent, trench tramway ditto — accommodation so bad that we have to reduce battn. trench strength'. He could foresee only a 'great deal of work' ahead.[1]

The first task was taking Polderhoek Spur with its pillboxes and ruined chateau, to prevent the Germans overlooking and enfilading some of the British trenches. Plans were in hand to take the ridge before the New Zealanders took over, and Russell had little choice but to push ahead. Mud was ever-present, and the Reutelbeek Stream created near-impassable bogs. But he was determined not to repeat the calamities of 12 October. Three artillery brigades were detailed for the operation, and special steps were taken to keep the men safe — including pulling them back from the front lines during a heavy cannonade against the chateau on 28 November. Sure enough, retaliatory German shells crashed down into the empty complex.

The attack went ahead on 3 December, a 'Fine clear windy morning' with light frost. Zero-hour was scheduled for noon, and the assault opened with a barrage by 18-pounders. It was a moment for heroism; the advancing 1 Canterbury Battalion were quickly held up by a machine-gun, and Captain G.H. Gray of 12 (Nelson) Company personally led a charge, capturing the gun. Wind blew away the smoke cover, and the flank came under heavy enfilade fire, but the men pushed on. Finally they were faced by another machine-gun position; and at this moment Private Henry Nicholas ran forward with part of his section, charging the post despite the bullets and taking it with Mills bombs. He won the VC for this action. However, the company was then held up by another pillbox, and had to dig in short of objective.

The other battalions were halted close to the chateau. Russell considered the casualties were 'excessive for ground gained' and blamed it on 'untrained men not following the officers boldly' — it was a 'mistake to attack frontally — prefer my idea of coming in on a flank — pillboxes too well sited'.[2]

Russell's winter priority was getting rid of 4 Brigade. He discussed the issue with Godley in London as early as 26 October, finding some opposition, although he was firm in his own mind 'that it be done away with'.[3] In November he raised it with Allen. 'After our losses in October,' he wrote, 'it seemed an opportune time … to break up the 4th Brigade.'[4] He did not quite win the argument; the brigade was disbanded the following February, but the men were sent to form three entrenching battalions — as Russell grumbled, this was 'hardly what was meant'.[5]

Christmas 1917 brought 'snow and sleet',[6] and some in the trenches had to make do with biscuits and bully beef in lieu of more festive fare. One unit lost its kitchen to artillery fire, though one man managed to get forward with a jar of rum.[7] Others enjoyed a more seasonal spread, 'pork and spuds', followed by 'old Plum Duff, then we had apricots & pineapples we bought ourselves'. To follow came 'plenty of cake & lollies we had got in parcels from home …'[8] It was the first white Christmas for many New Zealanders.

The division wintered at Ypres, and at the beginning of January 1918 was administratively shifted to 12 Corps, still under Godley. The men were desperately in need of a rest, but there was no respite. Stayte, part of a working party digging tunnels in Anzac Ridge, was haunted by the sight of dead horses and mules lining the roads.

> ... *men's helmets and equipment also tell a sad tale. Waggons and motor lorries and all kinds of War wreckage are strewn everywhere and also graves are scattered everywhere. Often a simple little wooden cross and more often, nothing at all but the poor soldier's steel helmet on the grave.*[9]

New Zealanders died amid the icy mud, among them Stayte's brother. 'I feel dazed and cannot get my mind on anything else,' Stayte wrote. 'May God help my poor Mother through her sorrow for I well know how the news will [be] received at home.'[10] Raids made life hazardous, and then in February the Germans began pounding communications tracks — this to the point where it was sometimes difficult to get hot food forward. Late in the month, 3 (Rifle) Brigade pushed their line out a further 200 yards to get a better view of the Keiberg valley, but the division was not relieved until the end of the month. They had suffered 2910 casualties since November, including 89 missing.[11]

## The Kaiser's Battle

By late 1917 there were signs that the Allies were worse off than their enemies. The French army had fought small offensives in August and October, but was still far from recovered. Britain reeled under the impact of U-boat warfare; the Third Battle of Ypres had been a disaster; and Russia had collapsed. Italy was shaky, while the United States was not expected to field a full expeditionary force until 1919.

Germany, too, bent before the storm, but the fall of Russia put the Kaiser's forces in a stronger position, and with the prospect of the war continuing for another two years, President Woodrow Wilson wondered about a negotiated peace. However, his 'Fourteen Points' of January 1918 were not acceptable to a German government flush with victory in the east, and Ludendorff's plans to renew the assault in the west were already well advanced. Fresh divisions had been trickling through as the Eastern Front ran down, becoming a flood when the war with Russia formally ended. Other divisions were brought up from Italy. A million men had moved west by March 1918, enough to produce numerical superiority over the Anglo-French armies.¹² They brought an arsenal of captured artillery, munitions and equipment.

Using them was another matter. Like the British, the Germans had been struggling with the thorny question of breaking the trench deadlock for some time, and the General Staff came up with a combined-arms approach that in many respects was prototypical of later warfare, lacking only effective tanks. Ludendorff insisted on pushing the commanders forward, demanding close air co-operation, lightning artillery bombardments with liberal use of gas, and swift follow-up by specially trained *sturmtruppen* (storm troopers). The whole tactic was designed to shatter Allied lines and exploit into open country. To compound the psychological blow Ludendorff even planned to bombard Paris from the unthinkable range of nearly 68 miles (109 km), deploying a new gun built for the purpose by Krupp.¹³

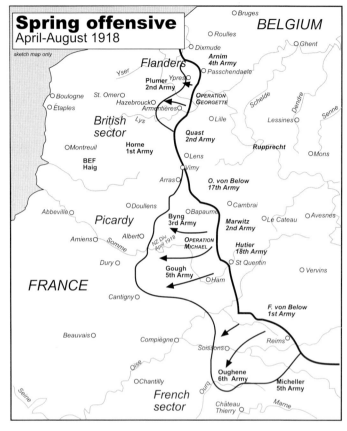

Everything hung off the offensive, and at a time of rising discontent in Germany the campaign was deliberately called the *Kaiserslacht*, the Kaiser's Battle. But Ludendorff had no strategic goals, and although he expected to springboard from any tactical success,¹⁴ the direction of attack was not well suited to such a move. Nor, in hindsight, had the logistics been properly considered, and to this was added the problem of quality. Like the British and French, the Germans had lost their best-trained soldiers on the bloody fields of Verdun, Ypres and the Eastern Front. There were still plenty of men in 1918, but Ludendorff considered them a militia.¹⁵

The fact that Germany planned an offensive was the worst-kept secret of the war.¹⁶ The transfer of forces alone sufficed to give away intentions; and to most Allied observers the arrival of US forces was going to force the German hand.

'She must realise how quickly America is assembling her men out here,' Birdwood declared to Allen as early as 31 January:

> … and I cannot help thinking she will try to give us a knock-out blow, before America's full weight can be felt. In this, I do not for one moment think she will succeed. With a tremendous offensive, she will undoubtedly … achieve some temporary and local success, but, after that, we should be able to get at her in sufficient strength to cause her enormous casualties, and I hope … to think more seriously about terms. This, at all events, is what I am instilling in all my men, urging them to regard a big German offensive as a thing not to be dreaded, but rather to be welcomed …[17]

In fact the British were more vulnerable than most commanders imagined. Haig wanted to renew the Passchendaele campaign, but the failures of the previous year had damaged his relationship with Lloyd-George. The half-million odd men he wanted were not provided. Any offensive was on hold until 1919, and Haig was forced to disband 141 battalions just to bring the rest up to strength.[18] Then Anglo-French politicking led to a demand for British forces to take up French lines south of the Ypres salient. He sent Lieutenant-General Ivor Maxse's 18 Corps to hold the stretch, further thinning the British position — they were left with but 59 divisions to hold nearly 130 miles (209 km) of front. Although four American divisions were on French soil, US General John J. Pershing refused to commit them until his whole army was fully formed and trained.

Haig's only other option was static defences, and Stayte joined New Zealand working parties building fortifications at the beginning of the month, a 'very long way' behind the line. The scale gave him confidence: '… if he does come over he will get an awful slathering up. The place is also heavily wired for miles.'[19] But these works looked better than they actually were. Some rearward areas were never completed, and in places commanders jammed up to a third of the infantry into the vulnerable forward zone.[20] Few British officers understood the weakness.

To top it off, many commanders had forgotten the techniques demanded of mobile warfare. The New Zealand experience was typical. The division began training for open-field warfare in late February — a novelty after so many years of static fighting. Russell was not enthused by the results. He went to see 1 and 4 Brigades on an 'abominably cold' 2 March and thought they were 'disappointing — Fire, discipline and control very poor, no difference between rapid and normal rates of fire — co-operation between movement and fire strictly limited'.[21] Two days later he inspected 1 and 2 Canterbury Battalions, finding 1 Canterbury 'good' and 2 Canterbury 'distinctly bad' — which he put down in part to a 'complete change of officers … In everything they require bracing up.' Ultimately, he felt, they had not recovered from Polderhoek.[22]

A rising tide of raids suggested to Russell that the 'pot is soon to boil', and he kept the pressure on, going to see more 'musketry school' work at Norbecourt on 7 March.[23] He was still unhappy; on the 15th he again decried the performance of 2 Canterbury Battalion — 'as usual poor fire control, and disappointing rate of fire'.[24] He was happier with the Wellington battalion next day; but thought 2 Auckland were 'not up to the mark' when he inspected them on the 18th.[25] Part of the problem was that Russell's standards were extremely rigorous, and the division was exhausted — though a few weeks' 'recreational training' had 'produced a very noticeable improvement in the physical and mental condition of the troops'.[26]

Neither Russell nor his divisional commanders knew quite when or where the blow would fall, but time was clearly running short. By early March, British intelligence had actually identified the point of attack — Gough's weakened army in the Somme region. A breakthrough here would split the French and British armies, allowing Germany to roll the British up against the Channel coast.[27] However, Ludendorff's feints convinced the French that the attack would be launched in Champagne, and the gigantic blow that fell against Gough's forces on 21 March came largely as a surprise.

## The Second Battle of the Somme

Operation MICHAEL opened with a paroxysmal eruption of more than 6500 guns, firing on well-registered targets along a 50-mile (80-km) front. This 'devil's orchestra' played for five hours, and then 43 German divisions slammed against the dozen of Gough's Fifth Army, driving a wedge between the British and French positions between Arras and St Quentin. A little further north, 19 German divisions tore into the 14 of General Sir Julian Byng's Third Army. In a day of hard fighting, the Germans destroyed or captured a fifth of the British artillery, inflicted around 38,500 casualties,[28] and pushed through two of the three defensive belts southwest of St Quentin.

The New Zealanders were still training when the offensive began. Russell watched 2 Brigade practise 'mad minute' rifle fire at Moulle,[29] but around 11.00 p.m. orders came to 'return to the line at once', and the brigade embarked in the early hours of the 22nd with the help of a hundred trucks.[30] Next day Russell was ordered to move the division 'at once' to the Somme. 'The men very pleased I hear,' he remarked in his diary.[31] This was not quite true. Some were; but others were gloomier. 'We will soon be into it again now,' Jesse Stayte remarked in his diary, adding: 'We seem to be always in the line.'[32] John Harcourt thought the news somewhat disquieting.[33]

Gough ordered his dwindling army to withdraw behind the Somme that day. Unfortunately these moves were not well co-ordinated with Byng's. Haig tried to urge his commanders to keep their flanks in contact, but he was too late. By the end of the day the British had suffered 100,000 casualties, and Ludendorff's forces pursued Gough's across the Crozat Canal on the 24th. Other units consolidated the lodgement over the Somme. New Zealand's destinations changed with the situation; they were first ordered to concentrate at Le Cauroy, then the 5th Army area around Corbie. In the early hours of the 25th they were told instead to head for Hangest, Ailly and St Roch 'owing to the railway to Amiens being damaged',[34] but four and a half hours later were swung to a fourth series of villages, joining Lieutenant-General Sir G.M. Harper's 4 Corps.

German forces took Albert late on the 25th, about the time that lead elements of the New Zealand Division arrived at Mericourt l'Abbe, Morlancourt and Denancourt. They were just in time to meet a fresh emergency. A gap had been blasted in the Allied line north of Hamel, and the New Zealanders were ordered to help plug it, giving the rest of Byng's army time to dig in on the Ancre.[35] Some of the men were lucky enough to be picked up by lorries, among them John Harcourt, who shared a box seat with Eric Waters during a grinding drive to the front.[36] But motor transport generally 'proved totally inadequate' and most units had to march from the stations, forcing Russell to 'send battalions into action irrespective of the Brigades to which they belonged'.[37] They left all but essential gear under guard at the rail-heads, moving forward in fighting rig with 220 rounds apiece and 'Lewis guns and Vickers up to maximum carrying capacity'[38] — but facing cold nights without enough blankets. Other equipment was sent ahead to Ville-souse-Corbie, and lost when the Germans took the village on the night of the 25th.

Russell set up his headquarters at Hédauville, four miles (6.5 km) back from the front. The situation was so dire that when the first unit arrived in the early hours of 26 March, Russell pushed them straight out to Mailly-Maillet after just a few hours' rest.[39] The men had already marched to Hédauville, and walked on through the night, knowing they might have to fight before they could sleep. 'The whole countryside is aglow with burning villages,' Stayte wrote of the march, 'and the roar of artillery is awful.'[40] Other battalions were pushed out next day as they arrived.

Desperate hours followed. 1 Brigade, under Brigadier-General Melvill, could deploy little more than the two Auckland battalions, 2 Rifle Battalion, and some machine-gunners. The general plan called for closing a gap with 4 Australian Brigade, part of 4 Australian Division. This unit had been given the task of taking Hébuterne, and the main New Zealand objective became a new line on higher ground between Hamel and Hébuterne, northeast of Mailly-Maillet.[41]

German forces were moving east over that ground as the New Zealanders arrived, and Stayte — now with 1 Auckland Battalion — was in no doubt they would be 'in action before night falls'. Sure enough, his unit was marching about 'half a mile beyond Mailly' along the Serre road when they reached a windmill where 'two 18 pounders' were 'being unlimbered as though they had only just arrived'. Minutes later the men were told to 'fix bayonets and get out into artillery formation'. They moved up a ridge and through a hedge:

> *and then all at once we were under artillery fire … The shells dropped right amongst us and we at once got the order to Charge. Many were hit before we left the assembly place, but soon we were off and got to the hedge and trees and it was here that we first got into the fight proper.*

> *Fritz seemed to have the range to a yard and his shells and bullets from machine-guns and rifles simply deafened one. The screech of bullets was awful and our men began to fall rapidly. We had 80 yards to go down a slope before we could get cover. Fritz was on the ridge in front. However we went on and got to the bottom where there was a trench which was our objective and we took it but we left a trail of dead and wounded all down that slope.*[42]

The Germans began massing for a second attack, which the New Zealanders deflected with a bayonet charge up a gentle slope. Stayte was amazed by his own reactions:

> *This was my first time over the top and I hope I may never again have to go over. We were all naturally nervous at the start, but once we started and saw our mates going down all fear vanished and our one aim was to get to them with our bayonets and when we did get there they ran like a flock of sheep and it was simply a matter of shooting them as they ran.*[43]

This action left the New Zealanders in possession of the ridge overlooking the Ancre Valley, near a prominent sugar refinery and stand of apple trees. However, the flank remained exposed and the line had yet to be extended to Hébuterne, some two miles (3 km) northeast. It also had to be pushed due southeast to Hamel. The division continued to pour in on the 26th amid a good deal of confusion; the 3rd Rifles arrived at 3.00 p.m., 2 Wellington Battalion turned up two hours later from Amiens, and 2 Otago Battalion reached the area at 7.30 p.m.[44]

Elements of 4 Australian Division took Hébuterne against light resistance, and by midnight on the 26th had a firm flank against which the New Zealanders could close. However, German forces were already in Colincamps; what was available of 1 Brigade had to divert forces to deal with them, and failed to get to their intended high-ground and the planned base at La Signy Farm. Units were still arriving in dribs and drabs from the stations, and Russell organised a composite brigade to move into the line on the night of 26/27 March.

The New Zealanders threw out flank guards from Colincamps, then pushed ahead through growing light, 3 Rifle Battalion on the left, heading for Hébuterne, and 2 Wellington Battalion on the right, with the aim of reaching the Hébuterne road and digging in. Despite coming under machine-gun fire, the rifle battalion brushed aside the forward German positions and contacted outlying Australian forces around 6.30 a.m. on the 27th. Meanwhile 2 Wellington took La Signy Farm, but in the face of heavy resistance had to dig in some 400 yards short of objective. It was nevertheless a remarkable effort. Some of the men had not slept for two days, all had marched at least 20 miles (32 km), and command lines worked despite the fact that many units were thrown into ad hoc formations.

The countryside was alive with advancing Germans, variously from the Second and Seventeenth Armies, who did not realise the gap had been plugged. One column advanced on 2 Auckland Battalion and was decimated at short range. Another walked into the jaws of 2 Canterbury Battalion positions and

New Zealand guns in action at Mailly-Maillet, 1 April 1918, during the height of Ludendorff's offensive. The return of open-field tactics changed the character of the war.

(Henry Armitage Sanders, RSA Collection, Alexander Turnbull Library, PAColl-5311, G-13077-1/2)

'Walking wounded' New Zealanders on the Somme, early April 1918. These exhausted men were among the thousands of Kiwi soldiers who plugged the gap blasted by Ludendorff's forces in the last week of March.

(Henry Armitage Sanders, RSA Collection, Alexander Turnbull Library, PAColl-5311, G-13097-1/2)

was repelled in bitter hand-to-hand fighting. Richard Tuckey wrote home a few days later that:

> *We could not make out their attacking us with full packs up, but on questioning some of the prisoners we found they had been told that they had only to attack & march right through us, that they would not meet with much opposition. They were fearfully disgusted to find it was the New Zealand opposed to them, so they thought we were still on the Belgian Front. Most of them were very glad to be taken prisoners, and one youth commented that he was only 20 and was too young to die yet.*[45]

Better-organised assaults developed during the afternoon. This time, however, most of the New Zealand forces had the advantage of ground. They could see the Germans coming, and attack after attack was repelled, leaving the landscape beyond the New Zealand positions scattered with bodies of German troops. Then a concerted assault developed against Hébuterne, which was pushed back by the Australians and New Zealanders. A final attack went in against 2 Wellington Battalion in the early evening, where they were dug in between the sugar refinery and Hébuterne, forcing them back over 500 yards. However, the impetus of the general German thrust fell off with nightfall, and Russell took the opportunity to reorganise the forces that had been thrown ad hoc into the breach, getting the units properly set out and command lines correctly established.

The crisis was far from over. Lieutenant-Colonel Edward Puttick was ordered to 'take up a certain line & to fight my way there if necessary' on the 28th. Time was short and he spent but 15 minutes detailing matters to his unit before pushing them out through a:

> *beautiful moonlight night, and as we marched forward covered by advance & flank guards we could see the fires of our shell dumps, set alight to save them from the Hun. A few Hun aeroplanes were about, and we could see one very plainly in the moonlight …*[46]

New Zealand forces in the front line, La Signy Farm, early April 1918. These new-dug trenches with notched firing steps and earth parapets were a far cry from the semi-permanent structures of earlier years, reflecting the shift to open-field warfare.

(Henry Armitage Sanders, gelatin dry plate negative, RSA Collection, Alexander Turnbull Library, PAColl-5311, G-13092-1/2)

Puttick's force took the position, but they had to fight on next day without their commander; soon after breakfast he walked to a support position where a 'machine-gun was turned on us, and I got a bullet thro' the chest, thro' the left lung'.[47]

Work began that day on reserve lines behind the new positions, and the artillery finally began arriving. It had been sent by rail to Amiens, and the first pieces — four 18-pounder batteries and a number of 4.5-inch howitzers — did not reach Hédauville until late on the 27th.[48] They were a substantial help, though, and by 28 March Russell felt the New Zealand position was a 'good deal steadier' and the defences were 'beginning to take good shape'.[49]

Rain fell steadily overnight, and the New Zealanders had no duckboards.[50] The pressure built up again next day, when New Zealand forces made an effort to close up the line from La Signy Farm to Hébuterne. The results were marginal against a superior enemy; and German fire caused casualties — among them Brigadier H.T. Fulton, who had only just taken 3 (Rifle) Brigade back from Lieutenant-Colonel A.E. Stewart. He and one of his staff, Major Purdy, were

Kiwi trench diggers, 6 April 1918. Mobile warfare did not reduce the need for protection — but did mean that today's trenches might be well in the rear by tomorrow. A typical digging squad could cut 400 yards of trench a day.

(Henry Armitage Sanders, RSA Collection, Alexander Turnbull Library, PAColl-5311, G-13731-1/2)

killed by an 'unlucky shell which fell at the mouth of their cellar' — both 'a severe loss to division'.[51] He was New Zealand's third general officer killed during the war. Stewart took over the brigade. Elsewhere the lines were quieter. At Mailly-Maillet there was a 'lot of sniping going on', but as Stayte remarked, 'not much shell fire'.[52]

The Germans advanced through Rossignol Wood on the 30th amid poor weather. Conditions were appalling; trenches became ditches, and the New Zealanders scrabbled to find duckboards left over from the Somme battles two years earlier. Much of the divisional equipment was still being brought up and they were also short on wet weather gear. But this did not prevent an effort being made that afternoon to straighten the line. The 2 Auckland and 4 Rifle battalions advanced through the mud to a spur overlooking the Serre road. Bryan McDermott died that day, one of nearly a dozen cut down by a single machine-gun burst.[53] There was stiff opposition — one German position fell only after three efforts. The New Zealanders poured into the new positions, finding an old and well-equipped trench. Russell thought the whole operation 'very successful'.[54]

A good deal of equipment fell into New Zealand hands, including 127 machine-guns, various machine-gun parts, a 'box for administering oxygen' — and one bicycle. Whippet tanks contributed to the outcome — as the official report remarked, the new vehicles 'did excellent work and very materially assisted the advance'. For all that, the 'want of divisional cavalry was especially felt during the first two days' fighting'.[55] Even this late in the war, horse remained the sole fast-moving punch. The logistics backup was also behind par, a sign of the speed with which both sides had been moving. This took some time to sort out, and as Tuckey put it:

> our men were getting very miserable not having the comfort of anything to smoke. The good old YMCA came to light as usual, and sent a free issue of cigarettes, tobacco & matches to the whole NZ Division. A few days afterwards they established a free canteen in a cellar in a village that is not only under shell fire day and night, but machine-gun fire as well. Here they issue hot bovril or cocoa, biscuits, and cigarettes at any hour of the day or night, and best of all, they are large minded enough

A 9.2-inch rail gun in action behind New Zealand lines, near Colgneux, at the end of April 1918.

(Henry Armitage Sanders, RSA Collection, Alexander Turnbull Library, PAColl-5311, G-13724-1/2)

New Zealand gunners fight their 18-pounder amid grassy landscape near Beaussart, 23 May 1918. The failure of Ludendorff's Operation MICHAEL did not much reduce the intensity of fighting afterwards.

(Henry Armitage Sanders, RSA Collection, Alexander Turnbull Library, PAColl-5311, G-13222-1/2)

*to include ALL troops, not only New Zealanders ... On top of all this they keep on sending up to the front line a supply of cakes, cigarettes, tobacco, matches & chocolate & writing material.*[56]

A few soldiers leavened their diet with booty; Stayte's unit discovered a 'lot of wine and cider' in a cellar near Mailly-Maillet, and made 'the best of it'.[57] The region was very different from the division's older digs to the north, and Russell contrasted it favourably with Ypres, a 'disgusting spot' by comparison with their new locale:

*Here we are on lovely open rolling country where wheeled transport can, by following the folds of the ground, get nearly up to the front line. The change of air and scene in itself is worth an enormous amount. The Spring is evident all round. Woods full of wild flowers, hedges looking green and the grass growing everywhere.*[58]

This idyllic setting soon deteriorated. 'Wet today,' Thomas Preston scribbled on 4 April. 'Had a rough night, I was put on outpost duty, had no sleep. Fritz raided us last night, but we beat him back & secured 2 officers & 2 men prisoners. We had about 10 killed, two wounded 5 killed in my company.'[59] They still had to fight, and by this stage nerves were getting strained; John Harcourt found himself trying to keep his men together in the face of a German assault on the 5th, despite feeling 'rather rattled' himself.[60] The weather got the New Zealanders down. 'Rain for days on end without a break,' Tuckey wrote home. 'Mud — well, I thought the Flanders mud the worst I had ever seen, but I think the liquid clay of Picardy puts it in the shade. It is one satisfaction to know that if we are having a bad time, Fritz is having a jolly sight worse. All the prisoners that came in pitch the same tale about the terrible hardships made worse by the deadly accuracy of our artillery.'[61] But such thought did not do much to relieve the New Zealand misery. Stayte described their plight on 4 April:

*We are still holding the front line at Mailly. There is nothing doing [during] the day only sniping so we live like wild beasts, we sleep in our holes or trenches at day and go out to maim and kill at night. I have to spend the night watching an old sap. We have a high block in it and for a step to stand on to watch over the block some clever fellow has made a platform of dead bodies and covered them with about 2 inches of earth. It is a good stand but rather gruesome when one is on guard standing on it through the night.*[62]

Russell still felt the Germans had fight left in them and went around the lines on a 'horribly rainy and cold' 8 April to stop working parties from getting 'run down before the next fight which cannot be far off'.[63] He was convinced the Germans had achieved their successes because on the whole they were 'better educated, more efficient and thorough' than the British — and 'because they have learnt to obey'. But he was in little doubt as to the outcome; 'at the end the wild beast will have exhausted itself, and we must then soberly … put our somewhat damaged house in order'.[64]

'Jumping Jennie', stuck in the New Zealand sector of the old Somme trench system near Gommecourt, July 1918.

(Henry Armitage Sanders, RSA Collection, Alexander Turnbull Library, PAColl-5311, G-13484-1/2)

By this time the impetus was swinging away from the New Zealand front, and they finally had time to draw breath after fighting for days in poor conditions against massive odds, without much equipment, and often without sleep. It was a remarkable performance; they had played a major role in stemming the German advance in the Somme sector, and the result was recognised by British command.[65] The soldiers were certainly well aware of what they had done. 'Our men were splendid,' Tuckey enthused in a letter home:

> *No sleep for three nights, a long forced march & then at the end of it, hopped into Fritz, checked his advance, drove him back & forced him to take up unfavourable positions & then held him there ... How appalling his losses must have been you can guess by the fact that his attack was stopped half way across no man's land, and what remained of his attacking force folded back to the shelter of his own trenches.*[66]

Further south, Ludendorff's forces took Albert and pushed towards Amiens. By 5 April they were approaching the junction of the Somme and the Oise, around 5 miles (8 km) from the town. As Birdwood admitted to Allen a few weeks later, these unprecedented advances gave them an 'anxious time', and he had not himself anticipated the way the line would 'bend to the extent it has'.[67] But the Germans were at the end of their tether. Supplies had to be brought up over country churned, dug and blasted by three years of positional warfare, and many soldiers succumbed to the lure of booty and wine.[68] Ludendorff was also running out of immediate forces. Although his men had pushed 40 miles (64 km) along a 50-mile (80-km) front by early April, nearly one in three became casualties. Finally he called the attack off. MICHAEL had made spectacular advances; but it had to be counted a failure, particularly as the direction mitigated against any bold strategic drive once the British line had been broken.

However, the Germans had yet to shoot their bolt; Ludendorff still had forces to work with, and as MICHAEL ground to a halt he launched a new operation around Armentières, pushing 35 divisions from his Sixth and Fourth Armies into the British First and Second Armies. The initial objective of Operation GEORGETTE was Hazebrouck, but again the BEF were the real target. Faulty defensive strategy quickly let the British down, and they were pushed into open country. New Zealanders were among them, including part of 6 Battery, which was detached from the division and dug in at 'Hyde Park Corner' near Ploegsteert Wood. Forces coming up to move the guns missed their destination, and battery commander Major R. Miles was ordered to hold on. He rallied infantry around his position and fought the guns until they were out of ammunition, even turning one to take on German positions in Ploegsteert village.

The situation looked grim. Haig issued a despairing 'no retreat' order on 10 April, but Messines Ridge fell to the German Fourth Army, and by 29 April the Germans had Ballieul, threatening to roll Plumer's Second Army up against the Belgians and the Channel coast. Pershing refused to allow his own forces to bolster the crumbling lines; but Ludendorff once again over-extended, and in the face of stiffening resistance, called off the offensive.

The Maori Pioneer Battalion welcome Sir Joseph Ward (left) and Prime Minister William Ferguson Massey near Bois-de-Warnimont, 30 June 1918.

(Henry Armitage Sanders, gelatin dry plate negative, RSA Collection, Alexander Turnbull Library, PAColl-5311, G-13284-1/2)

## Influenza and morale

The situation on the New Zealand front settled during April as the focus swung to GEORGETTE, but there were fears that Ludendorff might attack again around the Somme, and the pioneers dug fresh defences behind the new lines. Spring was 'well advanced', as Stayte put it. 'It is a very beautiful country only for the War one would enjoy it.'[69] Raiding again became a part of trench life, often led by Sergeant R.C. (Dick) Travis, with 2 Otago Battalion.[70]

The New Zealanders certainly made an impression. Prisoners revealed that they had been warned 'not to get captured alive' by New Zealanders, because 'New Zealanders were cannibals and would certainly eat them although initial kindness might be shown and cigarettes offered'. Russell took this as propaganda by the German officer corps 'to prevent Germans deserting',[71] and *The Times* report about the incident later turned up on New Zealand divisional Christmas cards.[72]

'Cannibal Paradise': rumour that New Zealanders ate their prisoners prompted great hilarity in mid-1918. These signs appeared in a trench near Gommecourt in early July, and the claim was dismissed by commanders as a German propaganda effort to reduce desertion. But it may have been founded in a general German ignorance of New Zealand and its peoples.

(Henry Armitage Sanders, RSA Collection, Alexander Turnbull Library, PAColl-5311, G-13460-1/2)

## The Commander

Major-General Sir Andrew Hamilton Russell.
(Photographer unknown, *Evening Post* Collection, Alexander Turnbull Library, PAColl-5927-29, C-22244-1/2)

The New Zealand Division was led by Major-General Sir Andrew Hamilton Russell (1868–1960), known as Guy to his friends and scion of one of Hawke's Bay's prominent pastoral families. He had impeccable credentials for the job: a Harrow old boy and Sandhurst graduate who served for five years in India during the high noontide of Queen Victoria's Imperial age. His career as a professional soldier was, however, short lived; in 1892 he returned to his native province to help run the family properties at Tunanui and Twyford, both near Hastings. But he retained his love for the military and took a significant role in the development of the Territorials. By 1914 he was commanding the 1st Wellington Mounted Rifle Brigade.

For Russell the war soon gained personal dimension. Some of the young men he led were from Hawke's Bay pastoral families, well known to the Russells; and as the Gallipoli campaign degenerated into muddy chaos he had the invidious task of passing on the worst news. 'I am so sorry for you,' he wrote to Mason and Margaret Chambers in August 1915, with the news that their son Selwyn had been killed by a sniper. 'For I knew and felt how you hated parting with him. One hardly cares to reckon any chance of getting out of this alive, or even untouched.'[73]

He took his responsibilities seriously when he became Major-General commanding the New Zealand Division in early 1916. His care for the men was legendary, but he was no slacker when it came to discipline,[74] and was determined to train the men to his exacting standards. By most accounts Russell displayed a flair for what was needed to succeed against the constraints of the Western Front, though by the early twenty-first century historical opinion was divided.[75] While his command was not flawless, he arguably put up a better showing than many of his peers, and better than many others in higher command.

Russell was awarded the DSO, made KCMG in 1915, and then KCB in 1917. He returned to New Zealand in 1919, and although he resumed his pre-war life as a pastoralist, retained a deep interest in the military and was a two-term president of the Returned Soldiers' Association. In 1940, as the twentieth-century struggle with Germany entered its second act, he came out of retirement to become Inspector-General of the armed forces. Afterwards he continued to live at Tunanui, where he died in 1960 at the age of 92.

Ludendorff launched another push against the French in late May, worrying Russell. 'Bosche offensive progressing down Soissons way too well,' he wrote in his diary, 'and fear it will draw reserves too far south.'[76] But in the end this too ran into trouble. Forty German divisions penetrated 40 miles (64 km) in three days; but by this time Pershing had relented and the US First and Second Divisions counter-attacked at Cantigny and Bellau Wood. Casualties were high; the 'Doughboys' were inexperienced, and it showed. But they halted the advance.[77]

The New Zealand Division was relieved in early June, withdrawing eventually to Authie, although one brigade was rotated into the Somme lines. They did so just as 'Spanish flu' erupted across the front, and although the mid-year variant of this disease was less lethal than the strain that emerged at year's end,[78] the sick lists flourished.

Richard Charles Travis (1884–1918), won a posthumous VC for his efforts on 23 July 1918. His day of action began when he walked into no-man's land with two Stokes mortar bombs to blow a path through the wire for his men. When one wing of the assault was held up by machine-gun fire, Travis took on a machine-gun post with a revolver, then shot four German soldiers running to rescue their fellows. He survived these actions only to be cut down later by shrapnel, mourned by his fellow soldiers and remembered by Major-General Sir Andrew Russell as the 'best all-round scout the division has produced'.

(Photographer unknown, Alexander Turnbull Library, F-103803-1/2)

The New Zealanders returned to the line in the first week of July, settling into a new sector running through Rossignol Wood to a point just east of Hébuterne, including what was left of Gommecourt. The weak point was the wood, where remaining trees provided cover for German troops, and early New Zealand operations were geared around eliminating the problem. First efforts focused on deepening the line around Hébuterne. Elements of 3 (Rifle) Brigade launched an operation south of Puisieux Road in the first week of July. Raids were also launched into the wood, but then the Germans withdrew under orders as Ludendorff straightened the line after GEORGETTE.

Plans were laid to raid the new German positions on the 23rd. The task went to Travis' battalion, 2 Otago, but the attack was delayed by rain and did not go ahead until late on the 4th — 'got 7 guns & 15 Huns killed', Preston wrote in his diary. 'Casualties light.'[79] Travis was awarded the Victoria Cross for his own efforts, but was cut down by shrapnel early on the 25th when a German artillery barrage hammered into the New Zealand front,[80] much to the dismay of everyone from Russell down. He was given a military funeral, attended by his battalion and Brigade staff.[81]

Ludendorff tried again in mid-July, but a swift French response on the Marne and German over-extension brought the push to an end. Germany had suffered more than one million casualties.[82] The line extended in several ragged salients, and Ludendorff pulled back from the Marne in the face of an efficient combined-arms offensive launched by the new French Commander in Chief, Ferdinand Foch.

Then on 8 August, Haig attacked from Amiens.

# 6

# ONE HUNDRED DAYS

The British assault on Amiens opened the 'hundred days' of action that brought the war to its end. The initial assault was prosecuted by the British First and French Fourth armies, using infantry, artillery, aircraft and tanks together in effective co-operation for the first time. Field wireless sets at Corps and Divisional command level helped the perennial problem of control. The campaign gained further impetus from another jump in scale; more than 530 tanks were deployed into the field, backed with monolithic artillery support. In the four weeks between 8 August and 6 September the British fired 5,372,000 rounds of 18-pounder ammunition, 1,443,400 rounds of 4.5-inch, and 1,566,800 rounds of 6-inch.

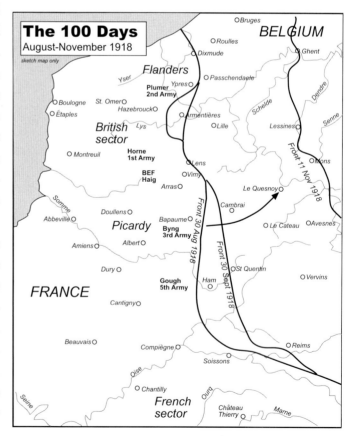

These advantages quickly told. British forces advanced 8 miles (13 km) on 8 August alone and inflicted more than 27,000 casualties. The main objective — the Paris–Amiens railway — fell into Allied hands, reducing German positions around Serre to an exposed salient, and Ludendorff's only sensible tactical option was withdrawal, though his direction was limited by the French capture of the Lassigny Range. Nor did the pace ease as the British

New Zealand forces near Bapaume, probably August 1918.

(Henry Armitage Sanders, RSA Collection, Alexander Turnbull Library, PAColl-5311, G-13608-1/2)

approached the old Somme trench systems. Haig now eschewed a frontal assault and launched a new offensive around Bapaume, in which Byng's Third Army played a lead role.

On 21 August the New Zealanders joined 42, 37, 5 and 63 (Royal Naval) divisions in a push from Puiseux towards the Albert–Arras railway and Irles-Bihucourt. The Kiwi force was — by plan — 'practically squeezed out' by the end of the day.[1] However, they took the valley east of Puiseux, topping the ridge beyond, where they came under machine-gun fire from German positions on the Ancre. Next morning 3 (Rifle) Brigade patrols came under heavy fire, and there was an attempted counter-attack from Miraumont. This was driven back by New Zealand machine-gunners, and around 300 Germans fell into New Zealand hands.

The division had a larger part in the Second Battle of Bapaume, which took the force a short distance north of their 1916 operations. Russell moved his advanced headquarters into a trench near Bucquoi,[2] and the Kiwis got the task of clearing Loupart Wood, Grévilliers, and the approaches to Bapaume. Russell pushed 1 and 2 Brigades forward with little gear, moving largely at night to escape detection. Darkness brought its own problems. By the early hours of

24 August, 1 Brigade was east of the Albert–Arras railway, but its commanders were uncertain where the front actually was.

The assault into Loupart Wood began in darkness at 4.15 a.m., but the tanks were hampered by foliage and 1 Wellington Battalion was beset by German machine-guns. Forces inside the wood were not subdued until around noon — and then only after the Wellingtons called up support. Meanwhile 1 Auckland Battalion walked into one side of Grévilliers as the Germans scurried out the other, only to run into wire 'gooseberries' and heavy machine-gun fire from trenches south of the town. Two tanks rumbled up, and the Kiwis waved their helmets to attract them. Although wounded, Sergeant Samuel Forsyth tried to lead one against anti-tank and machine-guns. A shell disabled the tank, but Forsyth then took the crew and several of his own men in an effort to flank the machine-guns, forcing them back — and at that moment he was killed by a sniper. He was awarded a posthumous Victoria Cross.

Forces from 2 Brigade pushed towards Biefvillers. The advance went smoothly until they reached a ridge southeast of the village, and German artillery opened fire. Four tanks were shattered, and then the infantry was enfiladed by the same machine-guns that were holding up the Aucklanders ahead of Grévilliers. That night 2 Brigade was relieved in line by part of 37

Laurie C. Mackie (left) and H.G. Wallace in what Mackie called a 'Fritzie dugout', Bapaume, August 1918.

(Photographer unknown, Alexander Turnbull Library, PA1-0-311-21-1)

Division, freeing the New Zealanders for a fresh attack on the 25th into Farreuil and Carresville, part of a wider push by Byng's forces to encircle Bapaume. But progress that day and the next was not great. At one point, German machine-guns situated in upper storeys of farm buildings were even able to enfilade the New Zealand trenches. Russell put a 'new plan' to 4 Corps command that day. Late on the 28th he heard of a fresh scheme at Corps level to 'rush Bapaume',[3] but the New Zealand troops found it was:

> … *not a hard nut. We bombarded it thoroughly, the Bosche walked out of it one end, and we walked into it at the other. As a matter of fact … the laugh was on his side, as he slipped out under our noses, and if we lost no men, neither did he …*[4]

The advance continued towards Fremicourt, which fell on the 30th. Russell thought it was an 'error not to have made [the] village [the] main objective', though he ruminated that 'villages are only obstacles — not ends in themselves'.[5] In the face of ongoing casualties he hoped his force might be 'worked quietly with a minimum expenditure of life, and a maximum of ammunition. The latter can be replaced, the former not so.'[6]

New Zealand Field Artillery near Grévilliers, 20 August 1918.

(Henry Armitage Sanders, RSA Collection, Alexander Turnbull Library, PAColl-5311, G-13582-1/2)

Part of the issue was that the British were in transition from a static war to one of movement. Lessons had to be learned, at times relearned. New Zealand shared the experience.

## Havrincourt to the Sambre

The New Zealand Division was in almost constant action during the last three months of the war. Germans surrendered in surprising numbers as divisional forces advanced beyond Fremicourt,[7] more than 200 on 2 September alone.[8] This matched similar experiences across the front, and one historian has argued that this predeliction to surrender, and not casualties or a decisive turn in the field, was what finally defeated Ludendorff's army.[9]

For some Kiwis the surrender of a long-time enemy created opportunity for revenge. Ormond Burton observed that some New Zealanders treated their prisoners well, but others even robbed ordinary German soldiery of watches, photographs of girlfriends, and cash.[10] Jesse Stayte was dismayed. 'I could not bring myself to rob a man's pockets even though he is a Fritz …. I don't mind looking him over after he is dead but not till then.'[11] Some went further; one New Zealand medical officer had to be threatened at gunpoint before he would treat a seriously wounded German.[12]

The New Zealanders pushed on. The barrage on 2 September went down in the wrong place, hampering the advance up a ridge ahead of Baencourt; and elements of 2 Otago Battalion had difficulty advancing on Haplincourt in the face of machine-gun fire from positions west of the village. The village fell next morning to 2 Brigade, supported by elements of the Scots Greys. The Germans pulled out of Havrincourt Wood on the 5th, which Russell felt was a 'relief'.[13]

Trescault Spur lay ahead, a vital ridge that overlooked the British advance on one side and the Hindenburg Line on the other. With the adjacent Canal du Nord the hill posed a formidable obstacle to the advancing 37th, New Zealand and 42nd divisions. A probing attack by 2 Rifle Battalion penetrated as far as the dense foliage of Gouzeaucourt Wood on 9 September, but was pushed back by an overwhelming number of green-clad *Jaeger*.

Russell went to a Corps conference that day in pouring rain — 'unfortunate as it means our new home is mud' — and 'arranged to take the ridge in front

At ease; officers of the Wellington Battalion near Gommecourt Wood, 10 August 1918.

(Henry Armitage Sanders, RSA Collection, Alexander Turnbull Library, PAColl-5311, G-13454-1/2)

The devastation of war: Puiseux, 21 August 1918. The original caption reads: 'In this advance as in every other the Germans shelled the villages from which they were pushed out although it would be impossible to cause any greater damage than had already been caused.'

(Henry Armitage Sanders, RSA Collection, Alexander Turnbull Library, PAColl-5311, G-13501-1/2)

of us'.[14] The plan that emerged was part of a wider effort by two British corps to crack the southern Hindenburg Line, throwing 37 Division, the New Zealand Division and part of 38 Division against the ridge. There were huge difficulties; the ridge was protected by a trench system dubbed Snap, flanked to the south by a further complex known as African. There was no doubt that the Germans intended to fight, and early on 12 September three battalions of 3 (Rifle) Brigade ran into 'stiff resistance' as they advanced towards Snap Reserve trench at the base of the ridge.[15]

One platoon on the right flank of the advance, under Sergeant Harry Laurent, ran across part of the African trench and pushed towards Gouzeaucourt. Just seven men were left when they reached their objective, but Laurent took both the position and 112 enemy soldiers. This performance won him the Victoria Cross. Snap Reserve fell to the New Zealanders, but the *Jaeger* holding Snap trench on the ridge began pasting the area with machine-gun fire. One small group of Kiwis eventually reached a crossroads, but while the New Zealanders 'eventually gained all the ground on [the] left', the objectives on the right remained elusive. Russell was dismayed, condemning 38 Division for doing 'nothing'.[16]

That night, 1 Brigade relieved the tired men of 3 (Rifle) Brigade amid pouring rain. They fought on next day under dismal skies and a steady sprinkle of gas shells, and the Kiwis were beaten back by resolute *Jaeger* armed with flame-throwers. On the 14th, the exhausted New Zealanders handed over to 5 Division and pulled back to Fabreuil for an overdue rest.

Haig launched his final opus on 26 September, a massive assault that involved virtually the whole Allied force in theatre. The tactics already tested at Arras were refined with 'bite and hold' techniques. Infantry tactics included 'diamond formation' advances in the lee of tanks; and the soldiers were lavishly equipped with Lewis guns, Stokes mortars and other portable weapons, firepower they had not enjoyed even two years earlier. Commanders had artillery tactics down pat; artillery fire-plans were co-ordinated on the 'hurricane' principle. Effective use was also made of aerial reconnaissance.[17] Munitions were available in huge quantities and used lavishly. Nearly a million rounds of all calibres were fired on 29 September alone.[18]

In this new environment of sweeping advances, small-scale movement

## Whippets

The New Zealanders first worked with Whippet medium tanks in March of 1918, near Mailly-Maillet, regarding the type with an affection that belied its many mechanical deficiencies.

Originally dubbed the 'Tritton Chaser', the Whippet was founded in a War Office demand for a breakthrough vehicle and weighed in at just over 14 tons. There was no requirement to cross trenches, which greatly eased the design constraints; the vehicle that emerged was capable of around 8 mph (13 kph) on the power of twin 45-hp Tylor motors, a great improvement over the rhomboids. However, the tracks were still unsprung and steering was achieved by differentially throttling the engines. In theory this avoided the power losses caused by the differential braking system used in the rhomboids, but it was not unknown for one engine to stall, leaving the Whippet spinning helplessly on its axis, shedding its tracks as it went. This was not the only deficiency. A range of 40 miles (64 km) was too limited for the breakthrough role, and the front-mounted fuel tank, though armoured, was in precisely the place where anti-tank fire was most likely to come in. Original plans for a revolving turret were scrapped because of the mechanical difficulties, and the resulting fixed structure with a gun in each quadrant was cramped.

All these problems were resolvable given time; but although a 360-hp aero-engined variant was built in 1918, better tanks were already on the drawing board and the 200-odd surviving Whippets were scrapped in 1919.

Mk A Whippet medium tanks in the mist on the New Zealand sector, August 1918.
(Henry Armitage Sanders, RSA Collection, Alexander Turnbull Library, PAColl-5311, G-13524-1/2)

became less crucial than the general thrust. Haig intended to partially flank the Hindenburg system with an advance towards Cambrai, combined with a frontal advance to take the outer defences. 4 Corps was expected to tackle the ridges ahead of the Hindenburg trench systems, and the New Zealanders were tipped to move if 5 or 42 Divisions broke through. Russell expected to be called on, but as late as 25 September was still 'very much in the dark', and went to see Harper next day in the hope of getting more information, without success.[19]

Battle opened on 27 September, though 4 Corps moves were 'not very successful'.[20] The New Zealanders launched an assault towards the Scheldt Canal. This was the essential key to the Hindenburg Line, and on the 28th the men of 1 and 2 Brigades 'attacked with complete success, overrunning the Boche as far as the Canal at Crevecour la racque bon Avir'.[21]

That day Ludendorff decided Germany had to seek terms. The central powers were collapsing; news arrived on the 29th that Germany's ally Bulgaria was seeking an armistice on the Salonika Front, and Ludendorff led a formal deputation recommending Germany follow suit on the basis of President Wilson's Fourteen Points. There was little dissent, but ructions followed among German government circles when it came to the details, and then Ludendorff backtracked amid apparently promising news from the front.[22] His men, by and large, were fighting on.

The extraordinary resistance put up by German armed forces during these last weeks of the war demands explanation in light of the way historians have usually interpreted the collapse of the Second Reich — arguments have ranged from the notion that the British defeated the German army in the field,[23] to the idea that Pershing's forces did the same.[24]

In fact, while both British and US armies scored a succession of victories, none was easy. Although briefly depressed by the late September experience, most of Ludendorff's men had plenty of fight left in them.[25] This point is borne out by the New Zealand experience as they squared up to the Crevecour Canal on 28 September. 5 Division was meant to come up on the flank, and when it did not the Kiwis were left in a difficult position. Evans recorded the frustration. In the early hours of the 30th he received orders to attack Crevecour, but 'As other boys were not up' they were changed to a limited objective to 'capture the bridgeheads over St Quentin and take the village'.[26] He 'marched off on a compass bearing' and 'captured and crossed the canal at 6.15 a.m.' — then ran into 'heavy MG fire' and his units were 'held up on River Escault'. Efforts to cross were foiled by 'MG fire from our front and right flank', and they held on to their slender bridgehead overnight in the face of heavy attack.[27] 'It's useless to depend on British divisions,' an exasperated Russell scribbled in his diary on the 30th, 'they may succeed or they may not.'[28]

British forces pushing into the Hindenburg Line beyond the Canal du Nord had better luck, helped by New Zealand engineering efforts; the Tunnelling Company threw a bridge across the canal in just four days from 28 September. The breakthrough threatened to collapse the German line, opening the way for the Second Battle of Le Cateau. Russell had the New Zealand part refined by 7 October, involving an advance of some 2.5 miles (4 km) to a plateau between the Schelde and Selle canals. He gave the task to 2 and 3 (Rifle) Brigades and scheduled a pre-dawn attack beginning at 4.30 a.m. on the 8th, grumbling that it was 'impossible to get British divisions … to attack in the dark', though the 'advantages are obvious and great in reducing casualties'.[29]

By 5.30 a.m. on 8 October the 1st and 2nd Rifle Battalions were on first objective on the Seranvilliers trench, then began advancing to the Cambrai road. Around a thousand prisoners fell into New Zealand hands, but what Russell called 'shilly-shallying' at command level gave the Germans time to regroup. There was a counter-attack around 5.00 p.m. that recovered part of Seranvilliers. Russell decided to push again next day, with the objective of the Le Cateau–Cambrai railway line, though he found the situation frustrating. 'Higher Command is oblivious of the difficulties of the lower ranks.'[30]

The second attack went in at 5.20 a.m. on 9 October, and in the face of a German retreat the New Zealanders were on the railway line by 9.00 a.m. The advanced forces reached the Selle River, 5 miles (8 km) ahead, before encountering any serious opposition. It appeared that the *Jaeger* had dug into the eastern slopes of the Selle River valley. The New Zealanders were about to hand over to 42 Division, but got the task of taking the enemy positions. There were several changes of plan during the day before an attack by the Wellington companies gained the heights.

The battle cost New Zealand 536 casualties, although they captured 1400 prisoners and took 13 guns.[31] It was an extraordinary 'bag', particularly given the way that other German forces were still fighting. Niall Fergusson has theorised that part of the reason was failure of morale. Some soldiers fought with undiminished resolve, but for others Ludendorff's moment of doubt was infectious, and the option of surrender was apparently validated when the Kaiser and his officials began looking for an armistice.[32] The hunger suggested by other historians seems to have been less of a factor. The Allied blockade reduced the German people to subsistence level,[33] but it appears some analysts have exaggerated deaths from starvation.[34] Certainly the soldiers had plenty of food. 'They do not look starved,' Russell remarked in one letter home.[35]

The more compelling issue was political. Germany had evolved into a military dictatorship, which was less stable than the democracies it was fighting, and a combination of casualty lists, hunger, shortages and social dislocation were finally translated into a recipe for state failure. Yet even in the third week of October 1918, as the High Seas Fleet succumbed to a communist-inspired mutiny, there was no clear sign that German leaders could agree on a ceasefire.

Haig did not let the pressure off. As fighting slowed around Le Cateau, he ordered a fresh assault on the Lys, which brought Lille into Allied hands by 18 October. A renewed thrust from Le Cateau began even before the northern push slowed, throwing much of the 4th Army and elements of the French into an attack on the Sambre-et-Oise Canal.

Anti-aircraft battery behind the New Zealand lines during the closing weeks of the First World War, 28 October 1918.

(Photographer unknown, Bruce Thomson Collection, Alexander Turnbull Library, PAColl-0197, F-92228-1/2)

The New Zealand Division led a general attack towards Beaurain on 23 October. The assault began on schedule at 8.20 a.m.,[36] but because of an artillery bombardment, 37 Division did not attack until 10.00 a.m., meaning the New Zealand right flank was exposed. In the end, elements of 2 Otago Company took some of the 37 Division objectives and cleared the way for the New Zealand advance. By nightfall, forces were in position near Beaudignies — a remarkable success which Russell credited to an 'exceptionally good performance' by the 'Bn. Cmdrs., [Lieutenant-Colonel A.D.] Stitt and [Lieutenant-Colonel J.] Hargest'.[37]

A good deal of equipment fell into New Zealand hands, and 2 Brigade commander, Brigadier-General R. Young, felt a further advance was possible. Russell concurred, and the New Zealand brigade pushed ahead at night — an unprecedented move that put the advanced elements within sight of Le Quesnoy. A series of small advances began on the 24th, partly to start encircling the town, partly to dislodge German forces from the flanks. There seemed little doubt that the German army largely retained its morale, however, and over the next few days the division was reorganised ready to renew the advance in strength. Russell tried to visit his sick brother in Switzerland, though in the event could get no further than Paris; and then news came that his brother had died. 'The war absorbs everyone entirely — not in part.'[38]

## The eleventh hour

The end came suddenly. Ludendorff's effort to discredit the pro-armistice faction backfired during the last week of October, and he tendered his resignation to the Kaiser on the 26th. Prince Max, the chancellor, appointed the moderate General Wilhelm Groener in his stead. The Kaiser was also under pressure to abdicate and left for Belgium on the 29th, ostensibly to be closer to his forces, wondering whether he could use the army to quell rebels in Verviers and Aix-la-Chappelle.[39]

Russell arrived in the French capital on 30 October amid rumour of peace.[40] Turkey signed an armistice that day, and Hungary declared itself independent on 1 November, signalling the collapse of the Austro-Hungarian Empire. Austria signed an armistice on 3 November. The British kept the pressure up on Germany with a fresh offensive into the region between the Sambre and Scheldt rivers. The New Zealand Division got the task of taking Le Quesnoy. This stood on high ground above the Ecallion and Rhonelle rivers, and retained its seventeenth-century ramparts, originally designed for Louis XIV by Sébastien Leprestre, Marquis of Vauban. These were ideal strongpoints for machine-gunners and a formidable barrier to infantry. The plan called for a heavy artillery barrage on and around the walls, accepting collateral damage to historic structures — a point that scarcely raised eyebrows.

The attack opened at dawn on 4 November with a hurricane barrage from artillery and mortars. By mid-morning Le Quesnoy was surrounded, but early efforts by Lieutenant-Colonel H.E. Barrowclough to break into the walled section came to nothing. The machine-guns on the walls posed a near insurmountable threat. One attempt to cross a bridge on the Landrecies road and tackle the wall was repelled by fire; however, as the day wore on mortars were brought up and began pasting the wall-top machine-gunners.

Around 4.00 p.m., Barrowclough found a rampart topped by a grassy bank. Barrowclough's intelligence officer, Second Lieutenant L.C. Averill, carefully climbed a ladder and poked his head over the top to see several Germans running away. He hastened them along with his revolver and then leaped to the

A New Zealand 4.5-inch howitzer in action near Le Quesnoy, late October 1918.

(Henry Armitage Sanders, RSA Collection, Alexander Turnbull Library, PAColl-5311, G-13698-1/2)

New Zealand transports at Le Quesnoy, late October 1918.

(Photographer unknown, RSA Collection, Alexander Turnbull Library, G-13696-1/2)

top, closely followed by Barrowclough and the men of the battalion. Soon afterwards, 3 (Rifle) Brigade began marching in through the Valenciennes gate.[41] Some 2000 prisoners and 60 guns fell into New Zealand hands.

Next day divisional forces began fanning beyond the town into stiff resistance, and took Mormal Forest on 5 November.

By this time it was obvious to most in the German government that the fighting had to be brought to an end.[42] Revolution simmered; there were red flags flying over 11 German cities and five of the harbours.[43] But until they formally agreed to armistice the war had to continue, and men still died, among them New Zealand gunner Frank Gardner, killed in action on the 7th.[44] He had survived almost to the end. On 9 November, 6 Corps took over the New Zealand sector. That day the Chancellor, Prince Max, handed power to socialist leader Frederich Ebert. Wilhelm abdicated next day, taking a train to 23 years of exile in Holland's Castle Doorn. The New Zealand Division was pulling back to reserve late on 10 November when word came that the 'Huns have until 11 am tomorrow to decide whether they will accept the Allies' armistice terms or not … Great joy amongst troops.'[45]

The armistice was signed in the early hours of 11 November, with effect from 11 a.m. Suddenly, on this 'very cold day' with 'every appearance of snow',[46] it was over, 54 gruelling months after the Germans first rolled into Belgium. The people of Britain, New Zealand, Australia, France, America and the other Allied nations flocked joyous into the streets,[47] but the response at the front was subdued. New Zealand's reaction was typical; some of the Kiwis expressed 'great joy and jubilation', but most — like Evans — also found it 'hard to realise that it is really here'.[48] N.E. Hassell heard someone mutter 'That's torn it.' Nobody appeared to know what to do next, and for the rest of the day 'we just wandered aimlessly about doing nothing'.[49] The response was noticed at command level. 'There has been little, if any, exuberant display of enthusiasm over the armistice here,' Russell wrote two days later.[50]

In hindsight it was perhaps predictable. The numbing environment of disease, mutilation, filth and mud could not be silenced with the stroke of a diplomatic pen. There had been too many air raids, whizz-bangs, gas shells, machine-guns, barrages, wire gooseberries and mines. Too many mates had died. Too many had been carried, screaming, choking or blinded, from the field. The names of the places where they fought and died were graven in the minds of the survivors: Flers, Messines, Passchendaele, Bapaume, Plogsteert Wood, Mailly-Maillet, Gommecourt, Rossignol, Le Quesnoy, words as poignant as the half-romanticised memories of home. Soldiers worn down by months and years of strain simply could not accept the moment when their personal hell came to an end; it had been too intense, too dominating, too enduring. Many simply gave silent thanks for their deliverance, Russell among them: 'Thank God!'[51]

There had been talk for weeks that the New Zealanders would be one of the occupying forces on the Rhine, and rumour flowed freely on 12 November.[52] Russell met his commanders next day to outline a demobilisation scheme, but that evening there was a 'very unfortunate occurrence' in the ranks.[53] Revolution had swept both Allied and Central powers in the last years of the war. Late on the 13th a 'mass meeting headed by a few Red Feds' was held in the New Zealand lines.[54] However, New Zealand's version of the movement was not particularly radical,[55] and Russell understood it was a 'friendly' assemblage, 'got up apparently by an agitator … who I understand has achieved notoriety in NZ'.

He was unconcerned: 'think no danger but must watch for Bolshevism'.[56] Evans, close to the cutting edge of the forces, was also relaxed. 'I don't think that we have anyone in the Batt. likely to support the ringleaders in last night's affair.'[57] This was typical of New Zealand; as always, Kiwis felt little need to revolt in the European sense; and even after four years of mind-shattering war, that fundamental value remained.

The division began marching through Belgium in mid-December. Evans' unit left on the 18th in 'rain which continued all day and made the march very heavy'. There were problems finding billets when they reached Liège. Evans looked at the fortifications with undisguised curiosity — concluding 'that these forts should have held up the German advance in 1914 much longer than what they did. Apart from the damage done by actually blowing up the gun pits, this fort is practically untouched.'[58]

The lead elements of 2 Brigade reached Cologne on 20 December, crossing

March on the Rhine: New Zealand forces on parade, part of the army of occupation, early 1919.

(Henry Armitage Sanders, RSA Collection, Alexander Turnbull Library, PAColl-5311, G-13768-1/2)

the Rhine on a wavering bridge supported by boats, and moving on to Mulheim amid the curious gazes of German people. It was a 'beautiful country & one regrets more than ever that it is not spring'.[59] Christmas came with a 'mantle of snow which made the region look extremely pretty and what one has always hoped Xmas in this hemisphere'. Food was short, but the men found what they could and 'considering the difficulties in getting supplies, we did exceptionally well'.[60] Many wondered what 1919 would bring. 'The future is a tough proposition,' Evans wrote in his diary, 'it is going to take some solving, as far as I am concerned. I wonder in what direction this day next year will find me.'[61]

The division spent three months in Germany. Fraternisation was strictly prohibited but it was impossible to avoid, and New Zealand chocolate won the hearts of hungry children. The one thing on the minds of most of the soldiers was demobilisation. The long process of disbanding the division began in late December; those sent on leave to England were kept there along with the Pioneer Battalion, which was despatched to England on 14 December. The 60 officers and 900 other ranks evacuated sick from Germany did not return either; and other units were steadily disbanded during the occupation period. One of the biggest initial problems was keeping the dwindling force ready for action in case peace negotiations failed.[62]

Demobilisation picked up in mid-March 1919, extending to the divisional animals. Some 3676 horses were sent back to base, 354 were sold to a local abattoir, and just five returned to New Zealand.[63] The artillery was disbanded on the 18th, and the remaining units, including divisional headquarters, were formally disbanded on 25 March,[64] relieved on the Rhine by 2 Division — though it was some time before all the men returned to New Zealand. Some were held up in Britain by a transport strike, and there were riots at Sling amid a sense of frustration.

The force spent its last two months without its wartime commander. Russell fell ill with a 'touch of bronchitis' on 26 January; but it developed into a more serious infection and he had to relinquish the division to Brigadier-General B. Napier Johnston. Russell got up on 1 February 'feeling very weak', but only to say goodbye to his brigadiers and commanders. In the early evening he took the train to Paris, the first leg of a journey to the warmer climes of Marseille.[65] He took passage back to New Zealand on the *Arawa* in April.[66]

## Passchendaele, Messines and Ypres today

*Top right*
Medical post at Essex Farm, north of Ypres. Canadian doctor John McCrae wrote the poem 'In Flanders Fields' while tending wounded in these tomb-like bunkers. (Matthew Wright)

*Top far right*
Deceptively ancient Ypres. Most of these buildings were constructed after the First World War. (Matthew Wright)

*Bottom right*
Ypres Cathedral: rebuilt at German expense after the First World War, part of the reparations levelled against the Weimar Republic by the victorious Allies. The last sections were completed in the 1960s. (Matthew Wright)

*Bottom far right*
Anzac Day ceremony at the Menin Gate, 2004. (Matthew Wright)

It's springtime in Belgium, the poppies are almost in bloom, and I stand in an old medical post near Essex Farm, two kilometres north of Ypres. Like all old fortifications the mouldering concrete bunker is faceless, damp, mustily redolent of decay. Canadian doctor John McCrae wrote 'In Flanders Fields' here during the second Battle of Ypres in March 1915, scribbling the words on a page ripped from an exercise book. This oft misquoted poem was not a lament for the dead, as might be thought from its first lines, but a call to arms for those who followed.

Nearby Ypres seems little different from any other Belgian town, complete with cathedral and magnificent medieval Grote Markt — the town square. But most of these buildings are less than half a century old. The central part of the cathedral, in all its Gothic magnificence, was finished in the mid-1960s.

The folk of Ypres do not forget the First World War. Menin Gate, arching over the Menin road out of town, carries 56,000 names engraved in Portland stone, soldiers known to have fought in the Ypres salient between November 1914 and August 1917 who

*Top far left*
Menin Gate; memorial to some 56,000 dead whose bodies were never found or identified. (Matthew Wright)

*Top left*
The view from Messines Ridge northwest. This entire area came under shellfire during 1915–18. Millions of live shells remain in Flanders' fields. Four or five Belgian farmers get unlucky every year, and so the death toll from the First World War continues to rise into the twenty-first century. (Matthew Wright)

*Bottom far left*
A British bunker on Messines Ridge, near the Hill 60 crater — built atop a German redoubt. (Matthew Wright)

*Bottom left*
Memorial to New Zealand dead at s'Gravenstafel, near Passchendaele. The inscription at the bottom reads 'From the uttermost ends of the Earth'. (Matthew Wright)

have no known grave. Every day since July 1927, buglers have played the 'Last Post' here at sunset. It will be 2078 before the trumpets have blown once for every soldier remembered here. That, alone, brings home the sheer scale of the First World War.

It is Anzac Day, and we stand in silence as New Zealand and Australian soldiers remember their dead. The 'Last Post' echoes through the arch and for a moment, it seems, this bustling Belgian town pauses in silence.

To the south lies Messines Ridge. We climb Hill 60 — hardly a hill by New Zealand standards. The mammoth gouge left by one of the giant mines used to take the ridge remains, a vast basin in the hillside that nearly 90 years of erosion has scarcely begun to fill. A moss-fringed bunker stands on the edge, British concrete poured over ruined German, a bullet still lodged in the aggregate.

Nearby Ploegsteert Wood — shattered stumps in 1917 — is once again a small and attractive European forest, and the April sun sprinkles through unfolding leaves. And beneath us lies one of the Messines mines, undetonated, precise location unknown. We pass through this delightful woodland quickly.

Near Wytschaete, we discover that enthusiasts have restored a section of former German trench. One

*Top right*
Tyne Cot, the world's biggest military cemetery. (Matthew Wright)

*Top far right*
The Memorial to the Missing stretches across the rear of Tyne Cot Cemetery; the New Zealand panels, seen here, list some 1166 names. (Matthew Wright)

*Bottom right*
Some of the 520 New Zealand graves at Tyne Cot Cemetery. (Matthew Wright)

*Bottom far right*
One of the panels in the New Zealand wall at Tyne Cot Cemetery. (Matthew Wright)

of them, incongruously dressed in coal-scuttle helmet and long greatcoat, smiles and waves as we approach. It is no ordinary trench. It was here that a young German messenger served for part of his war. Nobody knew him then, but by the time he returned to this place in 1940 — taking time out for a special visit to his old haunts — his Panzers had smashed France, and the name Adolf Hitler was on the lips of every European.

There are memorials to New Zealand scattered about the district. We pause briefly near the Passchendaele memorial at s'Gravenstafel before heading for nearby Tyne Cot, the biggest military cemetery in the world. Some 11,908 soldiers lie buried here. Around 70 percent are marked only by a stone and the poignant words 'A soldier of the Great War: known unto God'. A memorial wall at the rear records 34,927 names. New Zealanders take up a complete bay at the centre.

Out in the cemetery beyond, the graves of New Zealand soldiers are interspersed with the others, rank on rank. It seems almost strange to find them here in northwestern Europe, these men from the uttermost ends of the earth, their silent memorials a poignant reminder of the tragedy that shaped our twentieth century.

## Legacy of war

By 1918 many believed the First World War was the 'war to end all wars', a term reputedly coined by H.G. Wells.[67] But in fact neither the armistice nor the formal peace settlement seven months later brought fighting to a conclusion. As Niall Ferguson has shown, the world was not actually weary of all fighting in 1918, only of fighting on the Western Front. The cycle of warfare and civil disruption continued without pause in Bulgaria, Ireland, Egypt, Palestine and Iraq, among other places. In Russia more than six million people were wounded, became ill or died during the five years of brutal conflict that followed their largely war-induced revolution of 1917.[68] And in Paris, a former hotel kitchen hand working under the alias Nguyen Ai Quoc gave 1919 Peace Conference delegates demands for his native Vietnam which, as Ho Chi Minh, he was still fighting for in 1969.[69]

Nor was the struggle between the great powers really settled by the Treaty of Versailles. The German army had not been beaten in the field, as a number of German and Allied commanders realised at the time. A bitter Pershing felt another week's pasting would have made all the difference.[70] Humiliating terms set the seeds of dissent flowing in Germany, and the rise of Nazism was one product of the turmoil that followed. By the late twentieth century, most historians were swinging to the view that the Second World War was the inevitable second phase of the conflict that began in August 1914.[71] Arguably the third act was the Cold War — and New Zealand was in the forefront of the first collision.[72] On this basis the socio-political cycle that began in 1914 did not end until the collapse of the Soviet Union in 1991.[73] Certainly there is good reason to consider that the key social, economic and political trends characterising New Zealand's own twentieth century were refined and played out between 1914 and the mid-1980s.[74]

These broader patterns were not obvious in the 1920s. But the human legacy was clear enough; and the death toll did not end with the armistice. Some 227 New Zealanders were officially recorded as dying 'before discharge', though a number apparently succumbed to the influenza epidemic of late 1918.[75] New Zealand's hospitals were still treating around 3000 servicemen in 1920,[76] some of whom died. Others succumbed that decade. But we will never know the true

The First World War did not officially end until German negotiators agreed to Allied terms, including demands for reparations. It took just over six months; here, New Zealanders gather in Christchurch's Cathedral Square to celebrate the moment in July 1919.

(Photographer unknown, *The Press* (Christchurch) Collection, Alexander Turnbull Library, PAColl-3031, G-8741-1/1)

cost because many escaped the official record. There was also a financial legacy. Accountants had different ways of slicing up the pie;[77] but expeditionary force expenses alone, to the end of the 1921 financial year, came to just over £78.6 million. The same year there were 31,764 New Zealanders on a war pension — nearly double the number of old age pensions, at an ongoing cost of nearly £1.9 million.[78] Some 3215 New Zealanders were on the benefit for life.[79]

These experiences helped guide government policy when the twentieth-century struggle against Germany entered its second act in 1939. The Labour Government of Michael Joseph Savage and Peter Fraser, the latter a conscientious objector in 1916–18, did not shirk from sending men to war. But it was determined to look after them. There would be no more Passchendaeles.

The First World War — and particularly the Western Front experience — built the Anzac phenomenon, a complex and powerful cultural force that moulded New Zealand's twentieth-century society in complex ways. At military level, the Anzac ethos was founded in the reality of boisterous, young, male New Zealanders living and fighting overseas together. They were able to see themselves as a people for the first time, their thoughts, ideals and even dialect standing together in sharp contrast to the cultures in which they found themselves. This was further reinforced by the comradeship of battle, including the military performance of the division.

These same phenomena reinforced the ties with Australia. New Zealand had narrowly wobbled away from becoming the seventh state in 1900–1901.[80] Although Seddon pushed New Zealand down its own political path, social and economic ties kept the two Dominions close. On the Western Front the Australians usually fought on the New Zealand right, and off the front they found common social ground in the cafés and estiaments. Some of these ties

State efforts to rehabilitate returned soldiers focused on getting them on to the land. Slabs of back-country were offered at subsidised prices, fuelling brisk land speculation. These former soldiers practise shearing, probably around Christchurch, soon after the war.

(Steffano Francis Webb, Steffano Webb Collection, Alexander Turnbull Library, PAColl-3061, G-19506-1/1)

were more direct than we might imagine; more than 2000 of those serving in the AIF were New Zealanders, among them Napier's Percy Storkey, whose VC was claimed by both New Zealand and Australia.⁸¹ It was brotherly rivalry — servicemen from both sides of the Tasman joshed each other mercilessly. Sporting contact was as bitterly fought as any battle, such as the contest for the King's Cup in 1919.⁸² But when faced with a third party, be it enemy in the field or ally, they drew tight together.

To New Zealand civilians Anzac took different form, filtered through pre-war jingo thinking that intensified both New Zealand's sense of national identity and patriotism for Empire. It was tied with the sense of loss and the ideal of New Zealand's performance in the field, striking a chord with the public. There were unofficial celebrations on the first anniversary in 1916, and by 1923 Anzac Day had been adopted by government as a formal day of

Not all returned soldiers were able-bodied. These returned servicemen appear to be learning basket weaving as part of their state-sponsored rehabilitation programme.

(Photographer unknown, Health Department, Alexander Turnbull Library, F-944-1/4-MNZ)

remembrance. It remained a pillar of New Zealand's war history — taking a popular dent in the face of the post-Vietnam generation, but picking up again by the end of the twentieth century.

Both halves of the phenomenon helped shape New Zealand's concept of itself during the years after the First World War. Nor was this the only effect of the conflict. Pre-war social trends were sharpened, refined and accelerated both by the trauma of combat and by the unity that came to a people facing common grief. Those who grew up in the 1920s did so in the shadow of the war, when missing or disabled fathers and brothers were an ever-present reminder of the tragedy. There were two broad reactions. Some partied, among them still-youthful veterans who sought solace or forgetfulness, and youngsters who sought separation from something they had not experienced and which some preferred not to understand. Others found comfort, by contrast, in conservative social values.[83] This 'tightening' of society, as one historian has called it,[84] was not class-based but moral.[85]

The war also helped fuel new immigration. Post-war Britain was a dismal place where the economy was in recession and the disabled stumped the streets eking out a bare living from war pensions. Many left, a fair proportion heading to New Zealand where prospects initially seemed brighter. But post-war fortune in the Dominion did not last long. New Zealand, of course, had its own share of disabled. John Keating had been stunned by the plight of fellow wounded in one London hospital: '… my word there are a lot of cripples over here to go back to NZ,' he declared in a letter to a New Zealand colleague, 'chaps with legs off & arms off …'.[86] The gloom that swept New Zealand after 1922 was a direct outcome of the cancellation of the wartime 'commandeer', by which the British purchased virtually everything New Zealand could sell. That, too, shaped New Zealand, framing thought for a generation around the spectre of poverty and unemployment.[87]

Field comradeship resurfaced in unlikely places during the next decades. When Hawke's Bay was laid low by earthquake in 1931, the response was coloured by the Western Front. Many openly compared the destruction in Napier and Hastings with what they had seen around Ypres. Rescue efforts were also framed in military terms; old soldiers quickly rallied, and in Hastings one wartime unit was even resurrected — bringing organised help quickly to bear.[88]

The real cost, ultimately, was human. Survivors of Gallipoli and Flanders were often physically scarred; but all bore wounds that were never really identified at the time, still less cured. At a time when fearlessness was linked with honour, society provided a mechanism to ensure that those who suffered a stress reaction to battle were poorly treated. Their plight was belatedly identified, but even then given the vaguely deprecating term 'shell shock'. Symptoms varied. The worst wartime cases were usually — if inappropriately — committed to mental asylums, at the time as much mechanisms to enforce social conformity as therapeutic institutions. More functional victims sometimes absented themselves from the front, and a fair number were shot for desertion, including three of the five New Zealanders executed during the war.[89] They were pardoned by legislation in 2000. But it was all a question of degree. Many others did not display symptoms during the war itself, yet still suffered afterwards, silently, effectively alone.

These realities took decades to become first understood and then accepted. Time underpinned the depth of the human tragedy of the First World War. By the time the true personal cost was recognised by society at large, many of the veterans had passed away.

## CONCLUSION

# THE FIRST WORLD WAR AS HISTORY

Historians have been considerably exercised by the New Zealand performance on the Western Front, a theatre essentially synonymous with the First World War. The idea that the 'Silent Division' was the best in the field has been discussed, analysed, torn down and rebuilt. So too has the performance of its commanders.

In the wider sense the division could not make a huge impact on the campaign. Although it was the largest single formation in the field at one stage in 1917, the division was still but one of 60-odd British and Imperial divisions on the Western Front. This contrasted with the early Second World War experience, when the Second New Zealand Division was the largest of less than a dozen prosecuting Britain's land campaign in North Africa.[1] The New Zealanders did not have the numbers to exert decisive effect in 1916–18 France. Even the gap-plugging effort of March 1918 was not fought solo.

The question of quality therefore devolves to tactical performance. Here, the realities of the divisional efforts at Flers, Passchendaele, and during the offensives of 1918 are tangled with New Zealand's social Achilles heel — the 'cultural cringe' and its flip-side, the notion that we must, by definition, be world-beaters.[2] Settler-age New Zealand tottered to its feet in the 1880s, wavered, looked about at a seemingly dangerous world, and plunged for the bosom of mother England. Colonial pretensions to become a bigger or better Britain were transmuted into an ambition to become the greatest of Britain's children.[3] From this idea of capable inferiority emerged what one historian has called New Zealand's 'leading the bloody world' syndrome. In wartime this last idea fused with the image of rugged pioneering colonists, contributing to the notion that New Zealanders were natural soldiers, fuelling the myth of glorious failure at Gallipoli.

The use of the New Zealand Division as a spearhead in the difficult conditions of the Western Front provided further apparent proof of the point, and the origins of the late-twentieth-century idea that the division performed less well than legend attributes can also be found in this complex national self-view. Part of the problem has also been the difficulty of considering the First World War in its own terms. Academic studies of the war began appearing in the mid-1980s, at a time when some student communities defined themselves around a narrow and prescriptive ideology of post-Vietnam, post-colonial idealism, often confusing abstract analysis with personal advocacy.[4]

As always, the historical truths lie somewhere between the extremes. There is compelling contemporary evidence to suggest that the New Zealanders were genuinely good, achieving a performance in battle that drew admiration and respect. In part this was because Russell's exacting demands honed the skills of the men; in part because his hands-on style of field leadership — backed with the wider tactics demanded by talented senior commanders such as Plumer — lent itself to successful battles.

In part it was also because aspects of New Zealand's colonial 'bloke' culture actually did translate into better field performance, though not quite in the way that legend suggests. It is an overstatement to argue that New Zealanders were natural soldiers; like any citizen army they needed training to be effective, and there were good and bad soldiers among them. Nonetheless, the legacy of frontier ethos with its do-it-yourself idealism and tackle-anything mentality conferred some advantages in the field. When there was a job to do, New Zealanders usually went out and did it. To this extent, the division met the legend, punching above its weight and building a reputation that, by and large, was fulfilled through the campaign.

This highlights the point that the main effect of the war was social, and to understand the full extent of the war as both a social experience and social force we must disentangle the realities from the stereotype. The popular image of the Western Front as mindless slaughter ordered by stupid generals has been enduring, both in New Zealand and elsewhere. The concept struck a chord with the post-Vietnam generation, evidenced by popular satire such as the television series *Blackadder Goes Forth*. However, this image of vacuous tragedy — however wittily packaged — has merely contributed to a long-standing historical misconception, one often repeated even at academic level. At least one late-twentieth-century general history of New Zealand focused with a kind of academic voyeurism on the clichés, without really exploring the political, strategic and tactical realities of time and place.

Myth, in short, has persisted; yet, as Niall Ferguson has shown, many of the assumed realities of Britain's First World War, ranging from the 'anti-war' stance of its poets to an assumed revulsion by the soldiery at killing, do not stand up to closer analysis.[5] Some of Ferguson's arguments are compelling, and while he wrote in a British context, New Zealand's division fought as a British one. Similar questions could be asked. Did the New Zealanders become accustomed to this horror world of killing, death and mud?

This is the key historical question, though the answer is not always evident even in primary documents. Letters from the front — often self-bowdlerised for the benefit of both censor and family — seldom portray the realities, though

The unknown warrior returns. In November 2004, after 88 years under French soil, an anonymous New Zealander from the Western Front was selected to symbolise all our war dead. The soldier was brought back from the Caterpillar Valley cemetery near Longueval and received with full pomp and ceremony. Here the unknown warrior is carried into the legislative chamber.

(Matthew Wright)

many offer tantalising hints or say more by omission. Reminiscences come to us through the filter of years. But many diaries, penned in the heat of a moment or soon afterwards, do convey a gruelling and immediate picture of what we might call 'trench culture', the art of coping. Amid this world of new rules, often structured around the camaraderie of the field, revenge-fuelled killing became easy. To some extent it was a matter of getting the job done; but this behaviour also reflected the way the men coped with their environment, a technique fuelled in the New Zealand case by blokeish frontier mentality with its professed indifference to the visceral.[6]

There was a cost. Trench culture did not make the strains go away. The hidden tension often surfaced as hatred of the Germans — evidenced by the refusal by some New Zealand medical officers to aid dying 'Bosche'. It helped fuel a limitless appetite for alcohol and women. For some the penalty was 'neurasthenia' — shell shock. Others found that peace brought no relief, and their war lived on with them, often emerging as anxiety, rage, alienation or guilt. Some had trouble fitting into society. None entirely escaped, the worst

The unknown warrior on the way to his final resting place in the National War Memorial, 11 November 2004.

(Matthew Wright)

cases remembered in one post-war manuscript as 'restless, gas-drenched wrecks' who 'gradually sank lower and lower in the social scale' through no fault of their own.[7]

This was why few were prepared to talk afterwards, and the way that these realities quickly sank from public view is clear from the literature. Official photographs make clear that much of the nastiness was well known at the time.[8] Published accounts of the day were often frank about the harrowing realities.[9] However, accounts written in hindsight were more often abstracted.[10] This was probably inevitable. For participants the issue ran deeper than protecting the innocence of their wives and children. Some could not remember, victims of their own subconscious self-protection. Many relived the war whether they wanted to or not, suffering recurring nightmares for decades. This phenomenon was more sophisticated than simple reaction to the strains of being under fire. The 'post-traumatic' stress of the Western Front also rested in the general environment, and in the psychological games that had to be played to endure it.

Some of the estimated 100,000 Wellingtonians who lined the streets to watch the funeral procession of the unknown warrior in November 2004 — a number coincidentally similar to the number of New Zealanders who fought on the Western Front during the First World War.

(Matthew Wright)

None of this was entirely new. Soldiers the world over hated war, endured it, sought solace in the arms of women, drank themselves into oblivion whenever they could, and paid the price later. To this extent the soldiers of the First World War repeated the experiences of soldiers since Alexander's time or before. Even the scale was not new. While the First World War grew to encompass civilian populations, the Napoleonic Wars a century earlier had done something similar, if in a less well-organised sense. Nor was the destruction of civilian property and life exceptional. The religious wars that rent Europe asunder in the seventeenth century were, if anything, more devastating to the countries involved than the war of 1914–18. The Germans, for all their supposed *schrecklichkeit* — 'frightfulness' — to the Belgians and occupied French, did not repeat the performance of the Swedes at Magdeburg in 1635.

But in other ways the First World War was unique. It was fuelled by industrial-age technology, which gave long-term static warfare an endurance that even Napoleon's soldiers could not have envisaged. The weapons were lethal, sophisticated and wide-ranging, and their effects came as a popular surprise at a time when warfare had broadly lost its public horror. This social response, perhaps more than the military issues, remains one of the key factors that sets the First World War apart.

New Zealand, suffused in the hopeful ideals of its jingo age, shared that experience in almost every respect. The lesson that war was not glorious was abruptly learned at Gallipoli, which became the essential prelude to the experience of the Western Front. The New Zealanders who reached France in 1916 were well fitted to adopt local 'trench culture' as a result of their experiences on the peninsula. But this did not reduce the intensity and depth of the trauma. The Western Front was a shattering experience, and it was shared by a socially significant proportion of New Zealand's youth. The echoes of the campaign could be heard through the twentieth century, an imagery of horror that symbolised all New Zealand's wars. And the soldiers who fought it were not forgotten.

# NOTES

## Introduction

1. MS-Papers-3101, Richardson, George Spafford (Major-General Sir), 1868–1938, Letter to E.C. Walmsley re his war experiences, 4 February 1916.
2. Matthew Wright, *The Reed Illustrated History of New Zealand*, p. 255.
3. MS-Papers-2295, Hassell, N.E., 'Memories of 1914'.
4. Argued by Paul Fussell, *The Great War and Modern Memory*, p. 87.
5. Niall Ferguson, *The Pity of War*, p. 463.
6. Robert Cowley (ed.), *The Great War: Perspectives on the First World War*, p. xiv.
7. Carl von Clausewitz, *On War*, cited in J.F.C. Fuller, *The Decisive Battles of the Western World*, Vol. 2, p. 249.
8. See, e.g., Nicholas Boyack, *Behind the Lines*, p. 8.
9. AJHR 1921–22, H-19 'Defence Forces of New Zealand', report of General Officer Commanding, for period from 1st July 1920, to 30th June 1921', p. 2. See also M.F. Lloyd-Prichard, *An Economic History of New Zealand to 1939*, p. 266.
10. AJHR 1921–22, H-19 'Defence Forces of New Zealand', report of General Officer Commanding, for period from 1st July 1920, to 30th June 1921', p. 2.
11. David Thorns and Charles Sedgwick, *Understanding Aotearoa/New Zealand, Historical Statistics*, p. 53.
12. *The New Zealand Army*, New Zealand Army, Wellington, 1995, p. 103. (Author not stated.)
13. AJHR 1921–22, H-19 'Defence Forces of New Zealand', report of General Officer Commanding, for period from 1st July 1920, to 30th June 1921', p. 2.
14. Niall Ferguson, *The Pity of War*, p. 299.
15. Allen, J., Box 9, Correspondence with Colonels Birdwood and Russell, 1914–1920, Allen to Birdwood, 4 March 1918.
16. Figures in Ferguson, *The Pity of War*, p. 299.

## 1 In Flanders' fields ...

1. Matthew Wright, *Reed Illustrated History of New Zealand*, pp. 250–55.
2. A conspiracy to kill the Austrian royal couple misfired; but Gavrilo Princip, one of the conspirators, achieved the task when they drove past a café where he was commiserating the failure. See, e.g., A.J.P. Taylor, *How Wars Begin*, pp. 103–4; Martin Gilbert, *First World War*, p. 16.
3. Martin Gilbert, *First World War*, pp. 10–15.
4. J.F.C. Fuller, *The Decisive Battles of the Western World*, pp. 243–78.
5. R.F. Gambrill, *The Russell Family Saga*, Vol. II, typescript, Hastings Public Library, n.d., Diaries of General Sir Andrew Russell, 1 August 1914. Henceforth *The Russell Family Saga*. This is an unpublished collection of Russell family diaries, papers, notes and records collected by Gambrill as the basis of a biography.
6. W.S. Churchill, *The World Crisis*, p. 133.
7. Cited in Ferguson, *The Pity of War*, p. 163.
8. Argued by Ferguson, *The Pity of War*, p. 164.
9. Viscount Grey of Fallodon, *Twenty Five Years*, Vol II, Frederick Stokes, p. 20.
10. Matthew Wright, *Reed Illustrated History of New Zealand*, p. 260.
11. MS-Papers-2414, R.M. Watson, certificates of service.
12. MS-Papers-2295, Hassell, N.E., 'Memories of 1914'.
13. MS-Papers-2393, Aubrey Tronson, 'Soldier's Book of Life'.
14. *The Russell Family Saga*, Russell diary, 10 August 1914.
15. MS-Papers-2244, C.A. Healey Collection, Diary 11 January 1916.
16. Michael King, *Nga Iwi o Te Motu*, p. 89.
17. AJHR 1916 H-19D 'New Zealand Expeditionary Force: Return relative to Maoris and Half-Castes etc'.

18. MS-Papers-2477, Higginson, Louisa, diary 1914–18 (typescript).
19. Matthew Wright, 'Australia, New Zealand and Imperial Defence, 1909–1914', MA Thesis, Massey University 1986; Matthew Wright, *Reed Illustrated History of New Zealand*, pp. 247–48.
20. Matthew Wright, *Blue Water Kiwis*, pp. 26–28.
21. AD 10, 16/6, note by James Allen 'Defence: Proposed organisation for an expeditionary force'.
22. AD 10, 16/6, 'Scheme for the reorganisation of the military forces of New Zealand', August 1909, Appendix F.
23. See AD 10, 16/1, 'Defence Scheme — New Zealand, report by Lord Kitchener 1910'.
24. R.L. Weitzel, 'Pacifists and anti-militarists in New Zealand, 1909–1914', *New Zealand Journal of History*, Vol. 7, No. 2, October 1973, p. 129.
25. AD 10, 16/6, Godley to Allen, 9 October 1912.
26. AD 10, 16/6, 'Secret Memorandum for Hon. The Minister of Defence', 2 August 1912.
27. AD 10, 16/6, note by James Allen 'Defence: Proposed organisation for an expeditionary force'.
28. Quoted in Gilbert, *Atlas of the First World War*, p. 14.
29. H. Essame, 'The New Warfare' in Bernard Fitzsimons (ed.), *The Big Guns*, p. 5.
30. Lloyd Clark, *World War I: An Illustrated History*, p. 30.
31. E.g. the C.O. of 2 Battalion, Duke of Cornwall Light Infantry, F.C. Wright, pers. comm.
32. Edward Owen, *1914: Glory Departing*, pp. 53–54.
33. H. Essame, 'The New Warfare' in Bernard Fitzsimons (ed.), *The Big Guns*, pp. 6–7.
34. Clark, *World War I: An Illustrated History*, p. 12.
35. Edward Owen, *1914: Glory Departing*, p. 56.
36. Edward Owen, *1914: Glory Departing*, pp. 13–15; Lloyd Clark, *World War I: An Illustrated History*, pp. 9–10.
37. John Terraine, *White Heat: The New Warfare 1914–1918*, pp. 85–96. 'Big Bertha' was a less literal translation. Liége fell to older 11-inch weapons.
38. Malcolm Brown, *The Western Front*, Pan, London, 2001, p. 4.
39. Ibid., p. 8.
40. Terraine, *White Heat*, p. 110.
41. Owen, *1914: Glory Departing*, p. 77.
42. Terraine, *White Heat*, p. 103.
43. MS-Papers-3101, G. Richardson, letter to E.C. Walmsley, 4 February 1916.
44. H. Essame, 'The New Warfare' in Bernard Fitzsimons (ed.), *The Big Guns*, p. 6; see also Clark, p. 52.
45. Frank Mumby (ed.), *The Great World War*, pp. 29–31.
46. Terraine, *White Heat*, p. 158.
47. Ibid., p. 142.
48. Patrick Wright, *Tank*, p. 27.
49. Churchill, *The World Crisis*, pp. 349–52.
50. As noted by Terraine, *White Heat*, p. 148.
51. Arthur Marder (ed.), *Fear God and Dread Nought: Correspondence of Admiral of the Fleet Lord Fisher of Kilverstone*, Vol. III, 1959, Fisher to Churchill, 31 March 1915, p. 179.
52. Ibid., First Sea Lord to the Sea Lords, 8 April 1915, p. 190.
53. Churchill, *The World Crisis*, pp. 403–4.
54. Arthur Marder (ed.), *Fear God and Dread Nought: Correspondence of Admiral of the Fleet Lord Fisher of Kilverstone*, Vol. III, Fisher to Churchill, 20 March 1915, p. 167.
55. Ibid., Sea Lords to First Sea Lord, 7–8 April 1915, pp. 188–89.
56. MS-Papers-2295, Hassell, N.E., 'Memories of 1914'.
57. MS-2350 George Wallace Bollinger, diary, 15 December 1914.
58. MSX-4958, Frank Campbell, 1885–1944, papers.
59. MS-Papers-2295, Hassell, N.E., 'Memories of 1914'.
60. MS-2350 George Wallace Bollinger, diary, 6 December 1914.
61. MS-Papers-2295, Hassell, N.E., 'Memories of 1914'.
62. MS-2350 George Wallace Bollinger, diary, 3 January 1915.
63. Nick Boyack, *Behind the Lines*, pp. 21–22.
64. MS-2350 George Wallace Bollinger, diary, 6 December 1914.
65. MS-Papers-3914, E.P. Williams Collection, diary (transcript), 2 April 1915.
66. MS-2350 George Wallace Bollinger, diary, Good Friday, 1915.
67. Ibid., 15 December 1914.

68. MS-Papers-2393, Aubrey Tronson, 'A Soldiers' Book of Life'.
69. Allen, J., Box 9, Correspondence with Colonels Birdwood and Russell, 1914–1920, Birdwood to Bridges, 27 December 1914.
70. Ibid., 29 December 1914.
71. MS-Papers-4309, John W. Muldoon Collection, letter home 27 December 1914. John Muldoon was uncle of Robert Muldoon.
72. MS-2350 George Wallace Bollinger, diary, [n.d.] January 1915.
73. Ibid., 16 March 1915.
74. MSX-4958-4959, Campbell, Frank, 1885–1944, World War One diaries, 25 April 1915.
75. Ibid.
76. MS-Papers 2350, George Wallace Bollinger, diary, 26 and 27 April 1915.
77. MSX-4958-4959, Campbell, Frank, 1885–1944, World War One diaries, 25 April 1915.
78. Ibid., 29 April 1915.
79. MS-Papers 2350, George Wallace Bollinger, diary, 15 June 1915.
80. Location details were not in the letter.
81. MS-Papers-85-132, Fraser, John Roy, 1884–1936, World War One Papers, letter 13 February 1916.
82. Cited in *New Zealand Army*, p. 94.
83. Cited in Mumby (ed.), *The Great World War*, p. 145.
84. MS-Papers-2477-2, Higginson, Louisa, 1885–1978, Diaries/transcribed by Mrs R.L. Wilson.
85. MS-1172, McGilp, Clyde, Gallipoli historical records and war diary, 1st Battery, NZFA 1915–1916, diary, 1 January 1916.
86. Allen, J., Box 9, Correspondence with Colonels Birdwood and Russell, 1914–1920, Birdwood to Allen, 4 February 1916.
87. Allen, J., D1/6/5, 'Expeditionary Force: Establishment, history of changes in NZEF, reinforcements to, scale of reinforcements', report 28 July 1917.
88. AJHR 1915 H-19E, 'New Zealand Expeditionary Force: Provision of reinforcement drafts for the (Memorandum on)', p. 1.
89. Allen, J., Box 9, Correspondence with Colonels Birdwood and Russell Allen to Birdwood, 7 March 1916.
90. Allen, J., D1/6/3, 'New Zealand Division, Formation Of', Liverpool to Secretary of State for Dominion Affairs, 17 February 1916.
91. Allen, J., Box 9, Correspondence with Colonels Birdwood and Russell Allen to Birdwood, 7 March 1916.
92. Ibid., Birdwood to Allen, 4 February 1916.
93. Allen, J., D1/6/3, Birdwood to Allen, 11 March 1916.
94. Officially '3 (Rifle) Brigade'.
95. AJHR 1916 H-19D, 'New Zealand Expeditionary Force: Return relative to Maoris and Half-Castes etc'.
96. Christopher Pugsley, *Te Hokowhitu a Tu: The Maori Pioneer Battalion in the First World War*, p. 45.
97. See, e.g., Cecil Malthus, *Armentières and the Somme*, p. 83.
98. H. Stewart, *The New Zealand Division, 1916–1919*, p. 14.
99. MS-Papers-1439, Hankins Collection.

## 2 Trench culture

1. *The Russell Family Saga*, Russell diary, 21 April 1916.
2. Clark, *World War I: An Illustrated History*, p. 88.
3. Fuller, *The Decisive Battles of the Western World*, Vol. 2, p. 360.
4. Essame, 'The New Warfare' in Bernard Fitzsimons (ed.), *The Big Guns*, p. 7.
5. Cited in Terraine, *White Heat*, p. 203.
6. Churchill, *The World Crisis*, pp. 623–34.
7. Ferguson, *The Pity of War*, pp. 295, 297.
8. Churchill, *The World Crisis*, p. 633; Ferguson, *The Pity of War*, p. 297.
9. Ferguson, *The Pity of War*, p. 339.
10. Terraine, *White Heat*, p. 189.
11. Martin Marix Evans, *Passchendaele and the Battles of Ypres 1914–18*, p. 100.
12. Pugsley, *Te Hokowhitu a Tu: The Maori Pioneer Battalion in the First World War*, p. 211.
13. MS-Papers-3101, G.S. Richardson, letter to Walmsley, 4 February 1916.
14. *The Russell Family Saga*, Russell diary, 10 June 1917.
15. Allen, J., Box 9, Correspondence with Colonels Birdwood and Russell, 1914–1920, Allen to Russell, 28 August 1917.

16. Bernard Fitzsimons (ed.), *The Big Guns*, Phoebus, London, 1973, p. 27.
17. Ibid., pp. 28–29.
18. Pugsley, *Te Hokowhitu a Tu: The Maori Pioneer Battalion in the First World War*, p. 174.
19. MS-Papers-1439, Hankins Collection, diary, 21 June 1916.
20. Ferguson, *The Pity of War*, pp. 303–6.
21. See, e.g., Matthew Wright, *Desert Duel*, pp. 110–24.
22. Malcolm Brown, *Tommy Goes to War*, p. 194.
23. MS-Papers, Stayte, Jesse William, 1875–1918, rough notes from my diary, esp. 30 January 1918; also associated papers.
24. MS-Papers-4873, Bryan Peter McDermott Papers, attached notes.
25. 88-208, Spedding, Eric Claude, d. 1916, diary, entries 21 and 23 August 1916.
26. Ibid., entries 24 September 1916.
27. 91-319 Fama, Tano, d. 1940, Correspondence and newspaper clippings, letter 1 October 1916.
28. MS-Papers-7819-11, Tuckey, Frances Isobella, fl. 1870–1918; letters from Richard Septimus Tuckey, letter, 19 March 1918.
29. MS-Papers-2295, Hassell, N.E., 'Memories of 1914'.
30. MS-Papers-6293-2, Harcourt, John Gordon, fl. 1900–1960s, diary kept on active service in World War, 29 October 1917.
31. See also Ferguson, *The Pity of War*, p. 339.
32. Terraine, *White Heat*, p. 203.
33. *The Russell Family Saga*, Russell diary, 14 April 1916.
34. Ibid., A.H. Russell to A.H. Russell (father), 18 April 1916.
35. MSX-4131, A. Martin papers, diary, 1916, entry 5 May 1916.
36. *The Russell Family Saga*, Russell diary, 12 June 1916.
37. Ibid., 25 June 1916.
38. MS-2350 George Wallace Bollinger, diary, n.d. 1916.
39. *The Russell Family Saga*, Russell diary, 17 April 1916.
40. Quoted in H. Stewart, *The New Zealand Division 1916–1919*, p. 22.
41. MS-Papers-6027, Luke, Kenneth Ewart, d. 1965, Letters to his family, 28 October 1917.
42. Christopher Pugsley, *The Anzac Experience*, p. 152.
43. Allen, J., Box 9, Correspondence with Colonels Birdwood and Russell, 1914–1920, Allen to Russell, 7 November 1916.
44. MSX 4760 'Bently, Dawes', 'Doug Stark — Bomber with Otago on the Western Front', Vol. I.
45. Allen, J., Box 9, Correspondence with Colonels Birdwood and Russell, 1914–1920, Russell to Allen, 18 February 1917.
46. Ibid.
47. WA 5/1, 2, 'New Zealand Expeditionary Force; New Zealand Dental Corps'.
48. MS-Papers-7198, Stayte, Jesse William, 1875–1918, rough notes from my diary, 16 November 1916.
49. WA 5/1, 2, 'New Zealand Expeditionary Force; New Zealand Dental Corps'.
50. Allen, J., Box 9, Correspondence with Colonels Birdwood and Russell, 1914–1920, Russell to Allen, 17 September 1916.
51. See, e.g., concluding remarks in WA 5/1, 2, 'New Zealand Expeditionary Force; New Zealand Dental Corps'.
52. Weston, *Three Years with the New Zealanders*, p. 121.
53. Ormond Burton, *The Silent Division: New Zealanders at the front 1914–1919*, Angus and Robertson, Sydney, 1935, p. 222.
54. C.A.L. Treadwell, *Recollections of an Amateur Soldier*, p. 140.
55. MS 85-132, Fraser, John Roy, 1884–1936, World War One Papers, account of 1916 France.
56. Fussell, *The Great War and Modern Memory*, p. 49.
57. MSX-4131, A. Martin papers, diary, 1916, entry 21 May 1916.
58. MS-Papers-2244, C.A. Healey Collection, Diary 14 October, footnote.
59. MSX-4131, A. Martin papers, diary, 1916, entry 13 September 1916.
60. J.R.R. Tolkien, *The Two Towers*, p. 260.
61. Weston, *Three Years with the New Zealanders*, p. 104.
62. MS-Papers-7198, Stayte, Jesse William, rough notes from my diary, 12, 16 and 21 October 1917.
63. Ibid., 20 June 1918.

64. Noted by Ferguson, *The Pity of War*, pp. 359–60.
65. Matthew Wright, *Reed Illustrated History of New Zealand*, p. 297.
66. MS-Papers-4077-Folder 3, Peter Mathews Collection, Clark to his family 20 June 1917.
67. MS-Papers-6027, Luke, Kenneth Ewart, d. 1965, Letters to his family, 24 November 1917.
68. MS-Papers-1439, Hankins Collection, 12 October 1916.
69. Clark, *World War I: An Illustrated History*, p. 161.
70. MS-Papers-7198, Stayte, Jesse William, rough notes from my diary, 3 April 1918.
71. MSX 4337-4338, J.C. Heseltine, diaries, 1 August 1917.
72. Ferguson, *The Pity of War*, pp. 357–66.
73. MS-Papers-7198, Stayte, Jesse William, rough notes from my diary, 26 March 1918.
74. Micro MS 591, Kerse, Charles Allanton, 1894–1918, Diary 18 Aug 1914–22 July 1918, letter home 27 September 1916.
75. Possibly C. Murphy, see D.I.B. Smith, Introduction pp. x–xi, in Robyn Hyde, *Passport to Hell*.
76. MSX-4761, 'Doug Stark — Bomber, with Otago on the Western Front, Vol. 2'.
77. Micro MS 591, Kerse, Charles Allanton, 1894–1918, Diary 18 Aug 1914–22 July 1918, letter home 9 May 1917.
78. MS-Papers-7198, Stayte, Jesse William, rough notes from my diary, 20 June 1918.
79. 88-208, Spedding, Eric Claude, d. 1916, WWI Diary, 1 October 1916.
80. 91-319, Fama, Tano, d. 1940, correspondence and newspaper clippings, private letter 1 October 1916.
81. MS-Papers-6293-2, Harcourt, John Gordon, fl. 1900–1960s, diary kept on active service in World War, 25 March 1918.
82. MSX 4337-4338, J.C. Heseltine, diaries, 18 August 1917.
83. MS-Papers-2295, Hassell, N.E., 'Memories of 1914'.
84. MSX 4337-4338, J.C. Heseltine, diaries, 18 August 1917.
85. MS 85-132, Fraser, John Roy, World War One Papers, account of 1916 France.
86. MS-Papers-4077-Folder 3, Peter Mathews Collection, Clark to his family 20 June 1917.
87. MS 85-132, Fraser, John Roy, World War One Papers, account of 1916 France.
88. MSX 4337-4338, Heseltine, J.C., diaries, 5 June 1917.
89. MS-Papers-4077-Folder 3, Peter Mathews Collection, Clark to his family 20 June 1917.
90. MSX-2936-2938, Evans, J., diary, 2 August 1917.
91. See, e.g., MS-Papers-3952, C.S. Algie, diary, Brigadier-General W.G. Braithwaite to Mrs Algie, 21 July 1916.
92. MSX 4337-4338, Heseltine, J.C., diaries, 10 September 1917.
93. Allen, J., Box 9, Correspondence with Colonels Birdwood and Russell, 1914–1920, Russell to Allen, 19 June 1917.
94. Malthus, *Armentières and the Somme*, p. 69.
95. Patrick Wright, *Tank*, p. 42.
96. Matthew Wright, *The Reed Illustrated History of New Zealand*, pp. 268–69.
97. Allen Papers, DA/11, NZEF Rates of Pay, 20 August 1914.
98. MSX-4337-4338, Heseltine, J.C., diaries, 5 August 1917.
99. MS-Papers-2295, Hassell, N.E., 'Memories of 1914'.
100. C.H. Weston, *Three Years with the New Zealanders*, p. 211.
101. Allen, J., Box 9, Correspondence with Colonels Birdwood and Russell, 1914–1920, Russell to Allen, 18 February 1917.
102. MSX 4337-4338, Heseltine, J.C., diaries, 18 July 1917.
103. Ibid., 1 August 1917.
104. Ibid., 5 June 1917.
105. MS-Papers-2295, Hassell, N.E., 'Memories of 1914'.
106. Ibid.
107. Ibid.
108. Pugsley, *The Anzac Experience*, p. 156.
109. Preamble, (7) 'Pardon for Soldiers of the Great War Act, 2000'.
110. Stewart, *The New Zealand Division, 1916–1919*, p. 53.
111. MSX-4131, A. Martin papers, A Diary, 1916, entry 3 July 1916.
112. Stewart, *The New Zealand Division, 1916–1919*, pp. 16–19.

113. MS 188-146, Lynch, Thomas, d. 1954, letters home during World War One, October 1917 (n.d.).
114. Micro MS-832, O'Connor, Michael, Diary 1915–1917, 19 February 1916.
115. Allen, J., Box 9, Correspondence with Colonels Birdwood and Russell, 1914–1920, Birdwood to Allen, 6 May 1916.
116. MS-Papers-4873, McDermott, Bryan, service diary, n.d.
117. 88-208, Spedding, Eric Claude, d. 1916, diary, entry 21 August 1916.
118. See, e.g., Matthew Wright, *Reed Illustrated History of New Zealand*, pp. 108–11.
119. Norman Dixon, *On the Psychology of Military Incompetence*, Pimlico, London 1976, esp. pp. 176–89.
120. MS-Papers-4873, McDermott, Bryan, service diary, n.d.
121. Micro MS 593, Kerse, Charles Allanton, 1894–1918, Diary 18 August 1914–22 July 1918, 5 April 1918.
122. 88-208, Spedding, Eric Claude, d. 1916, diary, entry 23 August 1916.
123. WTu MS-Papers-7198, Stayte, Jesse William, 1875–1918, rough notes from my diary, 17 February 1917.
124. MS-Papers-7198, Stayte, Jesse William, 1875–1918, rough notes from my diary, 1 February 1917.
125. MS-Papers-4873, McDermott, Bryan, service diary, n.d.
126. MS-Papers-4077, Folder 3, Peter Mathews Collection, H.G. Clark [Edwin Clark], 23 June 1916.
127. Burton, p. 227.
128. MSX 4337-4338, Heseltine, J.C., diaries, 18 July 1917.
129. Micro-MS-591, Kerse, Charles Allanton, 1894–1918, Diary 18 Aug 1914–22 July 1918, 31 July 1917.
130. Allen Papers, Russell to Allen, 18 February 1917.
131. MSX 4337-4338, Heseltine, J.C., diaries, 18 July 1917.
132. Ibid.
133. MSX-2936-2938, Evans, J., diary, 24 May 1917.
134. MS-Papers-4077, Stayte, Jesse William, 1875–1918, rough notes from my diary, 3 February 1917.
135. Ibid., 5 Feb 1917.
136. MS-Papers-6027, Luke, Kenneth Ewart, d. 1965, letters to his family, 25 May 1917.
137. MS-88-208, Spedding, Eric Claude, WWI Diary, 7 and 9 September 1916.
138. MS-Papers-6027, Luke, Kenneth Ewart, d. 1965, letters to his family, 25 May 1917.
139. MS-Papers-2295, Hassell, N.E., 'Memories of 1914'.
140. Burton, p. 230.
141. MS-Papers-2295, Hassell, N.E., 'Memories of 1914'.
142. Ferguson, p. 353.
143. Allen, J., Allen to Russell, 19 July 1918, attached report.
144. WA 10/3, ZMR 1/1/40, letter fragment.
145. Ibid.
146. Allen, J., Box 9, Correspondence with Colonels Birdwood and Russell, Allen to Russell, 20 May 1918.
147. Ibid., Russell to Allen, 17 May 1918.
148. Ibid.
149. Ibid., Russell to Allen, 20 May 1918.
150. Ibid., Russell to Allen, 12 August 1918.
151. Ibid., Allen to Russell, 19 July 1918.

## 3 The Somme

1. Allen, J., Box 9, Correspondence with Colonels Birdwood and Russell, 1914–1920, Allen to Birdwood, 10 July 1916.
2. See, e.g., Allen, J., D1/6, Memo for the Governor, September 1915 (n.d.).
3. Gilbert, *The Atlas of the First World War*, p. 91.
4. 88-208, Spedding, Eric Claude, d. 1916, diary, entry 15 September 1916.
5. MS-Papers-2295, Hassell, N.E., 'Memories of 1914'.
6. MS-Papers-1439, Hankins Collection, diary 26 May 1916.
7. Allen, J., DA/11, 'NZEF Rates of Pay, 20 August 1914'. Not five shillings as usually stated; this was Lance-Corporal pay.
8. See, e.g., Robin Hyde, *Passport to Hell*, pp. 116–17.
9. Stewart, *The New Zealand Division, 1916–1919*, p. 52.
10. Donald Macintyre, *Jutland*, p. 187.

11. MSX-4131, A. Martin papers, A Diary, 1916, entry 4 June 1916.
12. MS-Papers-2295, Hassell, N.E. 'Memories of 1914'.
13. Ibid.
14. Brown, *The Western Front*, p. 114.
15. Clark, *World War I: An Illustrated History*, p. 111.
16. Brown, *The Western Front*, p. 115.
17. Ibid.
18. MSX-4131, A. Martin papers, diary, 1916, entry 3 July 1916; see also Stewart, p. 45.
19. *The Russell Family Saga*, Russell diary, 29 June 1916.
20. Ibid., 2 July 1916.
21. Stewart, *The New Zealand Division, 1916–1919*, p. 38.
22. Malthus, *Armentières and the Somme*, pp. 77–78.
23. Ibid., p. 81.
24. *The Russell Family Saga*, Russell diary, 19 August 1916.
25. Stewart, *Armentières and the Somme*, p. 58.
26. 88-208, Spedding, Eric Claude, d. 1916, diary, entry 2 September 1916.
27. Patrick Wright, *Tank*, pp. 40–41.
28. David Miller, *Tanks of the World*, p. 302; Patrick Wright, *Tank*, pp. 28–29.
29. 91-319 Fama, Tano. d. 1940, correspondence and newspaper clippings, letter 1 October 1916.
30. Churchill, *The World Crisis*, pp. 358–59.
31. Clark, *World War I: An Illustrated History*, p. 115.
32. *The Russell Family Saga*, Russell diary, 7 August 1916.
33. Ibid., 8 September 1916.
34. MS-85-132, Fraser, John Roy, 1884–1936, World War One papers, account of 1916 France.
35. Stewart, *The New Zealand Division, 1916–1919*, p. 72. Theoretically the tanks were good for 3.7 mph (6 kph), but this was not achievable in battlefield conditions. See Miller, *Tanks of the World*, p. 302.
36. Stewart, *The New Zealand Division, 1916–1919*, pp. 69–70.
37. *The Russell Family Saga*, Russell diary, 13 September 1916.
38. MS-85-132, Fraser, John Roy, 1884–1936, World War One papers, account of 1916 France.
39. MSX-4131, A. Martin papers, diary, 1916, entry n.d. mid-September 1916.
40. Ibid.
41. *The Russell Family Saga*, Russell diary, 14 September 1916.
42. MS-85-132, Fraser, John Roy, 1884–1936, World War One papers, account of 1916 France.
43. Stewart, *The New Zealand Division, 1916–1919*, p. 75.
44. Cited in ibid., p. 75.
45. Cited in ibid., p. 75.
46. G. Bryant, *Where the Prize is Highest*, p. 58.
47. Rhomboidal tanks were steered by a driver and two 'gearsmen', who differentially braked the tracks. Miller, *Tanks of the World*, p. 304.
48. *The Russell Family Saga*, Russell diary, 15 September 1916.
49. MS-Papers-2295, Hassell, N.E., 'Memories of 1914'.
50. Ibid.
51. 91-319 Fama, Tano, d. 1940, correspondence and newspaper clippings, letter 1 October 1916.
52. Ibid.
53. Ibid.
54. MS-Papers-2295, Hassell, N.E. 'Memories of 1914'.
55. MS-85-132, Fraser, John Roy, 1884–1936, World War One papers, account of 1916 France.
56. Ibid.
57. Ibid.
58. Weston, p. 104.
59. *The Russell Family Saga*, Russell diary, 20 September 1916.
60. Ibid., 21 and 22 September 1916.
61. 88-208, Spedding, Eric Claude, d. 1916, 26 September 1916.
62. *The Russell Family Saga*, Russell to Milly, 29 September 1916.
63. *The Russell Family Saga*, Russell diary, 30 September 1916.
64. 88-208, Spedding, Eric Claude, d. 1916, diary, entry 1 October 1916.
65. Bryant, *Where the Prize is Highest*, pp. 59–60.
66. 88-208, Spedding, Eric Claude, d. 1916, Wilfred Kellow to Fred Irwin, 28 May 1917.
67. *The Russell Family Saga*, Russell diary, 2 October 1916.
68. Stewart, *The New Zealand Division, 1916–1919*, p. 119.

69. Matthew Wright, *Freyberg's War: The Man, the Legend and Reality*, p. 20.
70. *The Russell Family Saga*, Russell diary, 21 October 1916.
71. Ibid., 23 October 1916.
72. Stewart, *The New Zealand Division, 1916–1919*, p. 137.
73. MS-Papers-2244, C.A. Healey Collection, Diary, 14 November 1916.
74. MS-Papers-2295, Hassell, N.E., 'Memories of 1914'.
75. MS-Papers-8090, Foley, Harold, fl. 1916–1918, diary, 25 December 1916.
76. *The Russell Family Saga*, Russell diary, 20 and 21 February 1917.
77. Ibid., 12 March 1917.
78. MS-Papers-2295, Hassell, N.E., 'Memories of 1914'.
79. Allen, J., Box 9, Correspondence with Colonels Birdwood and Russell, 1914–1920, Allen to Russell, 27 March 1917.
80. *The Russell Family Saga*, Russell diary, 28 February, 1917.
81. Allen, J., Box 9, Correspondence with Colonels Birdwood and Russell, 1914–1920, Russell to Allen, 3 April 1917.
82. *The Russell Family Saga*, Russell diary, 31 March 1917.
83. Ibid., 15 March 1917.
84. Allen, J., Box 9, Correspondence with Colonels Birdwood and Russell, 1914–1920, Allen to Russell, 27 March 1917.
85. See, e.g., Matthew Wright, *Desert Duel*, pp. 13–14, 19–20.

## 4 Passchendaele

1. Roger Parkinson, *Tormented Warrior*, p. 109.
2. Ibid., p. 122.
3. Leon Wolff, *In Flanders Fields*, p. 35.
4. Ibid., p. 41.
5. Allen, J., Box 9, Correspondence with Colonels Birdwood and Russell, 1914–1920, Birdwood to Allen, 17 January 1917.
6. Ibid., Russell to Allen, 19 June 1917.
7. Ibid., Russell to Allen, 10 February 1917.
8. *The Russell Family Saga*, Russell to Gwen Russell, 13 March 1917.
9. Wolff, *In Flanders Fields*, pp. 55–56.
10. Ibid., pp. 61–62.
11. Parkinson, *Tormented Warrior*, p. 130.
12. Wolff, *In Flanders Fields*, p. 64.
13. *The Russell Family Saga*, Russell diary, 7 March 1917.
14. WA 2/3, Box 13, No. 241, 'Magnum Opus'.
15. *The Russell Family Saga*, Russell diary, 21 March 1917.
16. Ibid., 30 April 1917.
17. Wolff, *In Flanders Fields*, pp. 91–93.
18. *The Russell Family Saga*, Russell diary, 25 March 1917.
19. Ibid., 2 April 1917.
20. WA 20/3, Box 13, No. 241, 'Outline of Plan for Offensive Against Messines', 3 April 1917.
21. *The Russell Family Saga*, Russell diary, 6 April 1917.
22. WA 20/3, Box 13, No. 241, Russell to ANZAC Corps, 11 May 1917.
23. Ibid., Braithwaite to Russell, 15 May 1917.
24. Allen, J., Box 9, Correspondence with Colonels Birdwood and Russell, 1914–1920, Russell to Allen, 19 June 1917.
25. *The Russell Family Saga*, Russell diary, 14 May 1917.
26. WA 20/3, Box 13, No. 241, NZ Divisional letter to 2 Anzac Corps, 27 April 1917.
27. WA 20/3, Box 13, No. 257, 'Secret Orders 2 Brigade, Preliminary Instructions, 31 May 1917'.
28. *The Russell Family Saga*, Russell diary, 5 June 1917.
29. Allen, J., Correspondence with Colonels Birdwood and Russell, 1914–1920, Russell to Allen, 19 June 1917.
30. *The Russell Family Saga*, Russell diary, 5 June 1917.
31. MS-Papers-3951, Michael Corrigan Papers, diary 7 June 1917.
32. MS-Papers-2244, C.A. Healey Collection, Diary, 7 June 1917.
33. Wolff, *In Flanders Fields*, p. 100; Fussell, *The Great War and Modern Memory*, p. 14.
34. Gilbert, *The Atlas of the First World War*, p. 90; Clark, *World War I: An Illustrated History*, p. 152.
35. Bryant, *Where the Prize is Highest*, p. 78.
36. WA 20/3, Box 13, No. 241, 'Report on the Capture of Messines by 4th Battalion, 3rd NZ (Rifle) Brigade, together with One Coy (Captain Free), 2nd Canterbury Regiment'.

37. *The Russell Family Saga*, Russell diary, 8 June 1917.
38. Allen, J., Box 9, Correspondence with Colonels Birdwood and Russell, 1914–1920, Russell to Allen, 19 June 1917.
39. WA 20/3, Box 13, No. 241, 'Report on the Capture of Messines by 4th Battalion, 3rd NZ (Rifle) Brigade, together with One Coy (Captain Free), 2nd Canterbury Regiment'.
40. Allen, J., Box 9, Correspondence with Colonels Birdwood and Russell, 1914–1920, Allen to Russell, 23 June 1917.
41. *The Russell Family Saga*, Russell diary, 10 June 1917.
42. Ibid., 14 June 1917.
43. Ibid., 16 June 1917.
44. Ibid., 21 June 1917.
45. Stewart, *The New Zealand Division, 1916–1919*, p. 222.
46. MS-Papers-4077, Folder 3, Peter Mathews Collection, letter Edwin Clark to mother and sisters, 20 June 1917.
47. MS-Papers-188-146, Lynch, Thomas, letters home during WWI, letter [n.d.] October 1917.
48. 88-208, Spedding, Eric Claude, d. 1916, diary, entry 16 September 1916.
49. MSX-4131, Martin A., Diary 1916.
50. WA 20/5, 50 'Notes on Use of Gas', report by Lt-Colonel Hartley.
51. Ibid.
52. MSX-2936-2938, Evans, J., diary, 16 and 17 October 1917.
53. Wolff, *In Flanders Fields*, p. 110.
54. Ibid., p. 123.
55. Clark, *World War I: An Illustrated History*, p. 152.
56. Wolff, *In Flanders Fields*, p. 82.
57. Ibid., pp. 128–29.
58. Bryant, *Where the Prize is Highest*, pp. 82–83.
59. MSX-2936-2938, Evans, J., diary, 1 August 1917.
60. J.F.C. Fuller, *The Decisive Battles of the Western World*, p. 360.
61. Wolff, *In Flanders Fields*, pp. 173–74.
62. Ibid., pp. 180–84.
63. MSX-4337-4338, Heseltine, J.C., diaries, 26 September 1917.
64. Stewart, *The New Zealand Division, 1916–1919*, pp. 248–49.
65. Ibid.
66. MS-Papers-2295, Hassell, N.E., 'Memories of 1914'.
67. MSX-4337-4338, Heseltine, J.C., diaries, 28 September 1917.
68. Ibid., 29 September 1917.
69. MS-Papers-2295, Hassell, N.E., 'Memories of 1914'.
70. MSX-4337-4338, Heseltine, J.C., diaries, 7 August 1917.
71. MS-Papers-8090, Foley, Harold, fl. 1916–1918, diary 30 September 1917.
72. *The Russell Family Saga*, Russell diary, 25 September 1917.
73. Ibid., 27 September 1917.
74. Ibid., 2 October 1917.
75. MSX-4337-4338, Heseltine, J.C., diaries, 3 October 1917.
76. Ibid., 6 October 1917.
77. MSX-2936-2938, Evans, J., diary, 3 October 1917.
78. Ibid.
79. *The Russell Family Saga*, Russell diary, 4 October 1917.
80. MSX-4337-4338, Heseltine, J.C., diaries, 4 October 1917.
81. MSX-2936-2938, Evans, J., diary, 3 October 1917.
82. MSX-4337-4338, Heseltine, J.C., diaries, 4 October 1917.
83. MSX-2936-2938, Evans, J., diary, 3 October 1917.
84. MSX-4337-4338, Heseltine, J.C., diaries, 3 October 1917.
85. MS-Papers-5629-2, Preston, Thomas Reginald (1896–1918), diary and papers, diary 4 October 1917.
86. MSX-2936-2938, Evans, J., diary, 4 October 1917.
87. *The Russell Family Saga*, Russell diary, 4 October 1917.
88. MS-Papers-4077, Folder 3, Peter Mathews Collection, attached papers.
89. MS-Papers-2512-1, H.T. Boscawen Collection, letter 2 March 1978.
90. Stewart, *The New Zealand Division, 1916–1919*, p. 271.
91. MSX-2936-2938, Evans, J., diary, 4 October 1917.
92. Ibid.
93. MSX-4337-4338, Heseltine, J.C., diaries, 6 October 1917.
94. Matthew Wright, *Wings Over New Zealand*, p. 126.

95. Wolff, *In Flanders Fields*, p. 195.
96. Ibid., p. 200.
97. Stewart, *The New Zealand Division, 1916–1919*, pp. 274–75.
98. MSX-4337-4338, Heseltine, J.C., diaries, 4 October 1917.
99. WA 10/3, Box 2, ZMR 2/1/9, Report on Operations of New Zealand Division from October 1st–31st 1917.
100. WA 20/3, Box 9, 25/88, '3 NZ (Rifle) Brigade Order No. 114', 10 October 1917.
101. Stewart, *The New Zealand Division, 1916–1919*, p. 276.
102. Wolff, *In Flanders Fields*, p. 223.
103. *The Russell Family Saga*, Russell diary, 7 October 1917, 11 October 1917.
104. MSX-4337-4338, Heseltine, J.C., diaries, 3 October 1917.
105. Stewart, *The New Zealand Division, 1916–1919*, p. 278.
106. MSX-4337-4338, Heseltine, J.C., diaries, 4 October 1917.
107. MS-Papers-7198, Stayte, Jesse William (1975–1918), 'Rough notes from my diary', 11 October 1917.
108. WA 20/3, Box 9, 25/88, '3 NZ (Rifle) Brigade' Order No. 114', 10 October 1917.
109. MSX-2936-2938, Evans, J., diary, 12 October 1917.
110. Stewart, *The New Zealand Division, 1916–1919*, p. 293.
111. MS-Papers-7198, Stayte, Jesse William, 1875–1918, 'Rough notes from my diary', 12 October 1917.
112. Ibid.
113. MSX-2936-2938, Evans, J., diary, 13 October 1917.
114. Ibid.
115. WA 10/3, Box 2, ZMR 2/1/9, Report on Operations of New Zealand Division from October 1st–31st 1917.
116. MSX-2936-2938, Evans, J., diary, 16 October 1917.
117. MS-Papers-7198, Stayte, Jesse William (1875–1918), 'Rough notes from my diary', 11 October 1917.
118. Ibid., 21 October 1917.
119. Ibid., 26 October 1917.
120. *The Russell Family Saga*, Russell diary, 11 and 12 October 1917.
121. Ibid., 24 October 1917.
122. Ibid., 31 October 1917.
123. Wolff, *In Flanders Fields*, pp. 194–95.
124. Fuller, *The Decisive Battles of the Western World*, Vol 2, p. 360.
125. Pugsley, *The Anzac Experience*, pp. 237–39.
126. Allen, J., Box 9, Correspondence with Colonels Birdwood and Russell, 1914–1920, Allen to Russell, 28 January 1918.
127. See, e.g., Clark, *World War I: An Illustrated History*, pp. 179–180.

## 5  Spring offensive

1. *The Russell Family Saga*, Russell diary, 13 November 1917.
2. Ibid., 4 December 1917.
3. Ibid., 26 October 1917.
4. Allen, J., Box 9, Correspondence with Colonels Birdwood and Russell, 1914–1920, Russell to Allen, 7 November 1917.
5. *The Russell Family Saga*, Russell diary, 8 February 1917.
6. Ibid., 25 November 1917.
7. MS-Papers-2295, Hassell, N.E., 'Memories of 1914'.
8. MS-Papers-5629-2, Preston, Thomas Reginald (1896–1918), diary and papers.
9. MS-Papers-7198, Stayte, Jesse William (1975–1918), 'Rough notes from my diary', 8 January 1918.
10. Ibid., 24 January 1918.
11. Stewart, *The New Zealand Division, 1916–1919*, p. 327, note 1.
12. Clark, *World War I: An Illustrated History*, p. 196.
13. Jean Hallade, 'Big Bertha Bombards Paris' in Fitzimonds (ed.), *The Big Guns*, pp. 54–55.
14. Parkinson, *Tormented Warrior*, p. 150.
15. Terraine, *White Heat*, p. 279.
16. Stewart, *The New Zealand Division, 1916–1919*, p. 331.
17. Allen, J., Box 9, Correspondence with Colonels Birdwood and Russell, 1914–1920, Birdwood to Allen, 31 January 1918.
18. Terraine, *White Heat*, p. 278.
19. MS-Papers-7198, Stayte, Jesse William, 1875–1918, 'Rough notes from my diary', 1 March 1918.

20. Clark, *World War I: An Illustrated History*, p. 198.
21. *The Russell Family Saga*, Russell diary, 2 March 1918.
22. Ibid., 4 March 1918.
23. Ibid., 6 and 7 March 1918.
24. Ibid., 15 March 1918.
25. Ibid., 18 March 1918.
26. WA 10/3, Box 2, ZMR 2/1/3, 'Summary of Operations of NZ Division, 1 March–30 April 1918'.
27. Terraine, *White Heat*, p. 282.
28. Ibid., p. 285.
29. *The Russell Family Saga*, Russell diary, 22 March 1918.
30. MS-Papers-7198, Stayte, Jesse William (1875–1918), 'Rough notes from my diary', 21 March 1918.
31. *The Russell Family Saga*, Russell diary, 22 March 1918.
32. MS-Papers-7198, Stayte, Jesse William (1875–1918), 'Rough notes from my diary', 22 March 1918.
33. MS-Papers-6293-2 Diary, Harcourt, John Gordon, fl. 1900–1960s, diary kept on active service in World War, diary 24 March 1918.
34. WA 10/3, Box 2, ZMR 2/1/3, 'Summary of Operations of NZ Division, 1 March–30 April 1918'.
35. Ibid.
36. MS-Papers-6293-2, Diary, Harcourt, John Gordon, fl. 1900–1960s, diary kept on active service in World War, diary, 25 March 1918.
37. WA 10/3, Box 2, ZMR 2/1/3, 'Summary of Operations of NZ Division, 1 March–30 April 1918'.
38. Ibid.
39. *The Russell Family Saga*, Russell diary, 26 March 1918.
40. MS-Papers-7198, Stayte, Jesse William (1975–1918), 'Rough notes from my diary', 26 March 1918.
41. WA 10/3, Box 2, ZMR 2/1/3, 'Summary of Operations of NZ Division, 1 March–30 April 1918'.
42. MS-Papers-7198, Stayte, Jesse William, 1975–1918, 'Rough notes from my diary', 26 March 1918.
43. Ibid.
44. Stewart, p. 349.
45. MS-Papers 7819-11 Letters written during World War One; Tuckey, Frances Isobella, fl. 1870–1918; letters from Richard Septimus Tuckey, letter 11 April 1918.
46. Puttick 2, 3 Personal Diary Vol. IV, 27 March 1918.
47. Ibid.
48. Stewart, *The New Zealand Division, 1916–1919*, p. 255.
49. *The Russell Family Saga*, Russell diary, 28 March 1918.
50. WA 10/3, Box 2, ZMR 2/1/3, 'Summary of Operations of NZ Division, 1 March–30 April 1918'.
51. *The Russell Family Saga*, Russell diary, 28 March 1918.
52. MS-Papers-7198, Stayte, Jesse William (1975–1918), 'Rough notes from my diary', 27 March 1918.
53. MS-Papers-4873, McDermott, Bryan, notes in MS packet.
54. *The Russell Family Saga*, Russell diary, 28 March 1918
55. WA 10/3, Box 2, ZMR 2/1/3, 'Summary of Operations of NZ Division, 1 March–30 April 1918'.
56. MS-Papers 7819-11 Letters written during World War One; Tuckey, Frances Isobella, fl. 1870–1918; letters from Richard Septimus Tuckey, letter 11 April 1918.
57. MS-Papers-7198, Stayte, Jesse William (1975–1918), 'Rough notes from my diary', 30 March and 3 April 1918.
58. Allen, J., Box 9, Correspondence with Colonels Birdwood and Russell, 1914–1920, Russell to Allen, 3 April 1918.
59. MS-Papers-5629-2, Preston, Thomas Reginald (1896–1918), diary and papers, 4 April 1918.
60. MS-Papers-6293-2, Diary, Harcourt, John Gordon, fl. 1900–1960s, diary kept on active service in World War, 5 April 1918.
61. MS-Papers 7819-11 Letters written during World War One; Tuckey, Frances Isobella, fl. 1870–1918; letters from Richard Septimus Tuckey, letter 11 April 1918.

62. MS-Papers-7198, Stayte, Jesse William (1975–1918), 'Rough notes from my diary', 3 April 1918.
63. *The Russell Family Saga*, Russell diary, 8 April 1918.
64. Ibid., Russell to his sisters, 13 April 1918.
65. Stewart, *The New Zealand Division, 1916–1919*, p. 372.
66. MS-Papers 7819-11 Letters written during World War One; Tuckey, Frances Isobella, fl. 1870–1918; letters from Richard Septimus Tuckey, letter 11 April 1918.
67. Allen, J., Box 9, Correspondence with Colonels Birdwood and Russell, 1914–1920, Birdwood to Allen, 28 April 1918.
68. Terraine, *White Heat*, p. 288.
69. MS-Papers-7198, Stayte, Jesse William (1975–1918), 'Rough notes from my diary', 2 May 1918.
70. Stewart, *The New Zealand Division, 1916–1919*, pp. 385–86.
71. *The Russell Family Saga*, Russell diary, 6 June 1918 — extract.
72. Ibid., 1918 divisional Christmas card.
73. Quoted in Matthew Wright, *Havelock North — The History of a Village*, p. 131.
74. See, e.g., *The Russell Family Saga*, Russell diary, 13 February 1916.
75. See, e.g., Pugsley, *The Anzac Experience*, pp. 204–44.
76. Ibid., Russell diary, 30 May 1918 — extract.
77. Clark, *World War I: An Illustrated History*, p. 205.
78. See, e.g., Matthew Wright, *The Reed Illustrated History of New Zealand*, pp. 269–72.
79. MS-Papers-5629-2, Preston, Thomas Reginald (1896–1918), diary and papers, 25 July 1918.
80. James Gasson, *Travis, VC: Man in No Man's Land*, pp. 120–27.
81. MS-Papers-5629-2, Preston, Thomas Reginald (1896–1918), diary and papers, 27 July 1918.
82. Terraine, *White Heat*, p. 324.

## 6 One Hundred Days

1. Russell diary, 21 August 1918.
2. Ibid., 22 August 1918.
3. Ibid., 28 August 1918.
4. *The Russell Family Saga*, Russell to Milly Russell, 31 August 1918.
5. Ibid., Russell diary, 30 August 1918.
6. Ibid., Russell to Milly Russell, 30 August 1918.
7. Burton, p. 303.
8. Stewart, *The New Zealand Division, 1916–1919*, p. 463.
9. Ferguson, *The Pity of War*, pp. 447–48.
10. Burton, p. 303.
11. MS-Papers-7198, Stayte, Jesse William (1975–1918), 'Rough notes from my diary', 1 April 1918.
12. Burton, p. 303.
13. *The Russell Family Saga*, Russell diary, 6 September 1918.
14. Ibid., 9 September 1918.
15. Ibid., 12 September 1918.
16. Ibid.
17. See Terraine, *White Heat*, p. 307; Fergusson, *The Pity of War*, p. 310.
18. Terraine, *White Heat*, p. 308.
19. *The Russell Family Saga*, Russell diary, 25 and 26 September 1918.
20. Ibid., 27 September 1918.
21. Ibid., 28 September 1918.
22. John Keegan, *The First World War*, p. 442.
23. Ferguson, *The Pity of War*, p. 311; Terraine, *White Heat*, pp. 312–14.
24. John Mosier, *The Myth of the Great War*, esp. pp. 327–36.
25. Keegan, *The First World War*, p. 443.
26. MSX-2936-2938 Evans, J., diary, 30 September 1918.
27. Ibid.
28. *The Russell Family Saga*, Russell diary, 30 September 1918.
29. Ibid., 7 October 1918.
30. Ibid., 8 October 1918.
31. Stewart, *The New Zealand Division, 1916–1919*, p. 539.
32. Ferguson, *The Pity of War*, pp. 316–17.
33. Clark, *World War I: An Illustrated History*, p. 80.
34. Ferguson, *The Pity of War*, p. 276.
35. *The Russell Family Saga*, Russell to family, 25 October 1918.
36. Ibid., Russell diary, 23 October 1918. Stewart, p. 546 states 8.40 a.m.

37. *The Russell Family Saga*, Russell diary, 24 October 1918.
38. Ibid., Russell to Milly Russell, 31 October 1918.
39. Martin Gilbert, *First World War*, p. 497.
40. *Russell Family Saga*, Russell diary, 11 November 1918.
41. Stewart, *The New Zealand Division, 1916–1919*, p. 592.
42. Argued by Ferguson, *The Pity of War*, p. 368.
43. Martin Gilbert, *First World War*, p. 497.
44. MS-Papers-7440, Gardner, Frank Warren, 1890?–1918, Papers, death notice and enclosed letter.
45. MSX-2936-2938, Evans, J., diary, 10 November 1918.
46. Ibid., 11 November 1918.
47. Churchill, *The World Crisis*, p. 949.
48. MSX-2936-2938, Evans, J., diary, 11 November 1918.
49. MS-Papers-2295, Hassell, N.E., 'Memories of 1914'.
50. *The Russell Family Saga*, Russell to family, 13 November 1918.
51. Ibid., Russell diary, 11 November 1918.
52. MSX-2936-2938, Evans, J., diary, 12 November 1918.
53. Ibid., 13 November 1918.
54. Ibid.
55. See Matthew Wright, *The Reed Illustrated History of New Zealand*, pp. 250–54.
56. *The Russell Family Saga*, Russell diary, 13 November 1918.
57. MSX-2936-2938, Evans, J., diary, 13 November 1918.
58. Ibid., 18 December 1918.
59. Ibid., 22 December 1918.
60. Ibid., 25 December 1918.
61. MSX-2936-2938, Evans, J., diary, 31 December 1918.
62. WA 22/6, Box 5, No. 50 'Report on Demobilisation'.
63. Ibid.
64. Stewart, *The New Zealand Division, 1916–1919*, p. 607.
65. *The Russell Family Saga*, Russell diary, 26 January, 1 February 1919.
66. Ibid., 1 April 1919.
67. Ibid., p. 233.
68. Ferguson, *The Pity of War*, p. 391.
69. Martin Gilbert, *First World War*, p. 510.
70. Ibid., p. 503.
71. See, e.g., John Bourne, Peter Liddle, Ian Whitehead, *The Great World War, Vol I*, pp. 13–26; Keegan, *The First World War*, p. 453.
72. Matthew Wright, *Italian Odyssey*, pp. 160–65.
73. This was the thesis of Eric Hobsbawm, *Age of Extremes*, esp. pp. 5–11.
74. My argument. See Matthew Wright, *Reed Illustrated History of New Zealand*, p. 255.
75. AJHR 1921–22, H-19, p. 2.
76. M.F. Lloyd-Prichard, *An Economic History of New Zealand to 1939*, p. 266.
77. See, e.g., AJHR 1920 H-19a 'War Expenses Account', 'Detailed statement of expenditure from the beginning of the war to the 31st March, 1920'; AJHR 1921-22, H-19 'Defence Forces of New Zealand', report of General Officer Commanding, for period from 1st July 1920, to 30th June 1921', p. 4.
78. AJHR 1921-22, H-18 'Twenty third annual report of the pensions department', p. 1.
79. Ibid., p. 7.
80. Matthew Wright, *The Reed Illustrated History of New Zealand*, pp. 243–44.
81. Matthew Wright, 'Napier VC winner slept through "off"', *Hawke's Bay Today*, 1 February 2003. Storkey's VC is on display in the Queen Elizabeth II Army Museum, Waiouru.
82. Pugsley, *The Anzac Experience*, pp. 33–34.
83. Matthew Wright, *The Reed Illustrated History of New Zealand*, pp. 287–302.
84. James Belich, *Reforging Paradise*, pp. 157–88.
85. Argued by Matthew Wright, *Reed Illustrated History of New Zealand*, p. 287.
86. MS-Papers-6887, Keating, John Joseph, letter 'Jack' to 'Jack', 7 July 1918.
87. Argued by Matthew Wright, *The Reed Illustrated History of New Zealand*, pp. 308–18.
88. Matthew Wright, *Quake — Hawke's Bay 1931*, pp. 88, 142; Matthew Wright, *Town and Country*, pp. 444–45.
89. Pugsley, *The Anzac Experience*, pp. 156, 163.

**Conclusion**
1. See, e.g., Matthew Wright, *Desert Duel*, pp. 169–70.
2. Matthew Wright, *Reed Illustrated History of New Zealand*, pp. 239–44.
3. Ibid., pp. 232–35.
4. Ibid., p. 429.
5. Ferguson, *The Pity of War*, pp. 442–56.
6. Matthew Wright, *Reed Illustrated History of New Zealand*, p. 297.
7. MSX-4760, 'Bentley, Dawes', 'Doug Stark — Bomber with Otago on the Western Front'.
8. See, e.g., Ferguson, *The Pity of War*, photo essay, pp. 178–79.
9. See, e.g., Weston, *Three Years with the New Zealanders*, p. 104.
10. See, e.g., Treadwell, *Recollections of an Amateur Soldier*, esp. pp. 114–48, Burton, e.g. pp. 146–47, 218–21.

# GLOSSARY

| | |
|---|---|
| ANZAC | Australian and New Zealand Army Corps, initially coined on a rubber stamp in 1914–15. |
| Army | A formation of two or more corps, usually led by a full General or Field Marshal. |
| *bataille d'usure* | Wearing-out battle. |
| battalion | A formation usually comprising three or four companies. |
| Bosche/Bosch/Boche | Slang for Germans or German soldiers. |
| brigade | A formation usually comprising three or four battalions, usually led by a Brigadier-General during the First World War. |
| bunker | Fortified concrete position, usually housing a machine-gun position. |
| CIGS | Chief of the Imperial General Staff, the senior British military officer. |
| company | A formation usually comprising three or more platoons. |
| corps | A formation of two or more divisions, usually led by a Lieutenant-General. |
| digger | Slang for New Zealand soldiers, reputedly deriving from their trench-digging abilities. Used afterwards to mean Australian troops. |
| division | A formation usually comprising three brigades, led by a Major- or Lieutenant-General. |
| enfilade | Fire entering a position from an angle. |
| estiament | Small public bar. |
| fire trench | The very front trench in a defensive complex. |
| Fritz | Slang for German soldiers. |
| GOC | General Officer Commanding, term given to the officer in charge of a significant military formation such as a division or expeditionary force, usually a Major- or Lieutenant-General. |
| gooseberry | A nest of wood and wire designed to obstruct advancing infantry. |
| Hindenburg Line | Allied term for the Siegfried Line, to which Germany retreated in early 1917. |

| | |
|---|---|
| Hun | Slang for German soldiers. |
| iron rations | Slang for shells or bombs. |
| Mills bomb | Known on the Western Front as 'bomb'; the classic 'pineapple' grenade, patented in 1915. |
| mustard gas | Dichlorodiethyl sulphide, a vesicant used by the Germans on Allied forces from 1917 onwards. |
| NCO | Non-commissioned officer. |
| New Zealand and Australian Division | Original name of the division assembled to fight on Gallipoli. |
| no-man's land | Territory between the front trenches of each side, varying from under 100 to more than 200 metres. |
| NZEF | New Zealand Expeditionary Force. |
| pillbox | British term for bunker. |
| platoon | A formation, introduced to the British in the early twentieth century, comprising two or three sections. |
| Plug Street Wood | Slang for Ploegsteert Wood. |
| *poilus* | French private soldiery. |
| Rifle Brigade | Pre-1916 name of 3 (Rifle) Brigade; still used informally afterwards. |
| salient | The protruding part of a line. |
| section | The basic military unit, comprising 16 or 20 men and usually under a Lance-Corporal or Corporal. |
| SMLE | Short Magazine Lee Enfield; the bolt-action infantry rifle used by the New Zealanders. |
| stunt | Western Front slang, usually meaning a planned military action. |
| tank | Code name for the armoured 'land ships' developed in 1915–16, later adopted as the generic term for the type. |
| Tommy | Slang for British soldier. |
| walking barrage | Artillery fire directed so as to advance, in planned stages, ahead of infantry. |
| Wipers | Slang for Ypres. |

# BIBLIOGRAPHY

## Alexander Turnbull Library

85-132, Fraser, John Roy, 1884–1936, World War One papers.
88-208, Spedding, Eric Claude, d. 1916, World War One diary.
91-319, Fama, Gaetano J. d. 1940, Correspondence and newspaper clippings.
Micro-MS-591, Kerse, Charles Allanton, 1894–1918, diary 18 Aug 1914–22 July 1918.
Micro-MS-832, O'Connor, Michael, diary 1915–1917.
MS Papers 2244, C.A. Healey Collection, Diary.
MS-1172, McGilp, Clyde, Gallipoli historical records and war diary, 1st Battery, NZFA 1915–1916.
MS-88-146, Lynch, Thomas, d. 1954, letters home during World War One.
MS-760, Parmenter, N.E., Diary.
MS-copy-micro-0528, Kinsey, Sir Joseph James Papers, 1869–1935.
MS-Papers-1439, Hankins Collection.
MS-Papers-2094, E.R. Sutton, diary.
MS-Papers-2295, Hassell, N.E., 'Memories of 1914'.
MS-Papers-2350, Bollinger, George Wallace 1890–1917, diary and letters.
MS-Papers-2393, Tronson, Aubrey de Coudrey 1892–1957, 'A soldier's book of life'.
MS-Papers-2414, Watson, R.M., certificates of service.
MS-Papers-244, C.W. Melvill Collection.
MS-Papers-2477, Higginson, Louisa, diaries/transcribed by Mrs R.L. Wilson.
MS-Papers-2481, Bourke, Harry O'Donel, diary and memoirs.
MS-Papers-2512-1, H.T. Boscawen Papers.
MS-Papers-3101, Richardson, George Spafford (Major-General Sir), 1868–1938, Letter to E.C. Walmsley re his war experiences.
MS-Papers-3914, Williams, Ernest Percival, 1883–1917, diary.
MS-Papers-3951, Corrigan, Michael, 1885–1918, diaries.
MS-Papers-3952, Algie, Colin Stewart (Lieutenant), 1887–1916, papers.
MS-Papers-4077, Folder 3, Peter Mathews Collection, Research from Northern Wairoa Gazette, and WWI letters.
MS-Papers-4309, John W. Muldoon Collection.
MS-Papers-4873, McDermott, Bryan Peter, d. 1918, diary.
MS-Papers-5334, Clift family papers.
MS-Papers-5629-2, Preston, Thomas Reginald (1896–1918), diary and papers.
MS-Papers-6027, Luke, Kenneth Ewart, d. 1965, letters to his family.
MS-Papers-6293-2, Harcourt, John Gordon, fl. 1900–1960s, diary kept on active service in World War One.
MS-Papers-6406-3, McLean, Douglas Rawei, 1892–1976, World War One papers, letters to family.
MS-Papers-6476, Tompkins, Lance. b. 1896, letters from Helen Crabb.
MS-Papers-6887, Keating, John Joseph, 1881–1955, inward correspondence.

MS-Papers-7198, Stayte, Jesse William, 1875-1918, rough notes from my diary.

MS-Papers-7768, Anderson, Lars Stanley, 1879-1918, Papers relating to his life.

MS-Papers-7819-11, Tuckey, Frances Isobella, fl. 1870-1918, letters from Richard Septimus Tuckey.

MS-Papers-8090, Foley, Harold, fl. 1916-1918, Diary/transcribed.

MSX 4760-4671, Bently, Dawes, fl. 1920, 'Manuscript of Doug Stark — bomber with Otago on the Western Front.

MSX-2936-2938, Major James Evans, MC and Bar, diary.

MSX-4337-4338, Heseltine, J.C., diaries.

MSX-4958, Frank Campbell (1885-1944), diary.

MSX-5130, McLaren, George, fl. 1919, World War One letters and diaries.

qms-SMI 1829, Smith, Ralph, 'Retrospection'.

## National Library of New Zealand

*Appendices to the Journal of the House of Representatives (AJHR)*

1915 H-19E 'New Zealand Expeditionary Force: Provision of reinforcement drafts for the (Memorandum on)'.

1916 H-19D 'New Zealand Expeditionary Force: Return relative to Maoris and Half-Castes etc'.

1920, C-9, 'Discharged Soldiers Settlement for the year ending 31st March 1920'.

1920, H-19a 'War Expenses Account'

1921-22, H-18 'Twenty third annual report of the pensions department'.

1921-22, H-19 'Defence Forces of New Zealand', report of General Officer Commanding, for period from 1st July 1920, to 30th June 1921'.

## Archives New Zealand/Te Rua Mahara o Te Kāwanatanga, Wellington Office

*War Archive*

SERIES 5

5/1, 2 Reports (historical) during war period NZ Dental Corps

SERIES 10

10/3, ZMR 1/1/40, NZEF HQ War Records Section — Registered files — ZMR System — Miss E.A. Rout, Mar-Jun 1917.

10/3, Box 2, ZMR 2/1/9, NZEF HQ War Records Section — Registered files — ZMR System, Report on Operations of New Zealand Division from October 1st-31st 1917.

10/3, Box 2, ZMR 2/1/3, NZEF HQ War Records Section — Registered files — ZMR System, Summary of Operations of NZ Division, 1st March-30th April 1918.

SERIES 20

20/3, Box 9, 25/88 HQ NZ&A Division — NZ Division General Staff — Registered Files — Miscellaneous Series — NZ Rifle Brigade, Orders/Operations October 1917.

20/3, Box 13, No. 241, HQ NZ&A Division — NZ Division General Staff — Registered Files — Miscellaneous Series — General Corps plans, instructions No. 1-8 (Attack on Messines-Wytschaete Ridge), Apr-Jun 1917.

20/3, Box 13, No. 257, HQ NZ&A Division — NZ Division General Staff — Registered Files — Miscellaneous Series — Tanks, May–June 1917.

20/5, 35, HQ NZ&A Division, NZ Division General Staff — Unregistered Files — Gravenstafel.

20/5, 50, NZ&A Division, NZ Division General Staff — Unregistered Files, Notes on Use of Gas.

Series 22

22/6, Box 5, No. 50 NZ&A Division, NZ Division General Staff — Unregistered Files, Report on Demobilisation.

*Army Department*

Series 10

10/16/1, Secret Registry: Confidential Series — New Zealand defence scheme, report by Lord Kitchener, 1910, March–April.

10/16/6, Secret Registry: Confidential Series — New Zealand defence scheme Expeditionary action by territorial force, August 1912–June 1913.

10/16/12, Secret Registry: Confidential Series — New Zealand defence scheme, Reinforcements for service abroad, predictions as to requirements, August 1914–October 1918.

*Personal Papers*

Lieutenant-General Sir Edward Puttick

Series 2/3, Personal Diaries whilst a member of the New Zealand Rifle Brigade, 8 October 1915–21 October 1918.

Hon. James Allen

'Correspondence with Colonels Birdwood and Russell, 1914–1920', from 'Miscellaneous files and papers'.

D1/6/3 'Expeditionary Force: New Zealand Division, Formation Of', from 'Defence Files'.

D1/6/5 'Expeditionary Force: History of Changes in', from 'Defence Files'.

D1/6 'Expeditionary Force, Reinforcements for', from 'Defence Files'.

DA/11 'Instructions of General Commanding Officer relating to the NZEF', from 'Defence Files'.

## Hastings Public Library

Gambrill, R.F. (ed.), *The Russell Family Saga* (5 vols).

## Secondary sources

Belich, James, *Reforging Paradise*, Penguin, Auckland, 2001.

Bourne, John; Liddle, Peter; Whitehead, Ian, *The Great World War*, Vol I., HarperCollins, London, 2002.

Boyack, Nicholas, *Behind the Lines*, Allen & Unwin, Wellington, 1989.

Brown, Malcolm, *Tommy Goes to War*, J.M. Dent & Sons Ltd, London, 1978.

——, *The Western Front*, Pan, London, 2001.

Bryant, G., *Where the Prize is Highest*, Collins, Auckland, 1972.
Burton, Ormond, *The Silent Division, New Zealanders at the front 1914–1919*, Angus and Robertson, Sydney 1935.
Churchill, W.S., *The World Crisis*, Four Square, London, 1960.
Clark, Lloyd, *World War I: An Illustrated History*, Helicon, Oxford, 2001.
Cowley, Robert (ed.), *The Great War: Perspectives on the First World War*, Random House Trade Paperback, New York, 2004.
Dixon, Norman, *On the Psychology of Military Incompetence*, Pimlico, London, 1976.
Essame, H., 'The New Warfare' in Bernard Fitzsimons (ed.), *The Big Guns*, Phoebus, London, 1973.
Evans, Martin Marix, *Passchendaele and the Battles of Ypres 1914–18*, Osprey, London, 1997.
Ferguson, Niall, *The Pity of War*, Allen Lane, London, 1998.
Fitzsimons, Bernard (ed.), *The Big Guns*, Phoebus, London, 1973.
Fuller, J.F.C., *The Decisive Battles of the Western World, Vol. 2*, Paladin, 1970.
Fussell, Paul, *The Great War and Modern Memory*, Oxford University Press, Oxford, 1975.
Gasson, James, *Travis, VC: Man in No Man's Land*, A.H. & A.W. Reed, Wellington, 1966.
Gilbert, Martin, *The Atlas of the First World War*, Dorset Press, London, 1970.
———, *First World War*, HarperCollins, London, 1994.
Grey of Fallodon, Viscount, *Twenty Five Years*, Vol II, Frederick Stokes, New York, 1925.
Hallade, Jean, 'Big Bertha Bombards Paris' in Fitzsimons, Bernard (ed.), *The Big Guns*, Phoebus, London, 1973.
Hobsbawm, Eric, *Age of Extremes*, Abacus, London, 1995.
Hyde, Robin, *Passport to Hell*, Auckland University Press, Auckland, 1986.
Keegan, John, *The First World War*, Hutchinson, London, 1998.
King, Michael, *Nga Iwi o Te Motu*, Reed, Auckland, 1997, revised edition 2001.
Lloyd-Prichard, M.F., *An Economic History of New Zealand to 1939*, Collins, Auckland and London, 1970.
Macintyre, Donald, *Jutland*, Evans Brothers, London, 1957.
Malthus, Cecil, *Armentières and the Somme*, Reed, Auckland, 2002.
Marder, Arthur (ed.), *Fear God and Dread Nought: Correspondence of Admiral of the Fleet Lord Fisher of Kilverstone*, Vol. III, Jonathan Cape, London, 1959.
Miller, David, *Tanks of the World*, Greenwich Edition, London, 2001.
Mosier, John, *The Myth of the Great War*, HarperCollins, New York, 2001.
Mumby, Frank (ed.), *The Great World War*, Vol. III, Gresham, London, n.d. [1915–17]
Owen, Edward, *1914: Glory Departing*, Buchan and Enright, London, 1986.
Parkinson, Roger, *Tormented Warrior*, Hodder & Stoughton, London, 1978.
Pugsley, Christopher, *Te Hokowhitu a Tu: The Maori Pioneer Battalion in the First World War*, Reed, Auckland, 1995.
———, *The Anzac Experience*, Reed, Auckland, 2004.
Stewart, H. *The New Zealand Division, 1916–1919*, Whitcombe and Tombs, Auckland, 1921.
Taylor, A.J.P., *How Wars Begin*, Book Club Associates, London, 1979.
Terraine, John, *White Heat: the New Warfare 1914–1918*, Sidgwick and Jackson, London, 1982.
*The New Zealand Army*, New Zealand Army, Wellington, 1995.

Thorns, David, and Sedgwick, Charles, *Understanding Aotearoa/New Zealand, Historical Statistics*, Dunmore Press, Palmerston North, 1997.
Tolkien, J.R.R., *The Two Towers*, Unwin Paperbacks, London, reprint 1982.
Treadwell, C.A.L., *Recollections of an Amateur Soldier*, Wellington 1936.
Weston, C.H., *Three Years with the New Zealanders*, Skeffington & Son, London, n.d.
Wolff, Leon, *In Flanders Fields*, Longmans Green & Co, London, 1959.
Wright, Matthew, 'Australia, New Zealand and Imperial Defence, 1909–1914', MA Thesis, Massey University 1986.
———, *Havelock North: The History of a Village*, HDC, Hastings, 1996.
———, *Blue Water Kiwis: New Zealand's Naval Story*, Reed, Auckland, 2001.
———, *Quake: Hawke's Bay 1931*, Reed, Auckland, 2001.
———, *Town and Country: The History of Hastings and District*, HDC, Hastings, 2001.
———, *Desert Duel: New Zealand's North African War 1940–43*, Reed, Auckland, 2002.
———, *Wings Over New Zealand: A Social History of New Zealand Aviation*, Whitcoulls, Auckland, 2002.
———, *Italian Odyssey: New Zealanders in the Battle for Italy 1943–45*, Reed, Auckland, 2003.
———, 'Napier VC winner slept through "off"', *Hawke's Bay Today*, 1 February 2003.
———, *Reed Illustrated History of New Zealand*, Reed, Auckland, 2004.
———, *Freyberg's War: The Man, the Legend and Reality*, Penguin, Auckland, 2005.
Wright, Patrick, *Tank*, Faber and Faber, London, 2000.

# INDEX

1 Anzac Corps   35, 103, 105, 106, 107, 121
2 Anzac Corps   65, 90, 102, 103, 106, 112

1 Auckland Battalion   107, 108, 128, 146
2 Auckland Battalion   83, 108, 126, 130, 134
3 Auckland Battalion   107, 108, 115

1 Australian Division   30
3 Australian Division   103, 112, 116
4 Australian Division   96, 129
5 Australian Division   82

1 Brigade   33, 65, 74, 96, 106, 107, 108, 126, 128, 129, 145, 146, 150, 152
2 Brigade   33, 43, 65, 79, 88, 115, 118, 127, 145, 146, 148, 152, 153, 155, 159
3 (Rifle) Brigade   33, 42, 66, 69, 72, 74, 75, 81, 83, 84, 115, 116, 118, 123, 133, 143, 145, 150, 153, 157
4 Brigade   97, 110, 106, 107, 122, 126

1 Canterbury Battalion   116, 122, 126
2 Canterbury Battalion   81, 93, 97, 126, 130

1 Otago Battalion   97, 115
2 Otago Battalion   82, 98, 115, 129, 140, 143, 148, 155
3 Otago Battalion   107, 108
4 Otago Battalion   41

1 Wellington Battalion   78, 94, 107, 108, 146
1 Wellington Mounted Rifle Brigade   141
2 Wellington Battalion   69, 76, 82, 108, 129, 130, 131

3 Corps   78
12 Corps   122
15 Corps   72
18 Corps   105, 112
20 Corps   88

2 Bavarian Corps   82
3 Bavarian Division   93
4 Bavarian Division   106
13 Bavarian Division   80

9 Division   116
17 Division   65
18 Division   69
25 Division   89, 94
33 Division   103
41 Division   78, 81
48 Division   109
49 Division   110, 112
57 Division   83, 84
66 Division   112

2 Rifle Battalion   74, 128, 148
4 Rifle Battalion   93, 134

12 Nelson Company   122
36 (Ulster) Division   84
40 (Saxon) Division   93
51 (Highland Territorial) Division   69
63 (Naval) Division, *see also* Royal Naval Division (RND)   82

Abbeville   69
Abraham Heights   108, 109, 116
Aisne   86
Albert   72, 127, 138
Allen, Sir James   10, 32, 33, 38, 54, 63, 64, 85, 87, 96, 119, 122, 125, 138
Allenby, General Edmund   87
Alsace-Lorraine   20
Amiens   138, 143, 144
Ancre River   68, 70, 127, 145
Ancre Valley   129
Andrew, Lance-Corporal Leslie Wilton   102
Anzac Day   7, 162, 167
Anzac Division   31, 32, 34

Anzac phenomenon  31, 165, 166, 167
Armentières  34, 35, 45, 46, 47, 65, 66, 69, 97, 138
Arnim, General Sixt von  101, 107
Arras  65, 127
Asquith, Herbert  12, 32
Austria-Hungary  12
Averill, Second Lieutenant L.C.  156

Baker-Carr, Colonel C.D.  102
Ballieul  139
Bapaume  70, 144, 147, 158
Barrowclough, Lieutenant-Colonel H.E.  156, 157
Basseville  102, 109
bataille d'usure  36
Bellevue  113, 115
Below, General Fritz von  21, 36, 38
Berlin Farm  108
Berlin Wood  108
Bethman-Hollweg, Theobald von  86
Biefvillers  146
Birdwood, Lieutenant-General Sir William Riddell  30, 32, 33, 43, 65, 86, 112, 125, 138
Bleuwen Molen  94
Boer War  38
Bollinger, George  25, 27, 28, 30
Boscawen, Hugh  109
Braithwaite, Brigadier-General W.G.  42, 76, 88, 89, 97, 116
Bridges, Major-General W.T.  28
British Expeditionary Force (BEF)  19, 20, 21, 22, 23, 138
Broodseinde  106, 109
Broodseinde Ridge  103
Brown, Brigadier-General C.H.  96
Brown, Sergeant Donald Forrester  75, 81
Burton, Ormond  60, 62, 148
Byng, General Sir Julian  127, 145, 147

Cairo  25, 27, 28, 32
Calais  87
Cambrai  120, 152, 153
Campbell, Lance-Corporal Frank  30
Canal du Nord  148, 153
Caterpillar Valley  172
Chambers, Selwyn  30

Champagne  87
Chappell, Sergeant F.E.  108
Charge of the Light Brigade  15
Chateau Wood  102
chlorine  100
Chunuk Bair  31
Churchill, Winston  12, 24, 36, 39, 72
Clark, H. George  40, 48, 52
Clark, Sergeant Edwin  40, 60, 99, 109
Clausewitz, Carl von  8
Cockerell, Second Lieutenant A.R.  116
Colgneux  135
Cologne  159
Courtney, Sergeant J.  69
Crevecour Canal  152
Crozat Canal  127
'cultural cringe'  170

Dardanelles  24
de Lisle, General Sir Beauvoir  82
Defence Act 1909  17
Defence Amendment Act 1910  17
Delville Wood  50, 72
Douvre River  84
Douvre Valley  102
Duigan, Major J.E.  65

Egypt  17, 42
Estaires  65, 100
Étaples  45, 65, 100
Evans, James  52, 61, 101, 108, 109, 116, 118, 152, 158, 159, 160
Expeditionary Force  65

Fama, Tano  41, 51, 70, 78
Fernandez, Corporal J.  94
Fircourt Wood  74
First World War  8, 9, 111, 164, 165, 168, 169, 171, 172, 174, 175
Fisher, Admiral Sir John  24
Flanders  9, 10, 35, 48, 58, 84, 169
Flers  39, 70, 71, 72, 76, 78, 80, 103, 188, 170
Foley, Harold  82, 105
Forsyth, Sergeant Samuel  146
Franco-Prussian War (1871)  11, 18
Fraser, John  46, 72

Fraser, Peter   165
Fremicourt   147, 148
French, General Sir John   19, 12, 21
Freyberg, Lieutenant-Colonel Bernard   82
Frickleton, Lance-Corporal Samuel   93
Frost, Sergeant-Major W.E.   69
Fuller, J.F.C.   103, 119
Fullerphones   36
Fulton, Brigadier H.T.   133

Gallipoli   9, 25, 31, 32, 34, 35, 42, 45, 50, 66, 141, 169, 171, 175
Geange, Private T.   108
Gheluveldt Plateau   103
Gibbon, Colonel C.M.   32
Godley   122
Godley, Major-General Alexander   17, 18, 30, 35, 69, 83, 97, 98, 103, 119, 122
Goldingham, Sergeant K.A.   108
Gommecourt   137, 143, 158
Gordon, Brigadier-General J.M.   18
Goudberg Spur   115, 120
Gough, Lieutenant-General Sir Hubert   68, 100, 102, 126, 127
Gouzeaucourt Wood   148, 149
Gravenstafel   105, 106, 108, 109
Grévilliers   146, 147
Grey, Edward (British Foreign Secretary)   13
Grove Alley   74
Group Wytschaete   103
Gueudecourt   70, 78, 80

Haig, Field Marshal Sir Douglas   23, 35, 36, 38, 42, 44, 68, 86, 100, 102, 103, 111, 112, 119, 125, 127, 143, 145, 150, 152
Hamel   127
Hanebeeck Stream   107
Hankins, Clarence   34, 40, 66
Harcourt, John   42, 127, 136
Hargest, Lieutenant-Colonel J.   155
Harper, Lieutenant-General Sir G.M.   127
   4 Corps   127
Hassell, N.E.   25, 41, 54, 76, 78, 158
Havrincourt Wood   148
Hawke's Bay Regiment   70
Hazebrouck   106, 115, 138

Healey, Clarence   82
Hébuterne   128, 129, 131, 132, 133, 143
Hédauville   128, 133
Heliopolis   25
Heseltine, J.C.   52, 53, 54, 55, 60, 105, 106, 109, 110, 111, 113
Higginson, Louisa   14, 32
High (Foreaux) Wood   72, 74
Hill 60   89
Hill 63   89, 91
Hindenburg, Field Marshal Paul von   86
Hindenburg Line   87, 88, 148, 150, 153
Hohenzollern, Kaiser Wilhelm II   20
   and Kaiser's Battle   124, 155, 157
Holmes, Brigadier-General Harry   43
Horne, Major-General G.S.   70
Houplines   47, 65
Houthulst Forest   112

'incorrigibles'   44
Institution Royale   93, 95

Jellicoe, Admiral Sir John   101
Joffre, Marshal Joseph   20, 21, 23, 86
Johnston, Brigadier-General B. Napier   38, 88, 105, 113, 160
Jutland, Battle of   67

Kansas Farm   117
Keating, John   168
Kemmel Hill   92
Kerensky, Alexander   87
Kerse, Charles   60, 61
King, Colonel George   116
Kitchener, Lord Herbert Horatio,   16, 17
   and New Army,   35, 38
Kluck, Colonel-General Alexander von   20, 21
Kronprinz Farm   108

l'Epinette sector   65
Langemarck, Battle of   102
La Signy Farm   129, 130, 132, 133
Laurent, Sergeant Harry   150
Le Cateau,   First battle of   21
   Second battle of   153-154
Le Quesnoy   155, 156, 157, 158

Lee, Private John A.  94
Liège  20
Lille  67, 154
Lloyd-George, David  86, 92, 101, 103, 125
London  7, 8, 54, 62, 64, 69, 122
Loupart Wood  146
Ludendorff, Field Marshal Erich von  86, 123, 124, 126, 127, 130, 131, 135, 138, 139, 140, 142, 143, 144, 148, 152, 155
Luke, Kenneth  43
Lynch, Thomas  57, 100
Lys River  42, 65, 84, 97, 154

Mackenzie, Major A.G.  83
Mackenzie, Private D.  107
Mackie, Laurie C.  29, 67, 146
Mailly-Maillet  128, 129, 130, 134, 136, 151, 158
Malone, Colonel William  31
Malthus, Cecil  54, 69
Marne  21, 143
Martin, Dr A.  47, 48, 67, 74, 78
Massey, William Ferguson  11, 17, 64, 85, 139
Maxse, Lieutenant-General Sir Ivor  112, 125
McDermott, Bryan  58, 134
Mediterranean Expeditionary Force (MEF)  24
Melvill, Brigadier-General  128
Menin Gate  7, 161
Menin Road  22, 53
Mericourt l'Abbe  127
Messines 'Magnum Opus' plan of attack on  88, 93, 94, 95, 98, 99, 100, 101, 103, 158, 161
Messines Ridge  88, 89
  mines  91-92, 97, 139, 162
Miles, Major R.  139
Miraumont  145
Moascar  32, 33
Moltke, Field Marshal Helmuth von  20, 21
Monash, Major-General Sir John  37, 66, 119
Mons  21
Mormal Forest  157
Mounted Brigade, The  34
Muldoon, John W.  28
Murray, General Sir Archibald  32
Mushroom, The  69
mustard gas  100, 101

Namur  20
National War Memorial, New Zealand  173
New Zealand and Australian Division  30, 31
New Zealand Division  8, 9, 10, 36, 37, 44, 45, 57, 65, 70, 76, 81, 82
  4 brigade formed  85, 89, 103, 109, 127, 134, 141, 142, 148, 150, 155, 156, 157, 171
New Zealand soldiers
  trench life  45–48
  adaptation to trenches  48
  attitudes to death  50
  attitudes to killing  51–52
  conditions  53–54
  leave  55–58
  prostitution  63–64
  early attitudes to Germans  67–68
New Zealand Soldiers' Club  62
New Zealand Tunnelling Company  66, 87
Ngata, Apirana  14
Nicholas, Private Henry  122
Nicholson, General Sir William  16
Nimot, W.P.  57
Nivelle  87
No. 1 General Hospital, Brockenhurst  57
Norbecourt  126

Oise  138
Ontario Farm  92
Operation GEORGETTE  138, 140, 143
Operation MICHAEL  126, 135, 138
Ostende  88, 101
Otago Mounted Rifles  33, 34

Palestine  34
Pals Battalions  40
Paris  8, 21, 54, 61, 64, 87, 124, 155, 160
Paris, Major-General Sir Archibald  68
Passchendaele  9, 88, 100, 101, 103, 104, 106, 109, 110, 112, 115, 116, 118, 120, 121, 125, 158, 161, 163, 170
Perenchies Ridge  67
Pershing, General John J.  125, 139, 142, 152, 164
Petain, Marshal Henri  87
phosgene  100
Picardy  9, 10, 34, 84, 136

Piccadilly Stunt  59
Pilckem Ridge  102
Pioneer Battalion  29, 33, 72, 113, 139, 160
Ploegsteert Wood  96, 139, 162
Plumer, Lieutenant-General Sir Herbert  35, 88, 89, 91, 94, 102, 103, 111, 139, 171
Poelcapelle  106
Polderhoek Spur  121
Polygon Wood  102, 103, 107, 109, 121
Poperinge  104, 115
Powley, Captain A.J.  69
Preston, T.R.  109, 136, 143
Puiseux  143, 145, 149
Puttick, Lieutenant-Colonel Edward  115, 132, 133

Ravebeek Stream  112
Ravebeek Valley  115, 116
Rawlinson, General Sir Henry  35, 68, 70
Reutelbeek Stream  121
Rhine  158, 159, 160
Richardson, Brigadier-General G.S.  21, 37, 63
Robertson, General Sir William ('Wully')  103
Rossignol  84, 158
Rossignol Wood  134, 143
Rout, Ettie  63
Royal Naval Division (RND)  21, 24
Royal Overseas Officers Club  62
Russell, Major-General Sir Andrew Hamilton ('Guy') 12, 13, 31, 33, 35, 37, 38, 42, 43, 44, 45, 54, 63, 64, 69, 72, 74, 80, 83, 84, 85, 87, 89, 89, 90, 91, 96, 97, 98, 106, 109, 113, 115, 116, 118, 119, 121, 122, 126, 126, 127, 128, 129, 132, 133, 134, 136, 137, 140, 141, 142, 142, 143, 145, 147, 148, 150, 152, 153, 154, 155, 158, 160, 171
Rifle Brigade *see also* 3 (Rifle) Brigade  33, 58
Russo-Japanese War  16

Sailly  82
Salonika Front  152
Sanctuary Wood  102
Savage, Michael Joseph  165
Scheldt Canal  152
Scheldt River  156
Schlieffen, Count Alfred von  20
Schlieffen plan, the  21
Second New Zealand Division  170
Second World War  85, 164
Seddon, Prime Minister Richard John  166
Selle River  153
Seranvilliers  153
Serre road  134
Shrewsbury Forest  102
Sling Camp  41, 57, 58, 60, 69, 100
Smith-Dorrien, General Sir Horace Lockwood  21, 22, 23
Somme, The  7, 35, 38, 38, 40, 42, 48, 52, 68, 72, 77, 79, 84, 126, 127, 130, 134, 137, 138, 142, 145
Spedding, Eric  51, 58, 62, 69, 70, 80, 81, 100
St Quentin  127, 152
Stark, Doug  51
Stayte, Jesse  40, 41, 48, 51, 59, 62, 115, 118, 122, 125, 127, 128, 129, 134, 136, 140, 148
Stayte, Oliver  40, 123
Stewart, Lieutenant-Colonel A.E.  133, 134
Storkey, Percy  167
Suez Canal  32

tanks developed  23, 38–39, 76, 91
    deployed with New Zealanders  70–72, 102, 120
Tennyson-D'Eyncourt, Sir Eustace  39
Third Battle of Ypres  100, 123
Travis, Sergeant R.C. (Dick)  140, 142, 143
Treaty of Versailles  164
trench foot  46, 48
Trescault Spur  148
Tritton, Sir William  39
Tronson, Aubrey  13, 28
Tuckey, Richard  41, 131, 134, 136, 138
Turkey  24, 155
Turner, Major W.W.  115
Tyne Cot Cemetery  163

Unknown Warrior, The  7, 172, 173, 174

Verdun  42
Ville-souse-Corbie  128
Vimy Ridge  87

Ward, Sir Joseph  11, 15, 17, 139
Warneton  98, 102
Wateau  106
Waters, Eric  127
Wazir, Battle of the  28
Wellington Battalion  126
Wells, H.G.  8, 39, 164
Weston, C.H.  48, 80
Westroosebeke  112
Whippet medium tank  134, 151
Wilson, President Woodrow  86, 123, 152
Wolf Farm  115
Wolseley, Major-General Sir Garnet,  15

YMCA  62
Young, Brigadier-General R.  155
Ypres  7, 21, 110, 119, 120, 121, 122, 124, 125, 136, 161, 168

Zeebrugge  88, 101, 102
Zeitoun Camp  25
Zonnebeke Stream  109

## Battle for Crete
### New Zealand's Near-run Affair 1941

New Zealand soldiers arrived in Crete during early May 1941, short of equipment after a hasty evacuation from Greece. Three weeks later, the Germans attacked, and for a while, the fate of New Zealand's active armed force lay in the balance on an island a world away from home.

Today Crete continues to prompt intense debate. British historians writing during the 1990s have argued that both New Zealand soldiers and the island commander, Major General Bernard Freyberg, fell short of the mark during the battle, resulting in the German victory.

Matthew Wright draws on a wide range of archival sources to refute this criticism, arguing that in the face of total German air superiority, the battle was unwinnable. The fact that the British came so close to successfully holding the island can be largely credited to Freyberg's outstanding abilities as a commander, and to the quality of the men he led.

The battle for Crete was very much a 'near-run affair' and remains a crucial part of the annals of New Zealand's military history.

ISBN 0 7900 0732 0

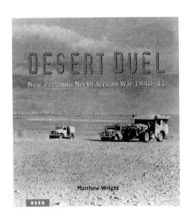

## Desert Duel
### New Zealand's North African War 1940–43

In June 1942, Field Marshal Erwin Rommel's Panzerarmee Afrika surged into Egypt. It was his second effort to take the Nile delta, and within a few days the main intact force standing between the Axis army and Cairo was the Second New Zealand Division, classified by Rommel as the elite of the British Army.

A few days later, the Panzerarmee surrounded the New Zealanders at Minqar Qaim. Outnumbered and cut off, the Kiwis should have surrendered. Instead, they smashed their way out through a Panzer division.

*Desert Duel* tells the story of New Zealand's four-year war in North Africa. In a lively and well-illustrated account, making extensive use of original source material, Matthew Wright argues that, in part thanks to Lieutenant-General Sir Bernard Freyberg's leadership, the division put up a performance well in excess of what might have been expected from a small and youthful South Pacific nation.

ISBN 0 7900 0852 1

## Pacific War
### New Zealand and Japan 1941–45

In December 1941, Japan attacked the British Commonwealth and the United States. For a few desperate months in early 1942, New Zealand faced down the threat of blockade and, ultimately, invasion. Despite a heavy commitment to the European war, New Zealanders fought the Japanese on land, sea and in the air, from Malaya to the Solomons and, finally, in Japanese home waters. New Zealand also provided bases and recreation facilities for US forces, food for the whole campaign, and even physicists for the atomic bomb project.

In *Pacific War*, Matthew Wright recounts the story of New Zealand's Pacific struggle, focusing particularly on the politics of war and the short-lived army contribution to the Pacific islands. Diaries and letters from the front, some previously unpublished, help bring New Zealand's war experience alive.

ISBN 0 7900 0908 0

## Italian Odyssey
### New Zealanders in the battle for Italy 1943–45

In September 1943, the Second New Zealand Division landed in Italy, beginning a 20-month campaign that took the New Zealanders from Taranto to Trieste. It was dominated by the two-month siege of Cassino, a bitter struggle in the depths of winter that remains controversial today.

In this illustrated account of the campaign, Matthew Wright argues that adverse weather, the politics of the Anglo–American alliance, and sheer lack of numbers on the ground, stacked the odds against 2 NZ Division. Ultimately, the question is not whether New Zealand failed, but how they achieved as much as they did under the circumstances.

ISBN 0 7900 0897 1